Promoting professionalism, innovation and transnational collaboration: a new approach to foreign language teacher education

Edited by Götz Schwab, Mareike Oesterle, and Alison Whelan

Published by Research-publishing.net, a not-for-profit association
Contact: info@research-publishing.net

© 2022 by Editors (collective work)
© 2022 by Authors (individual work)

Promoting professionalism, innovation and transnational collaboration: a new approach to foreign language teacher education
Edited by Götz Schwab, Mareike Oesterle, and Alison Whelan

Publication date: 2022/07/25

Rights: the whole volume is published under the Attribution-NonCommercial-NoDerivatives International (CC BY-NC-ND) licence; **individual articles may have a different licence**. Under the CC BY-NC-ND licence, the volume is freely available online (https://doi.org/10.14705/rpnet.2022.57.9782383720041) for anybody to read, download, copy, and redistribute provided that the author(s), editorial team, and publisher are properly cited. Commercial use and derivative works are, however, not permitted.

Disclaimer: Research-publishing.net does not take any responsibility for the content of the pages written by the authors of this book. The authors have recognised that the work described was not published before, or that it was not under consideration for publication elsewhere. While the information in this book is believed to be true and accurate on the date of its going to press, neither the editorial team nor the publisher can accept any legal responsibility for any errors or omissions. The publisher makes no warranty, expressed or implied, with respect to the material contained herein. While Research-publishing.net is committed to publishing works of integrity, the words are the authors' alone.

Trademark notice: product or corporate names may be trademarks or registered trademarks, and are used only for identification and explanation without intent to infringe.

Copyrighted material: every effort has been made by the editorial team to trace copyright holders and to obtain their permission for the use of copyrighted material in this book. In the event of errors or omissions, please notify the publisher of any corrections that will need to be incorporated in future editions of this book.

Typeset by Research-publishing.net
Cover theme by © 2022 Editors
Cover layout by © 2022 Raphaël Savina (raphael@savina.net)

ISBN13: 978-2-38372-004-1 (Ebook, PDF, colour)
ISBN13: 978-2-38372-005-8 (Ebook, EPUB, colour)
ISBN13: 978-2-38372-003-4 (Paperback - Print on demand, black and white)
Print on demand technology is a high-quality, innovative and ecological printing method; with which the book is never 'out of stock' or 'out of print'.

British Library Cataloguing-in-Publication Data.
A cataloguing record for this book is available from the British Library.

Legal deposit, France: Bibliothèque Nationale de France - Dépôt légal: juillet 2022.

Table of contents

v   Notes on contributors

ix   Acknowledgements

1   Introduction
Götz Schwab, Mareike Oesterle, and Alison Whelan

Part 1.

15   Continuing professional development: key themes in supporting the development of professional practice
Steve Mann and Katie Webb

45   Developing a framework of CPD for the context of foreign language teaching
Mareike Oesterle and Götz Schwab

Part 2.

83   Getting curious and gaining knowledge through transnational collaboration in foreign language teacher education
Ulrich Hoinkes and Kyra Clausen

107 The proPIC study weeks: experiencing transnational exchange
Götz Schwab and Mareike Oesterle

131 Student reactions to using interactive tutorials as part of the proPIC study programme
Richard Baldwin and Tobias Ruhtenberg

147 Developing an innovative and collaborative assessment framework for proPIC Europa
Alison Whelan and Paul Seedhouse

Table of contents

191 Approaches to the development of pre-service language teachers' e-portfolios
Azahara Cuesta, Jaume Batlle, Vicenta González, and Joan-Tomàs Pujolà

Part 3.

215 Personal pronouns as linguistic features in the construction of pre-service language teacher identity
Azahara Cuesta and Jaume Batlle

223 Images to foster student teachers' reflective practice and professional development
Joan-Tomàs Pujolà and Vicenta González

233 Filmmaking by students or rethinking thinking
Kyra Clausen and Ulrich Hoinkes

243 Impact beyond the project: exploring engagement in proPIC Europa and potential lasting impact on teaching studies and professional development
Alison Whelan and Richard Baldwin

253 How can teacher educators benefit from participating in a transient transnational community?
Mareike Oesterle

Part 4.

263 proPIC student vignettes
Alison Whelan, Götz Schwab, and Mareike Oesterle

287 Author index

Notes on contributors

Richard Baldwin is a senior lecturer at the Faculty of Librarianship, Information, Education, and IT at the University of Borås, Sweden. He defended his PhD thesis in 2013, which looked at the recontextualisation of the Bologna process in teacher education in Sweden. His research interests include aspects of change in higher education as well as issues relating to second language learning.

Jaume Batlle holds a PhD in didactics of language and literature at the University of Barcelona. He is currently a lecturer at the Department of Language Education in the Faculty of Education at the University of Barcelona. His research interests focus on classroom interaction in second language teaching from a conversation analysis perspective, as well as on gamification in education. He is an investigator in the realTIC research group.

Kyra Clausen is a PhD student in French didactics at the University of Kiel. As a research assistant, she is currently working in the international project *Ed-In-Mov* on digitisation and internationalisation in teacher education funded by the Federal Ministry of Education and Research. She conducts research on filmmaking in higher education using the methodological approach of design-based research. Her research interests focus on didactics and internationalisation in foreign language teacher education.

Azahara Cuesta is a PhD student in didactics of language and literature at the University of Barcelona. She is currently teaching at the Department of Language Education in the Faculty of Education at the University of Barcelona. Her research interests focus on reflective practice, e-portfolios, and internationalisation projects in teacher education. She takes part in the realTIC research group as a PhD researcher.

Vicenta González holds a PhD in education sciences at the University of Barcelona. She is currently Associate Professor at the Department of Language Education in the Faculty of Education at the University of Barcelona. She collaborates in teacher training courses for several international institutions, such as Instituto Cervantes, Universidad Internacional Menéndez Pelayo, or SDI

München, among others. Her research interests focus on different topics related to reflective practice in teacher education, gamification in second language teaching, and the use of ICT tools in second language teaching and learning processes. She is an investigator in the realTIC research group.

Ulrich Hoinkes is a professor of Romance studies and teacher education at the University of Kiel, Germany. His main professional profile is that of a linguist specialised in several fields. He received his doctorate at the University of Münster in 1990 with a thesis on philosophy and grammar in the French Enlightenment. He subsequently habilitated in 1999 with a thesis on regional bilingualism and technical language use. Since his appointment at Kiel University, he has turned his attention to educational science and foreign language didactics. As a university teacher, Hoinkes built long-term projects on student filmmaking and international exchange in teacher education. Since 2015, he has been dedicated to building an international and interdisciplinary research project on anxiety culture.

Steve Mann (Professor of applied linguistics) currently works at the Department of Applied Linguistics at the University of Warwick. He previously lectured at both Aston University and the University of Birmingham. He has experience in Hong Kong, Japan, and Europe in both English language teaching and teacher development. Steve supervises a research group of PhD students who are investigating teachers' education and development. The group's work considers aspects of teacher development, teacher beliefs, and the development of knowledge, the first year of teaching, reflective practice, mentoring, blended learning, and the use of technology in teacher development. His most recent books are '*The Research Interview: Reflexivity and Reflective Practice in Research Processes*' (Palgrave), and '*Reflective Practice in English Language Teaching: Research-Based Principles and Practices*' (Routledge).

Mareike Oesterle is a PhD student and research assistant at the University of Education Ludwigsburg, Germany. She has a degree in primary and secondary teaching and has been involved in a number of different projects (e.g. proPIC,

Notes on contributors

VEO Europa and Beyond School), currently being involved in the digiTED@EU project at the University of Education Ludwigsburg. All the projects mainly aimed at developing innovative formats to support (future) teachers and teacher educators in their own continuing professional development. In her PhD, she currently investigates a transient professional community of teacher educators and explores possible ways to foster professional learning in a transnational context. Further interests include language learning and teaching, and the use of mobile technologies in teacher education.

Joan-Tomàs Pujolà holds a PhD in applied linguistics at the University of Edinburgh. He is currently Senior Lecturer at the Department of Language Education in the Faculty of Education at the University of Barcelona. He collaborates in teacher training courses at the Institute of Professional Development. His research interests focus on different topics related to computer assisted language learning such as m-learning, telecollaboration, tandem learning, LMOOCs, e-portfolios for teacher education, and active methodologies such as gamification. He is the principal investigator of the realTIC research group.

Tobias Ruhtenberg has an MA in educational work with focus on ICT. He teaches at the University of Borås, Sweden, on how to include ICT in all subjects in teacher education, and, also, is part of in-service training for teachers. He is involved in Edtech development in higher education and a former part of an Erasmus + project for engaging girls in STEM subjects with the help of mobile technologies.

Götz Schwab is Professor of applied linguistics at the Institute of English, Ludwigsburg University of Education, Germany. He worked as a secondary school teacher before starting a career at the university where he received his PhD in 2008. He is currently head of the institute and coordinates a number of transnational projects (e.g. DIVA, ETP, digTED@EU). Götz Schwab has a wide range of research interests. This includes conversation analysis for second language acquisition, virtual exchange/telecollaboration and the use of mobile technology, syntax, low achievers and students-at-risk, especially at secondary

Notes on contributors

schools, and ELT/FLT methodology in primary and secondary schools, as well as content and language integrated learning (CLIL).

Paul Seedhouse is Professor of educational and applied linguistics and Director of ilab:learn at Newcastle University, UK. With colleagues in computing science over 12 years, he has worked on four grants to use digital technology to teach users languages and cultural tasks simultaneously, resulting in the *Linguacuisine* and *ENACT* apps. He has also had five grants from the IELTS consortium to study spoken interaction in the IELTS Speaking Test. He has published ten books and over 70 articles and book chapters in the areas of spoken interaction, applied linguistics, and language teaching.

Katie Webb is currently undertaking a PhD at Warwick University, which explores the learning experiences, identities, and perceptions of a group of in-service teachers studying an MA TESOL. She has seven years of practical teaching experience in the UK, Europe, and Asia. She has recognised and well-respected ELT qualifications, including a CELTA, DELTA, and MA in ELT (with a speciality in teacher education). She has published articles on the themes of peer observation (*ELTED* journal) and dialogic approaches to feedback (*The Teacher Trainer* Journal), and has recently contributed a chapter on co-operative development for the book 'Teacher Reflection Policies, Practices, and Impacts: Studies in Honour of Thomas S.C. Farrell'.

Alison Whelan is Research Associate in the School of Education, Communication and Language Sciences at Newcastle University, UK. She has particular interests in language learning and teaching, project-based learning, teacher training and development, and the creation and implementation of research-based, innovative curricula at primary, secondary, FE and HE level. She is currently involved in several projects exploring the impact of collaborative learning, including an Erasmus+ project examining learning a second language through cultural activities; a National Lottery funded project looking at wellbeing through engagement in heritage workshops; and a UK Home Office funded project aiming to embed a PBL approach into North East Alternative Education settings.

Acknowledgements

The editors would like to express their gratitude for the generous grant funding received through the EU Erasmus+ programme KA203 (2017-1-DE01-KA203-003547), without which this project would not have been possible. We are grateful for their commitment to fostering transnational collaboration and European partnerships.

The academic and administrative staff at the five partner universities (Pädagogische Hochschule Karlsruhe, Germany; Christian-Albrecht-Universität zu Kiel, Germany; Högskolan i Borås, Sweden; Universitat de Barcelona, Spain; and Newcastle University, UK) have been invaluable in their support and assistance, allowing this project to continue even throughout the unexpected events which unfolded with the COVID-19 pandemic in early 2020. This forced us to radically change the project plans, and due to the continued support from our institutions, we persevered.

A fundamental aspect of this project was working with trainee teachers and students on education courses at each institution. We would like to thank each and every student who took part in the programme. Some students participated as a compulsory element of their course, some in an entirely voluntary capacity, but all of them showed enthusiasm, open-mindedness, and a willingness to learn from each other. They were a pleasure to meet and work with, and we wish them all every success in their future careers.

A special thanks goes to Stacey Wizner who contributed to this book with her outstanding proofreading of all the different chapters.

Finally, this book is about transnational partnerships and collaboration, and would not have come to fruition without the incredible partnerships developed between the project team members from each of the institutions involved. Some of these team members have been involved throughout the entire project, others joined us midway or left to go onto other projects, and we called on a range of colleagues and peers to provide support, guidance, and expertise. We are immensely grateful for the professional and personal relationships that have

Acknowledgements

evolved as a result of being involved in this project, and we hope to continue working together in some manner for many years to come.

Götz Schwab, Mareike Oesterle, and Alison Whelan

Introduction

Götz Schwab[1], Mareike Oesterle[2], and Alison Whelan[3]

The idea to develop the proPIC project[4] emerged in 2016. During this year, when travelling to conferences and other events was still possible, several authors of this edited volume found themselves drawn together, asking similar questions and raising related issues in regard to the education, training, and professional development of future language teachers. It struck us that the concept of Continuing Professional Development (CPD) had found its way into numerous curricula, research studies, as well as national and international projects (British Council, 2017; Caena, 2011; Day & Sachs, 2005; OECD, 2009). However, only a few of them, for instance Mann and Walsh (2017), gave any practical implications about how to update and change the current teaching and learning environments of teacher education to promote CPD that adapts to the rapid change which our education systems are facing. Today's teacher education is part of a vast and ongoing process of digitalisation and globalisation, demanding that professionals think out of the box, integrate digital tools, and engage in transnational networks. The COVID-19 pandemic has created even greater challenges, but also potentials for teacher education.

1. The proPIC project

The proPIC project ran from 2017 to 2020 and addressed Key Action 2 of the Erasmus+ programme on strategic partnerships for higher education.

---

1. University of Education Ludwigsburg, Ludwigsburg, Germany; goetz.schwab@ph-ludwigsburg.de; https://orcid.org/0000-0003-0939-3325

2. University of Education Ludwigsburg, Ludwigsburg, Germany; mareike.oesterle@gmx.de; https://orcid.org/0000-0002-9458-7927

3. Newcastle University, Newcastle-upon-Tyne, United Kingdom; alison.whelan2@newcastle.ac.uk; https://orcid.org/0000-0001-6272-6497

4. Promoting Professionalism, Innovation and Transnational Collaboration (Erasmus+, Strategic Partnerships, 2017-2020)

How to cite: Schwab, G., Oesterle, M., & Whelan, A. (2022). Introduction. In G. Schwab, M. Oesterle & A. Whelan (Eds), *Promoting professionalism, innovation and transnational collaboration: a new approach to foreign language teacher education* (pp. 1-11). Research-publishing.net. https://doi.org/10.14705/rpnet.2022.57.1381

Introduction

The abbreviation proPIC stands for *promoting professionalism, innovation, and transnational collaboration in foreign and second language learning and teaching – integrating research-orientation and mobile technologies in teacher education.* It brought together five European partners: Pädagogische Hochschule Karlsruhe (Germany), Christian-Albrecht-Universität zu Kiel (Germany), Högskolan i Borås (Sweden), Universitat de Barcelona (Spain), and Newcastle University (UK) with shared goals: (1) to empower both prospective teachers and themselves, the teacher educators, (2) to encourage teacher educators to actively become agents of their own CPD, and (3) to establish a culture of self-reflection and an intercultural network of professionals who creatively use mobile technologies and innovative ways of teaching and learning.

The aim of the project was to generate a framework for a study programme which promotes professionalism, innovation, and transnational collaboration in foreign language learning and teaching which uses and integrates a variety of mobile technologies. For this, the project built on an adaptable and innovative framework of a study programme, which was drafted prior to the start of the project at the University of Education Karlsruhe. Throughout the project, it was developed further by the whole consortium. For the partners, it was important to generate a programme with flexible and open elements, because the curricula and the conditions of the project partners involved were quite different to each other, as were some of the perspectives of the partners concerning the theories and models used as a basis for programme development.

The main outputs of proPIC were:

- a theoretical framework for CPD in the context of foreign and second language learning and teaching;

- an innovative, research-oriented study programme;

- a set of eight interactive tutorials in the form of iBooks introducing the use of innovative approaches and mobile technologies;

- a collection of creative products and e-portfolios of the participating prospective teachers; and

- an interactive webspace containing a reflective e-portfolio by the participating teacher educators.

Targeting future language teachers and teacher educators, the project's main objective was to define a theoretical concept for CPD in the context of developing, testing, and evaluating the above-mentioned adaptable research-oriented study programme comprising a variety of innovative elements. Crucial for this programme was the interplay between transnational collaboration, the use of mobile technologies, and the integration of research-oriented approaches and methods. As targeted, one group of participants of the project were prospective foreign and second language teachers, meaning graduate and undergraduate students who were enrolled at the partner institutions. The other group of participants were the project partners themselves, namely teacher educators working in the field of foreign and second language learning and teaching.

In line with the findings of this edited volume, the proPIC project has provided evidence of:

- enhanced openness and motivation to engage in transnational exchange;

- improved confidence in using mobile technologies in professional practices;

- increased motivation to engage in lifelong and innovative learning processes; and

- stronger existing and new ties between European institutions.

As the proPIC project aimed at promoting professionalism, innovation, and transnational collaboration in foreign and second language learning and teaching as a first priority, it was fully aligned with the Bologna Process and tools at opening higher education systems through mobility and internationalisation. By exploiting the benefits of new technologies to enrich teaching, improve learning experiences, enhance virtual mobility, and create new opportunities for research, the project further contributed to the modernisation of Europe's higher education systems as outlined in the renewed 2011 EU Modernisation Agenda and in the European Education Area (European Commission, 2021).

Targeting the second priority of supporting innovation and creativity through partnerships, the project helped increase professional, social, and intercultural skills and employability. In line with the European Qualifications Framework[5], the project promoted the development of valuable and creative learning outcomes (knowledge, skills, competences) by its participating students. As will be described in some chapters of this edited volume, the findings of the project indicate that it supported innovative and creative (professional) practices in language teacher education through something which turned out to be the most crucial element of the project on all levels: transnational partnerships and approaches.

Due to the project findings, we can further say that proPIC also addressed a third priority: open and innovative practices in a digital era. We believe that this aspect should represent a major component of how teacher education programmes ought to be designed in the future. Especially in a European context, resources, approaches, and theories, but also assessment criteria and curricula standards should become more open and innovative. Based on our experiences in creating common assessment criteria, including the exploration of new ways of assessment (i.e. video diaries, podcasts), we consider it crucial to gain a more open and flexible perspective, which we think can be supported through transnational partnerships and exchange on all levels in teacher education, if not beyond this discipline. From their very first steps in teacher education, trainee teachers have an impact on peers, colleagues, mentors, pupils at schools through placements, and their training providers. For every trainee teacher who was involved in the proPIC project, their new knowledge and skills benefitted

---

5. The Council of the European Union (2017)

all of these stakeholders. The outcomes of the project, which can be used by professionals from any country, address all three of the chosen priorities that were mentioned above.

2. Disseminating our outputs and findings through this edited volume

This book is the culmination of the proPIC project. It is based on its wide range of outputs, which can also be retrieved on the project's website[6]. All of the authors are experts in language teacher education at the primary and secondary level, adult education, educational technology, or applied linguistics. The book was written on the assumption that in current times, professionals in teacher education require concrete and hands-on good practice examples of how innovation, mobile technologies, and transnational collaboration can be incorporated in the concept of CPD. Moreover, we believe that these professionals have begun to ask more consciously for clear empirical evidence of what works, with whom in which context, and why. Furthermore, drawing on the experiences of authors from different countries (Germany, Spain, Sweden, and the UK), this book illustrates how CPD can be put into practice, by explaining and exemplifying various innovative elements of a comprehensive and overarching study programme developed over the course of three years. Although this study programme unites all of the resources, events, and case studies that are illustrated in the following chapters, each of them can be used as a stand-alone reference. As such, if a teacher from Croatia is interested in organising a study-abroad stay for students from one of her courses, she could consult Chapter 4 for general advice on how to plan, organise, and evaluate such an event. And even though this book has been composed in the context of language teacher education, most of the chapters generalise their findings. Therefore, this volume can also be used in a number of different settings, e.g. schools, as it helps to inspire in-service teachers by suggesting a large number of methods for blended teaching and learning, or by providing an innovative approach to assessing and giving feedback on

---

[6]. http://www.propiceuropa.com/

digital learning outputs. Moreover, this book can be used by policymakers as some chapters indicate strategies to improve teaching and learning on a more structural level to help rethink teacher education in a digital era.

The main argument of this book is that CPD must be seen as a collaborative and holistic endeavour. Education today needs to prepare students for changing tasks and roles in an increasingly digital and dynamic society. Teacher education needs to ensure that future teachers learn how to help their learners become critical and democratic citizens who are able to actively participate in a constantly changing society. For this, future teachers must be motivated and encouraged to engage in lifelong learning and become agents of their own professional development (European Commission, 2021). The necessity for the transformation of education systems has become even more visible due to the COVID-19 pandemic. Although this crisis has digitally transformed education, it has also put the deficits under a microscope and pointed out the basic problems and weaknesses – on local, national, and international levels. The way in which digitalisation and innovation are put into practice ranges widely across teacher education institutions, including the professional contexts of the authors of this book. However, the conclusions of all the chapters stress the need to connect and collaborate across borders and disciplines, inside and outside institutions, as well as the need to pool educational resources and create spaces for exchange of good practices and reflective dialogue. This is the exact need that this book intends to address. Drawing on the outputs and findings of the proPIC project, this book provides not only an innovative concept of how CPD works, but a unique collection of transnationally developed resources for teaching and learning. It includes not only the perspective of teacher educators, but also of students, i.e. prospective teachers and thus the main actors in the realm of the transformation of our educational systems.

3. The chapters in this volume

This volume, consisting of four parts, includes 13 chapters, each written to be relatively complete by itself. References are provided at the end of each chapter. **Part I** includes two chapters focusing on the concept of CPD. Both chapters serve as a theoretical basis for this edited volume. The main outputs of the project as well as related evaluative data are presented and discussed in **Part II**. In **Part III**, the authors of five chapters show and discuss empirical data that was collected throughout the project, putting the focus on different aspects of proPIC. **Part IV** includes the voices of some of the students that have participated in the proPIC project.

In **Chapter 1**, Mann and Webb introduce five key themes that they believe to be crucial to effectively support the professional development of teachers. Providing a detailed background on the topic of CPD, the authors further introduce a useful summary of good practice examples. In line with the findings of the proPIC project, they argue that professional development should be treated as an open, dynamic, and collaborative endeavour, which must be participatory and situated. **Chapter 2** adds to this, as it explicates the fundamental elements that underpin the CPD framework which was developed as part of the proPIC project. After reviewing relevant literature in this field, Oesterle and Schwab illustrate and exemplify the didactic elements, giving concrete examples and integrating relevant feedback from the students and teacher educators.

Although Chapters 2 to 7 include and refer to empirical evidence, the authors – some more than others – primarily use data to exemplify and evaluate the outputs that were developed in the proPIC project. In **Chapter 3,** Hoinkes and Clausen contribute to this volume by introducing the overall concept of the study programme that was developed in the project. In this context, the authors place an emphasis on the notion of transculturality, proposing that the study programme promotes intercultural understanding and can thus be viewed as an important contribution to the CPD of future language teachers. **Chapter 4** presents a more practical view, as Schwab and Oesterle concentrate on one core element of the project, which was the development and implementation of the so-called study week: a five day face-to-face stay abroad. In this chapter, the authors present and discuss the results and impact of these events which took place twice during the project. In order to do so, they include the overall framework of the events, as well as assorted materials and the feedback of the participating students. Additionally, an overview of relevant literature dealing with the concept of short stays abroad in teacher education programmes is provided. **Chapter 5** illustrates and explains a set of interactive tutorials that were produced in the proPIC project. These tutorials were in the form of interactive e-books and were created using the software iBook Author. In this chapter, Baldwin and Ruhtenberg explain each tutorial, give plenty of practical advice, and discuss both student and teacher educators' reactions to using interactive tutorials as part of a study programme. **Chapter 6** was written by Whelan and Seedhouse and focuses on the complex approaches to assessment in language teacher education in the context of a transnational partnership. Against this background, the authors address the question of whether commonality can be found across different institutions, and whether elements of individuality in these unique settings can be incorporated into a common framework which then could be used as a model to be adapted to suit each partner's needs and requirements. The chapter further illustrates and discusses the evaluation framework that was created in the proPIC project, using a variety of already existing frameworks. Cuesta, Batlle, González, and Pujolà concentrate on the concept of the e-portfolio in **Chapter 7**. Together, they describe the scope of the implementation of e-portfolios in language teacher education. The chapter uses empirical data that was collected during the project to analyse how the e-portfolios of 47 pre-service teachers were developed and adapted to their specific needs in the different educational institutions. The chapter is concerned with how the concept of e-portfolio was introduced to the students, describing the different didactic strategies and methods that were used in the process. Finally, the chapter presents a number of examples in relation to the different digital platforms used, the different didactic actions carried out, and the diverse assessment strategies applied in each institutional context.

In Part III, the authors draw more specifically on the data collected in the project in order to conduct small research investigations. **Chapter 8** offers an initial approach to understanding how future teachers construct and represent their teacher identities. Cuesta and Batlle base their study on a series of interactions designed to stimulate joint reflection in the context of the proPIC project, using corpus linguistics-conversation analysis to analyse their data. The authors were able to observe how the identity of a language teacher was established through the construction of epistemic arguments and standpoints in which the use of pronouns played a decisive role: Speakers use them to denote a position and to situate others in the arguments they construct. The study by Pujolà and González in **Chapter 9** analyses 17 images as visual metaphors. In the context of one project event at the University of Barcelona, student teachers had to depict their conceptions about teaching additional languages through an image together with an explanatory text. The authors aimed at finding out to what extent this task fosters a teacher's reflective practice in the process of building their teacher identity at pre-service stages of their professional development. The results establish five predominant conceptions of additional language teaching: openness, collaboration, process, construction, and challenge. In **Chapter 10**, Clausen and Hoinkes base their investigation on the assumption that students can acquire sustainable knowledge related to their subject through the process of filmmaking. Subsequent to giving a short theoretical input on filmmaking as an approach to learning, the authors investigate how foreign language students participating in the proPIC project evaluate this approach for their own future teaching practices. Based on their findings, the authors call for the implementation of filmmaking by students in teacher education in order to engage future teachers in rethinking education through an innovative and creative approach to learning and teaching. **Chapter 11** is a transnational contribution by Whelan and Baldwin and draws on data collected at two partner institutions in the UK and in Sweden. The authors explore the impact beyond the project, meaning the potential lasting impact the project had on some of the participating students, on their studies and their mindset, after the completion of the project. In **Chapter 12**, Oesterle presents interim findings of her doctoral thesis, for which the proPIC project was chosen as a single case study. In this chapter, the author deals with the complex challenges that teacher educators face in their professional environment. Using an auto-ethnographic approach to her investigation and drawing on qualitative data from the proPIC project, the author analyses the perceived benefits that the teacher educators describe when participating in a transient transnational community. The results indicate that fruitful communities are not emerging by chance, but need to be initiated and scaffolded. On an institutional level, this includes allocating time, space, and possibly finances to maximise their potential usefulness.

A major element of the proPIC project was the active and constant involvement of pre-service teachers. Throughout the project, 142 students took part and helped to develop various outputs and resources. Moreover, these students contributed to our research agenda by giving feedback, allowing us to record various sessions and meetings, and by producing a great number of diverse essays and papers. For us it was important to include the voices of at least some of the students in this edited volume. Therefore, **Chapter 13** in Part IV, combines extracts of student essays and includes a sample of vignettes that help examine the project from the inter- and transnational perspective of the students themselves, exploring their reflections on their participation and the impact it had on their studies and future careers as language teachers. As such, the chapter is structured according to the following three major topics: (1) teaching methodology, (2) digitisation, and (3) professionalism.

4. The funding

All practical implications and empirical evidence referred to in the following chapters, except Chapter 1, stem from the proPIC project. The resources that are mentioned in these chapters were developed as part of this project and are accessible on the project's homepage. As the project was an EU Erasmus+ funded project, all results are open-access items and publicly available.

5. Ethical implications

Throughout the book, there are numerous personal contributions from students or lecturers such as e-portfolios, images, or artefacts. All participants gave their consent to publish the data here or on our website.

References

British Council. (2017). *Frameworks of continuing professional development.* https://www.britishcouncil.in/teach/continuing-professional-development

Caena, F. (2011). Literature review. Quality in teachers continuing professional development. In European Commission (Eds), *Education and training 2020 thematic working group 'professional development of teachers'.* https://www.researchgate.net/publication/344906256_Literature_review_Quality_in_Teachers%27_continuing_professional_development

Day, C., & Sachs, J. (2005). *International handbook of the continuing professional development of teachers.* Open University Press.

European Commission. (2021). *European education area.* https://ec.europa.eu/education/education-in-the-eu/european-education-area_en

Mann, S., & Walsh, S. (2017). *Reflective practice in English language teaching. Research-based principles and practices.* Routledge.

OECD. (2009). Chapter 3. The professional development of teachers. In OECD (Eds), *Creating effective teaching and learning environments. First results from TALIS* (pp. 49-86). https://www.oecd.org/education/school/43023606.pdf

The Council of the European Union. (2017). Council recommendation of 22 May 2017 on the European Qualifications Framework for lifelong learning and repealing the recommendation of the European Parliament and of the Council of 23 April 2008 on the establishment of the European Qualifications Framework for lifelong learning. *Official Journal of the European Union, C 189/15.* https://eur-lex.europa.eu/legal-content/EN/TXT/HTML/?uri=CELEX:32017H0615(01)&from=EN

Part 1.

1 Continuing professional development: key themes in supporting the development of professional practice

Steve Mann[1] and Katie Webb[2]

1. Introduction

We would like to start with a statement about the importance of CPD. Julian Edge, in a lecture, once said that true teacher development is always a case of 'becoming'. In other words, a good teacher is always engaged, interested, and collaborative. The process of trying to be a better teacher, to understand learners just a little bit better, to develop materials that work just a little bit more effectively never really stops. If it did, then you might become stale, you might become self-satisfied, you might become disinterested. When you are new to the profession, there is by definition a lot to know, a lot to learn, and a lot to understand. However, the 'ing' in *becoming* and *continuing* is as important for 60-year olds as it is for 21-year olds. In fact, we believe, from our experiences of ageing, that the older you get, the more important this becomes. This chapter is admittedly personal and reflective, but we hope it can offer a few important touchstones for discussion, engagement, and comment.

In order to make this personal statement and provide a backdrop for the upcoming chapters in which the proPIC project[3] is the focus, in this introduction we consider five different dimensions of CPD (see Figure 1) that we believe are crucial to its effectiveness. CPD is ongoing in its efforts to promote professional

---

1. Warwick University, Coventry, England; steve.mann@warwick.ac.uk; https://orcid.org/0000-0002-6347-1614

2. Warwick University, Coventry England; katie.louise.webb@gmail.com; https://orcid.org/0000-0002-9068-5781

3. http://www.propiceuropa.com/

How to cite: Mann, S., & Webb, K. (2022). Continuing professional development: key themes in supporting the development of professional practice. In G. Schwab, M. Oesterle & A. Whelan (Eds), *Promoting professionalism, innovation and transnational collaboration: a new approach to foreign language teacher education* (pp. 15-44). Research-publishing.net. https://doi.org/10.14705/rpnet.2022.57.1382

learning and standards, and it fosters innovation, collaboration, and reflection. What follows is an attempt to make clear the value of the five dimensions. This chapter develops and extends arguments about CPD already made in Mann (2021) and some ground that was covered in Edge and Mann (2013).

Figure 1. The five dimensions of CPD

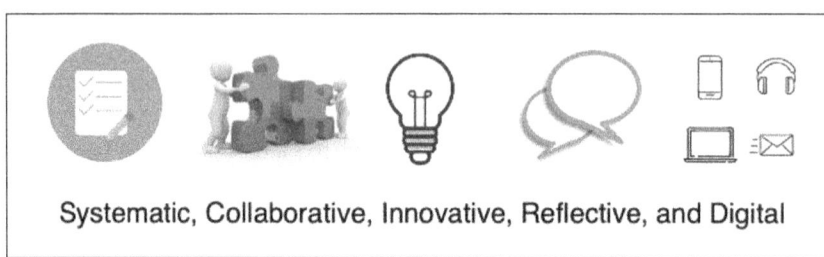

Systematic, Collaborative, Innovative, Reflective, and Digital

The first key dimension of CPD is that it should be systematic and ideally it needs to be introduced and fostered during pre-service teacher education. The second dimension is that CPD is usually more effective and valuable if it is collaborative. The third feature of CPD is that innovation is at its heart, but innovation is not applying others' new ideas; it is transformative, seeing innovation as something which starts with or at least involves practitioners. The fourth dimension is that Reflective Practice (RP) is essential and supports the first three dimensions mentioned above. The final dimension is that digital literacy and the appreciation of digital tools and platforms are now both inevitable and an integral dimension in the delivery and support of good quality CPD. This has been intensified and brought into sharp focus by COVID-19 which has turbocharged the necessity of digital options and practice.

2. CPD

Mann's (2005) article on teacher development for the Language Teaching Journal was a chance to take stock of those elements of professional development that were at the heart of the literature. We looked back on this and considered what is still the same and what is different today. Certainly, the sociocultural perspective, recognising the importance of context, and situated learning has become orthodox. The ideas of Prabhu (1990) and others (see Canagarajah, 2005; Holliday, 1994; Kumaravadivelu, 2001) have prevailed, and it is now common knowledge that there is no such thing as a 'one-size-fits-all' approach to teacher education or development. Perhaps the one area that seems different is the role that digital technology now plays in our practice and professional development because of its ubiquitous nature.

Today, teachers and stakeholders involved in teacher education recognise the importance of teachers' CPD. In theoretical terms, this has resulted in greater attention in the literature on the learning and teaching process and how this can best be supported. In practical terms, this means enabling teaching to continuously learn while they work (Mann, 2005). As evidenced by research, it is now understood that teachers' classroom practices are shaped by their beliefs about teaching (Tang, Lee, & Chun, 2012). That is to say, the decisions and actions of teachers in classrooms are influenced by their beliefs. Through CPD, teachers are exposed to new ideas and recent developments in the education field (Mann, 2021). As such, it is essential to ensure teachers' CPD experiences are positive because then it is more likely that they will want to continue to learn and try new things out in their classrooms (Mann, 2021).

Because of the demands of society, a great deal of attention has been paid to ensuring good quality education. Student learning gains are often seen as evidence of quality education (Mann, 2021). Because effective CPD can positively impact learning gains, it is, internationally, viewed as vital (Joyce & Showers, 2002) and seen by many as one of the best ways to improve the quality of teaching (Hayes, 2019). Many teachers who engage in CPD are more committed to the profession and to developing and extending their teaching skills (Day & Leitch, 2007). In addition, CPD can positively impact how teachers view themselves and their self-worth (Mann, 2021). The importance of ensuring CPD is designed in an effective way, is viewed positively by teachers, and functions to facilitate teachers' learning gains, is essential (Hayes, 2019). Yet, many CPD and In-Service Training Day (INSET) initiatives fail to do this. This is often because teachers' needs are not understood or taken into consideration by those designing the programmes (Borg, 2015b).

As we can see from the paragraph above, CPD for teachers has received a great deal of attention in the literature (see Hayes, 2019 for an overview). In particular, there has been a significant focus on teachers' beliefs and attitudes towards teaching and learning as this affects their decision to engage in CPD. Simon Borg has led the effort on this work (e.g. Borg, 2015a), but there have been other important contributions (e.g. De Vries, van de Grift, & Jansen, 2014) that have explored how teachers' beliefs about learning and teaching relate to their CPD. However, other advocates (Hayes, 2019; Maley, 2016; Prabhu, 1990) believe that good quality CPD means more than just exploring beliefs. While there has been much research into teachers' beliefs, very little has been published regarding the application of those beliefs to classroom practices. We have known for some time that espoused beliefs are not the same as beliefs in action (Argyris & Schön, 1980; Kane, Sandetto, & Heath, 2002; Kaymakamoglu, 2018). In simple terms, what a teacher says they do may not be the same as what they actually do. Stance, positioning, and identity are complex, and one aspect of our identity which may be foregrounded in an interview may not be so evident in classroom observation of more ethnographic data (Richards, 2003). This has implications for researching CPD as well.

3. Established good practices for CPD

Having provided some background on the topic of CPD, this section offers a summary of accepted good practices in promoting and supporting CPD, which has been drawn from Borg (2015a), Mann and Walsh (2017), Bates and Morgan (2018), Hayes (2019), and Walsh and Mann (2019).

It is crucial that transmissive and top-down approaches to CPD be avoided. Although a focus on content is vital because it "anchors everything" (Bates & Morgan, 2018, p. 623), it is essential that time is allocated for "collaboration, peer-talk, and connecting theory and input to classroom events and experiences" (Mann, 2021, p. 23). A didactic model "in which facilitators simply tell teachers what to do or give them materials without providing them opportunities to develop skills and inquire into their impact on pupil learning is not effective" (Cordingley et al., 2015, p. 8). When such approaches are avoided, trainers can focus on connecting input and tasks to teachers' context (Moon, 2001) with a view to bridging the gap between practice and theory (Wallace & Bau, 1991). This is important because the theory that teachers are presented with needs to be connected to their practice in a way that is visible and pragmatic (Edge & Richards, 1993). To establish a fuller understanding of an innovative professional practice (Hayes, 2014) and help cement this connection in CPD processes, opportunities for teachers to practise skills in a positive environment (perhaps through tasks or microteaching) should be created (Mann, 2021). New knowledge then needs to be linked to existing experiences, beliefs, and "personal theories" (James, 2001, p. 4) because this can help to ensure the content of a CPD course is relevant to teachers' actual roles (Weston, Hindley, & Cunningham, 2019).

CPD is stronger when it is example based and data-led (Mann & Walsh, 2017). To achieve this, vignettes, narratives, learner-feedback, transcripts, real teaching materials, demonstration lessons, peer observations, case studies of teaching, and videos can be included (Mann, 2021). In terms of the latter, short videos are preferred by teachers than whole lessons (see Mann et al., 2019). When teachers participate in the synchronous process, interactions need to be engaging (Mann, 2021). In addition, there should be further opportunity for follow-up reflection and communication between teachers (Wright & Bolitho, 2007). Approaches to professional learning, irrespective of how active, are only sufficient if they are sustained and reviewed (Darling-Hammond, 2010). Furthermore, CPD that is designed from the top-down is often limited in regard to its impact in the long term (see Joyce & Showers, 2002; Wedell, 2009). To put it another way, CPD is more effective when it is continuous and ongoing (Weston et al., 2019) and not one-off by design (Wedell, 2009). It can also be more successful if trainers, mentors, e-moderators, or coaches are supportive and encouraging (Lamb, 1995). One way this can be done is through the use of e-portfolios. Creating a collaborative or individual teacher (educator) e-portfolio is a possible way to make CPD more sustainable (see Gulzar & Barrett, 2019). Another way to make CPD sustainable is through collaborative reflection, as was used in the proPIC project[4].

An environment in which teachers are positioned as active participants in the learning process is also essential for effective CPD. To do this, learner data and classroom materials can be examined. In addition, it means helping teachers "grapple with aspects of practice (rather than prioritising theory and conceptual information)" (Mann, 2021, p. 23). Within such an environment, opportunities for sharing teacher knowledge can be created (Freeman, 2002). What teachers already know and believe will filter new information and thus needs to be acknowledged, otherwise it will form a basis of resistance. When teachers work in such a way, they establish what Desimone (2011) calls an "interactive learning community" (p. 69). Teachers are more likely to have positive experiences when a social environment is established where interaction is central and positive relationships are fostered (Hadfield, 1992; Moon, 2001). Creating an atmosphere where trusting relationships are built "is instrumental to creating a support group that works together to solve problems of practice" (Bates & Morgan, 2018, p. 624). When this is achieved, teachers will be more likely to discuss and address instructional issues or dilemmas with one another (Mann, 2021). CPD also works better when teachers have the chance to engage and interact collaboratively. Collaboration is necessary, but not sufficient (Cordingley et al., 2015) unless it is "closely aligned with structured input and appropriate and achievable goals" (Mann, 2021, p. 23).

While there is no one-size-fits-all approach to CPD, as we have highlighted above, and as a number of important reviews have shown (see for example, Broad & Evans, 2006; Orr et al., 2013; Timperley, Wilson, Barrar, & Fung, 2008), good practices for CPD have been identified. As is evident from these practices, when designing CPD, the teachers and the constraints of a particular context must be considered. This is something we feel is extremely important and is something

---

4. http://www.propiceuropa.com/teacher-educators.html

we want to reiterate to the reader before we move onto detailing and providing examples of the five dimensions of CPD that we consider core to effectiveness.

3.1. Systematic

CPD processes need to be structured, wide-ranging, and systematic. Evidence from Allier-Gagneur, McBurnie, Chuang, and Haßler (2020) highlight that 'effective teacher education programmes' are systematic. They argue that both face-to-face and online versions should concentrate on pupil learning outcomes; involve effective teaching practices using modelling; acknowledge teachers' existing knowledge, views, and experiences; and create opportunities for teachers to build on this existing knowledge (Mann, 2021). In addition, they argue for the development of practical subject pedagogy instead of theoretical general pedagogy and on "empowering teachers to become reflective practitioners" (Mann, 2021, p. 22). CPD should be designed in a way that it can be trialled and refined (see also Hayes, 2019). It is more effective when it involves peer-to-peer support and engagement and aims to motivate teachers (see Lamb & Wyatt, 2019). Embedded forms of CPD, in which teachers learn in their own contexts, are better (Allier-Gagneur et al., 2020; Borg, 2015a; Walsh, 2002). CPD is also more successful when it is supported by teachers' institutions and ministries of education and when there are clear policies in place to ensure it runs systematically (Mann, 2021).

One example of an attempt to channel teacher CPD through a workable framework that is adaptive enough to serve the above requirements is the British Council's (2016) Teaching for Success approach . The approach is structured around a unique CPD framework for teachers, teacher educators, and school leaders. Drawing on Evans (2002), the initial trials of the teacher framework reported in Bolitho and Padwad (2013), and the studies into English language teaching reported in Hayes (2014), the Teaching for Success framework divides teaching into 12 core professional practices representing the 'content' of teachers' knowledge (see Figure 2). It provides levels of attainment that map onto qualifications as well as descriptions of competency described as *awareness, understanding, engagement,* and *integration,* and to various levels

Chapter 1

of professional qualifications. As a 'legacy' of the implementation of an earlier model within language teaching contexts, the framework indicates levels of attainment in the Common European Framework of Reference for language (CEFR[5]) scheme for competency in a foreign language.

Figure 2. Teaching for Success framework (British Council, 2019[6], p. 5)

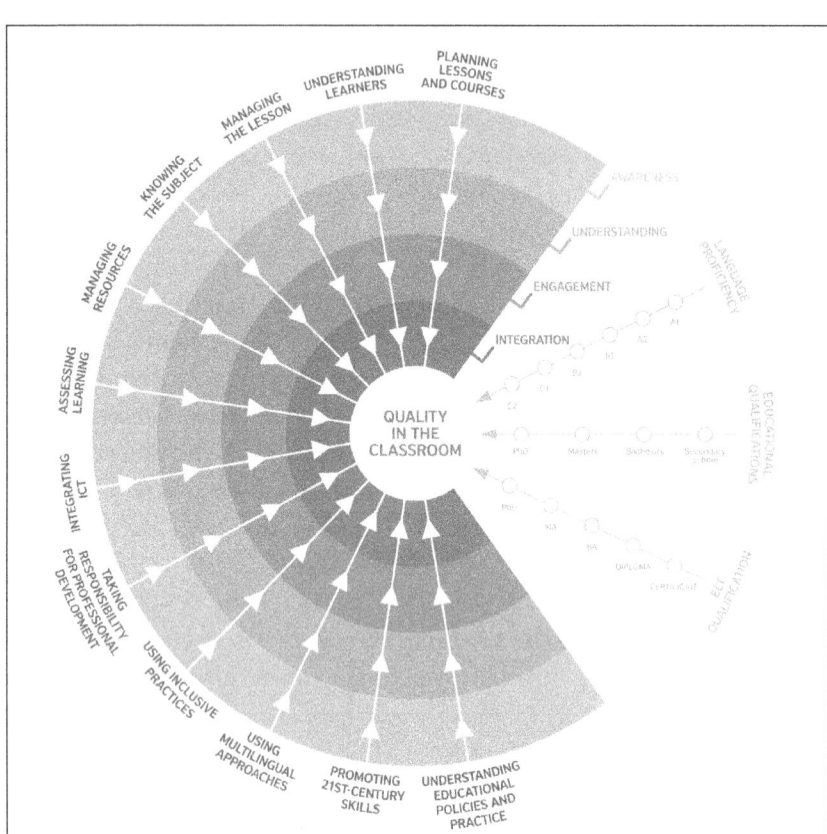

---

5. https://www.coe.int/en/web/common-european-framework-reference-languages/level-descriptions

6. © British Council licensed under CC-BY-NC-ND

The Teaching for Success framework has been successfully implemented in a range of contexts. For instance, as part of a larger ambitious educational reform programme, the Teaching for Success framework acted as conceptual grounding and a catalyst in establishing and improving teacher practices in Montenegro (Madzgalj & Kandybovich, 2018). The framework has been also proactively used in Armenia in recent years by the British Council Armenia office for developing and offering teacher development opportunities to English language teachers nationwide and has received positive reviews by the teachers. In addition, blended learning materials based on the Teaching for Success framework were evaluated very positively in a project for teachers in occupied Palestinian territories and particularly for teachers of English (British Council, 2019).

By utilising a framework such as the one above, teachers and teacher educators can map stages of development, identify needs, and decide on activities to engage in to develop the skills relevant to meeting these needs. When utilised to this effect, they can provide the pathways to achieve improvement in teaching and learning and, in turn, ensure that practice in the classroom demonstrates new professional learning and contributes to improved learning outcomes. That is to say, frameworks can help to ensure CPD is systematic. These lines of argument are similarly made by Oesterle and Schwab (2022) in Chapter 2 this volume, in which they offer a framework of CPD in the form of a multimodal online handbook that includes various linked documents and other external online resources.

3.2. Collaborative

Evidence shows that top-down approaches are less effective than programmes which are constructivist, dialogic, and actively include sharing between teachers (see Mann & Walsh, 2017). Wyatt and Dikilitaş (2016) show that engaging teachers in more constructivist CPD positions them as knowledge generators and makes them more likely to engage in research and gain deeper practical knowledge. Furthermore, when CPD is done collaboratively, it fosters an environment of openness, trust, and support among teachers, which facilitates the sharing of ideas, doubts, and difficulties (Forte & Flores, 2014). Collaborative CPD takes many forms, including team teaching; collaborative planning; peer coaching, mentoring and observation; collaborative project writing; and Co-operative Development (CD). While the context that teachers are working in may make one of these forms more appropriate than another, it is important that collaborative CPD is a bottom-up, teacher-led process, as this can help promote professional learning (Mann & Walsh, 2017). In other words, collaborative CPD is best when teachers in their own contexts decide how to work with one another (Desimone, 2011).

One type of collaborative CPD that we both have experience with is CD. CD typically involves two or more teachers meeting to develop a line of thought or argument, with a view to reflecting on and improving their individual professional practices (Edge, 2002). In CD meetings, one teacher takes on the role of 'Speaker' and the other of 'Understander' (Mann, 2002). The Speaker's role involves talking "through an idea or a personal concern" (Mann, 2002, p. 197), while the Understander's role is to remain non-judgemental and avoid giving advice or steering the talk towards their own agenda but instead to listen and assist the Speaker in articulating their own ideas as they clarify and discover where they lead (Edge, 1992). As the Speaker works on their own development (Edge & Attia, 2014), the Understander supports them by using a number of what are called 'Understander moves' (see Edge, 1992 for the CD framework). In this way, the impetus for development arises from the Speaker themselves through the support of the Understander.

CD has been established as a viable option for collaborative CPD and can be operalisationised in a number of ways (see Mann, 2002 for group development; Edge, 2006 for CD via email; Boon, 2005 for instant messenger CD; Webb, Mann, & Aqili-Shafie, 2022 for videoconferencing-mediated CD). It has been shown to enable teachers to achieve a greater awareness of their own strengths and skills and to support positive changes in teaching (Webb et al., 2022). For some text-based and video examples of CD, Edge's CD website[7] is a great

---

7. http://cooperative-development.com/?page_id=78

resource. Positive changes in teaching can also be brought about through peer observation, which is another type of collaborative CPD.

Although most teachers have, at some point in their careers, been observed, this is typically for assessment and/or appraisal purposes. Peer observation for development differs fundamentally from traditional types of observation because it is a non-judgemental, freestanding procedure that enables teachers to research areas of their choice (Mann, 2005). That is to say, it is not premised on the idea that the teacher being observed can be 'developed' by acting on or taking into consideration the suggestions of the observer (Webb, 2020). While there is a wide variety of models that teachers can adopt when engaging in peer observation (see Cosh, 1999; Freeman, 1982; Gosling, 2015), it is vital that there is mutual trust and respect among peers (Ahmed, Nordin, Shah, & Channa, 2018; Gosling, 2002; P'Rayan, 2013; Wang & Day, 2001) and that teachers are able to choose their partners (Carroll & O'Loughlin, 2013). Furthermore, because the most widespread use of observation is for the purpose of evaluation, teachers should be given the opportunity to engage in discussions that expose them to the type of developmental and/or reflective talk that the observations are aiming to promote (Webb, 2020).

Although research has yet to ascertain what, if any, benefit exists between peer observation and student learning/achievement (Donnelly, 2007; Gosling, 2015), teachers report that the process is useful for "self-assessment and improvement of teaching skills" (Donnelly, 2007, p. 127). While this may also be true with traditional types of observation, the collaborative element is important because teachers who engage in peer observation practice new skills and apply new strategies more frequently than colleagues who work alone (Showers & Joyce, 1996). Much like the case with CD, peer observation has a positive impact on camaraderie and collegiality (Atkinson & Bolt, 2010; Hamilton, 2013). Furthermore, it can be organised by teachers themselves, meaning that the teachers are centrally involved in decisions about the content and process of CPD, while being supported by the schools or education systems in which they work. When done in this way, CPD can achieve positive and sustained impacts on teachers (see Borg, 2015a).

Other forms of collaborative CPD are also valued by teachers themselves. For example, there has been a lot of recent attention on the benefits of Teacher Activity Groups (TAGs). The benefits of this kind of collaborative CPD are thus multifaceted (Borg, Lightfoot, & Gholkar, 2020). Through collaborative practices, teachers work together proactively to reflect on and respond to local problems, which, in turn, can enhance learning and promote collegiality. Communities of Practice (CoPs), TAGs, and Teacher Study Groups (TSGs) can have a positive impact on student learning gains (see Firestone, Cruz, & Rodl, 2020 for a fuller review) because teachers "work collaboratively on issues of contextual relevance, reflect on affordances and constraints and develop action plans to work towards solutions and innovation" (Mann, 2021, p. 24). This, in turn, promotes critical reflection among teachers and increases their agency (McAleavy, Hall-Chen, Horrocks, & Riggall, 2018).

TAGs and TSGs can be seen as forms of CoP. Internationally, CoPs are now viewed as a practical and efficient option for CPD (e.g. Al-Habsi, Al-Busaidi, & Al-Issa, 2021). People involved in CoPs "share a concern or a passion for something they do and learn how to do it better as they interact regularly" (Wenger, 2011, p. 1). The concept has been extensively embraced by professional groups of various kinds within language teacher education for various reasons (Hayes, 2019). For example, practising teachers involved in a CoP may be focused on classroom related issues and improving their practice. Teacher trainers, on the other hand, could be focused on feedback and want to learn how to provide it more efficiently. The CoP then would provide a place in these instances for teachers to share and discuss collaboratively. They afford the opportunity for professional development, while providing a space for teachers to engage socially and provide emotional support to one another (Mann, 2021).

3.3. Innovative

We believe that innovation is a key element of CPD goals and processes. When we talk about innovation, however, we usually think about new innovations which someone else (e.g. companies such as Sony, Apple, Cambridge English) makes available to us. However, in CPD terms, the powerful way to think about innovation is that it starts with or at least involves the practitioner. This view of CPD as an innovative process is reflexively tied to context and it is worth making some points about the importance of keeping a constant connection between innovation and context.

Innovations are not easily generalisable, because each context has its own constraints, affordances, and dynamics. This is something that Adrian Holliday recognised in his influential book on appropriate methodology' (Holliday, 1994). There is no point in adopting a 'best method' or 'innovation' from some organisation or expert if the context in which it is being used has not been considered. As was highlighted in Edge and Mann (2014), this means that:

> "an in-depth appraisal of the context is vital before introducing an innovation. The 'hybrid model' (Henrichsen, 1989) provides a useful system for identifying contextual factors likely to facilitate or hinder the change process and this gives us a good start in responding to Holliday's call for the recognition of the importance of a detailed, ethnomethodological understanding of the innovation situation in making judgements of appropriacy" (p. 38).

It is practitioners who have that detailed up-close understanding of a teaching context (both constraints and affordances).

When we strive for appropriate methodology in terms of what we aim for our teacher trainers to achieve, we move away from the idea of generalised 'best practice' towards 'praxis'. This is essentially where we are situated, functioning in a 'post-method condition' (Kumaravadivelu, 2001). In such a context, there needs to:

> "be a renewed and corresponding recognition of the importance of situated learning and appropriate methodology. In order for appropriate and situated methodology and learning to happen, tools need to be sufficiently flexible that they can be tailored to specific contexts and

> facilitate the kind of up-close professional understanding that CPD was originally designed to foster" (Edge & Mann, 2014, p. 36).

For example, Kurtoğlu-Hooton (2013) shows how innovative tools enable close-up and data-led attention to teaching and CPD potential. Furthermore, teachers need to develop a healthy degree of scepticism towards so called 'best practice' and more importantly, they need to be positioned as innovators and problem solvers.

In 2013, Edge and Mann published a book on innovation in teacher education. One of the key concepts was that a new idea is not the same as an innovation (Edge & Mann, 2013). To be considered an innovation, an action needs to have been taken. We argued that to be truly innovative as practitioners we must concentrate on the process, engage in ongoing self-evaluation and reflection and pay attention to "how we teach or train as to which topics get covered along the way, or the tools that we employ" (Mann & Edge, 2013, p. 5). For this reason, we requested that contributors outline the steps and details of how they introduced, implemented, and evaluated their innovations (Mann & Edge, 2013). For instance, Samb's (2013) article in the book on formative assessment would not be considered by many as a new idea. However, in the Senegal context it is an innovation (Mann, 2013). Similarly, Lesley Dick's (2013) work (see Edge & Mann, 2013) would not be seen as revolutionary. Many trainers and teacher educators have used 'top tips' with their trainees. What makes this an innovation is that Dick's top tips are formulated from trainee led discussions (Mann, 2013). Each time Dick (2013) works with a new group the tips are re-examined and renewed and this gives the feeling that the reflective process of stepping back has become embedded in the task itself. For Dick (2013): "I have used top tips in input sessions and in teaching practice feedback sessions for years but have never really taken a step back and queried why it worked and what it did" (p. 143). Of course, teacher educators can provide top tips, frameworks, models, and examples of good practice. However, at the same time, novice teachers need to be critical and prepared to adapt. Above all, in relation to CPD, they need to be realistic and sensitive to implementation and innovation in their context.

Above, we have highlighted that innovations are not the same as ideas; here, we wish to draw on the Japanese concept of 'kaizen', as we believe it is useful in understanding the kind of innovation that we should be promoting in our work as teacher educators. Kaizen is a Japanese management and business philosophy. It can be translated as kai ('change') and zen ('good') and together it has a metaphorical meaning of 'continuous improvement' and so is very close to the CPD concept (Mann, 2013). The objective of promoting kaizen is to involve and empower all workers in continuously improving the workplace in order to make it more efficient (Mann, 2013). Edge and Mann (2014, p. 40) argue that if we apply the same concept to CPD we can focus on the following:

- the practice of continuous quality improvement within one's teaching;

- innovation is based on many small changes rather than radical changes;

- ideas for change and improvement come from teachers and students themselves; [and]

- teachers take ownership for their work and related improvements.

We believe that focusing on innovation in CPD in this way can be powerful. As many teachers and teacher educators will know, it is not often practical or realistic to make big changes. Furthermore, it is not necessary. Making much smaller changes and adjustments can have a big impact on quality (Edge & Mann, 2014, p. 40). In fact, Jane Willis, (personal correspondence) once highlighted the significance of small tweaks in task-based learning and teaching. These small tweaks and adjustments are forefronted in kaizen as they can have a big future impact (Edge & Mann, 2014).

3.4. Reflective

We have already stated that a teacher becomes an active learner only by trying new things in the classroom as this creates an opportunity for reflection. This is important because RP is essential to teacher development (Farrell, 2019; Mann

& Walsh, 2017). Teachers learn about their own practice by systematically reflecting on their experiences (Richards & Farrell, 2005). While the latter has been known for some time, questions still remain over how opportunities for reflection can be *systematically* provided. In the words of Bailey and Springer (2013), developing "programmatically feasible forms of support for reflective practices that do not detract from a sense of personal initiative, autonomous choice, and ownership by teachers" (p. 120) is challenging. Yet, this is not the only challenge because transmissive styles of education, which were once prevalent, may have made it so that teachers are unfamiliar with reflecting in explicit ways (Mann & Walsh, 2017). In fact, in our experience, we have found that reflection can be difficult to get used to for both novice and experienced teachers. Thus, reflection needs to be appropriately operationalised and it needs to be supported and scaffolded. This is particularly important for novice teachers in pre-service teaching programmes. They need to understand that real reflection and not pseudo reflection (Hobbs, 2007) is an important part of their ongoing CPD. Therefore, before detailing some of the operational aspects of reflection for CPD, we think it is important to make clear that we believe that "reflection is a skill that should be fostered from the beginning of the learning-to-teach process" (Lee, 2007, p. 321). That is to say, it should happen in pre-service preparation programmes and is not only something in-service teachers should be encouraged to do. To highlight the importance of this, we would like to return to our earlier point about 'becoming' and 'continuing'. If teachers are familiarised with reflection from the beginning of their careers, then it is much more likely that they will understand the benefits of reflection, which, in turn, will increase the likelihood that they engage in it for their continuing development. Furthermore, proving this opportunity early on will enhance understanding of "what reflection is and how it might be enhanced for maximum effect" (Hammersley-Fletcher & Orsmond, 2005, p. 222). Russell Stannard provides an example of how screen-capture can be used to foster reflection in this video[8].

As mentioned above, embedding reflective elements in CPD can be challenging as it requires flexibility. If teachers are forced from the top-down to engage in

---

8. https://vilte.warwick.ac.uk/items/show/33

reflection in a prescribed manner, then it is likely that it will become a chore and the result will be superficial engagement and/or inauthentic reflection (Mann & Walsh, 2017). Furthermore, not all tools are sufficiently orientated to a teacher's particular contextual needs. As such, when possible, teachers should be given agency over the tools that they use to reflect. Some of the main reflective tools used to encourage and facilitate reflection are discussion (including teacher discussion groups and post-observation conferences), journal writing, classroom observations, video analysis, and action research (see Farrell, 2016 full range of reflective tools).

Giving teachers ownership over the way they engage in RP can help to ensure that it serves as a means for improving teaching and aiding teachers' professional development. However, when teachers reflect on their own, they face no challenges to their thinking and therefore their reflections can be superficial or shallow (Day, 1993). For this reason, we take the position that reflection is more effective when it is done collaboratively. As highlighted above, collaboration facilitates "new understandings to emerge, current practices to be questioned and alternatives to be explored" (Mann & Walsh, 2017, p. 190). It is also more effective when it is data-led and systematic.

Data-led reflection requires some kind of evidence. This does not have to be evidence from hours and hours of observation or weeks of research. In fact, the kind of data-led reflection we are proposing is "small-scale, localised, context-specific, and private, and conducted by teachers for their own ends" (Walsh & Mann, 2015, p. 354). One of the emerging and promising areas of developing RP is the use of e-portfolios (see also Cuesta, Batlle, González, & Pujolà, 2022, Chapter 7 this volume). In fact, this has the capacity to develop reflection and our next dimension, digital skills. Developing as a professional requires a lifelong commitment to learning and research (Day, 1999) and a portfolio approach to working with novice teachers helps with professional identity building and improvement of reflective skills. It provides a space for pre-service teachers to develop and document good teaching practices and innovation. It also encourages them to make connections between theory and applications, and to sustain professional networks and CoPs beyond the immediate education programme (see Gulzar & Barrett, 2019). Embedding tools like e-portfolios and CD helps foster reflection as an essential part of CPD. These tools also make evident that inquiry and reflection are valued as central professional learning processes by those organising CPD. This, as highlighted by Borg (2015a), can ensure that CPD achieves positive and sustained impacts on teachers, learners, and organisations.

3.5. Digital

Integration of Information and Communications Technology (ICT) is an important element of most recent approaches to CPD. ICT can help to shift the power, control, and agency to the teacher to make decisions about where to place their focus, and improve the inclusivity of professional development (Lightfoot, 2019). It can also make CPD more accessible, as it is not "constrained to a particular time or place" (Ally, Grimus, & Ebner, 2014, p. 48). To put it another way, it can facilitate the type of CPD that we have been promoting throughout this chapter, in the sense of being "site-based" and "self-directed" (Gaible & Burns, 2005, p. 15f.). Over the last few decades, as the world has become ever increasingly digitised, it has become more important to integrate technology in teacher education and development programmes. This is because exposing teachers to such technology will have the impact of improving their digital literacy, which, in turn, can facilitate effective use of technology with learners (Ally et al., 2014).

While there is a large variety of tools (e.g. e-portfolios, blogs, videos) and platforms (e.g. online, mobile, social media) that can be used in the delivery and support of good quality CPD, geographic factors and resources will need to be taken into consideration when deciding which is most suitable for a particular context. In higher resource contexts, there will be a greater opportunity to maximise those that are more complex and that require higher bandwidth whereas in lower resource contexts, the options will be more limited (Lightfoot, 2019). In terms of higher resource contexts, later in this book, in Chapter 7 this volume, Cuesta et al. (2022) discuss how interactive portfolios can be used as learning tools with prospective teachers in higher education institutions. In terms of the way digital tools can be utilised successfully in under-resourced and remote areas, Motteram, Adi, N'goran, and Dawson (2021) and the TATE (Technology Assisted Teacher Education) project are prime examples. In a series of schemes run under the TATE project, WhatsApp has been used to engage teachers, in different geographical areas, including Benin, Cameroon, Côte d'Ivoire (see Motteram & Dawson, 2019), and Jordan (see Motteram, Dawson, & Al-Masri, 2020) in developmental activities. As can be seen from the excerpt below (Table 1), teachers often use the chats to discuss issues they are facing in their classrooms.

Table 1. WhatsApp chat: Syrian teachers discussing a common classroom issue (Motteram et al., 2020, p. 5742)

04/05/2017	18:56	ML	I have many levels in one class .how I can help the weak students with out effect the good students
04/05/2017	19:01	ML	Some students don't know even the letters and some of them don't know the tenses
04/05/2017	19:02	ML	Reported speech for example.
04/05/2017	19:04	GY	So some are beginners and some have some language, is that what you mean?
04/05/2017	19:04	GY	So, what materials do you use with this class, now?
04/05/2017	19:04	GY	What teaching would you do?
04/05/2017	19:11	QM	I think we need more than one way to deal with that problem.
04/05/2017	19:17	ML	I tried to gave the weak students supporting lessons to explain the tense at the beginning then referred it to reported speach
04/05/2017	19:17	QM	We have to divide them and give every group what they need
04/05/2017	19:19	ML	I did it but the good students were not satisfied

As well as providing a space for teachers to expand their pedagogical content knowledge (Motteram et al., 2020), WhatsApp can connect teachers to a wider network who otherwise might be geographically isolated. Of course, there are many more examples of the ways in which digital tools can be incorporated to serve developmental purposes. For advice, activities, courses, and developing engaging materials, we recommend Peachey (2016, 2017).

Chapter 1

One specific tool for CPD that we would like to focus on is the inclusion of video for classroom observation (e.g. Schwab, 2020). This allows for demonstration of real-life situations, provides time for practice and feedback, and can provide ongoing opportunities for follow-up and coaching. When using video in this way, teachers can either watch videos of their own classes or those of others. The benefits of having teachers watch video-recordings of their own lessons is that it provides the opportunity for them to examine different aspects of their teaching (Lofthouse & Birmingham, 2010) and thus can act "as a stimulus for critical reflection" (Orlova, 2009, p. 30). It also enables them to identify any strengths and weaknesses in their teaching (Rich, Recesso, Allexsaht-Snider, & Hannafin, 2007; Tripp, 2009; Wu & Kao, 2008). The advantage of using a video of another teacher (rather than looking at oneself) is that the focus of attention is taken away from one's own pre-occupations and concerns.

When the focus is not on oneself and the teachers plan to meet up with others to discuss their observations (which given the above is unsurprising to find that we recommend), then it will be important to use a framework or checklist to focus the discussion and ensure the discourse is non-judgemental. This can have the benefit of being both collaborative and systematic. For example, the use of a framework such as Steve Walsh's SETT framework (Walsh, 2019) has the capacity to focus attention on a range of classroom interactive behaviours. The process builds awareness of classroom competence (e.g. giving instructions and feedback, and developing rapport). Used in conjunction with a digital tool such as VEO[9] (Seedhouse, 2021) or Swivl[10] (see Oesterle & Schwab, 2022, Chapter 2 this volume), pairs or groups can explore their own efforts in the classroom. Our experience suggests that it is often challenging for novice teachers to find the balance between their talk (teacher talking time), wait time, and other talk types. One of the challenges for teachers is developing sensitivity to both encouraging talking and allowing for silence. Navigating giving instructions, eliciting language and asking questions is not an easy matter, and video can certainly help build greater awareness of classroom options.

---

9. https://veo.co.uk/

10. https://www.swivl.com/

The use of digital video can also provide concrete examples of instructional practices that avoid much of the ambiguity of written descriptions (see Masats & Dooly, 2011). A video extract is not just a 'model' but can provide a strong stimulus for discussion and associated reflective thought for viewers. Hiebert and Hollingsworth (2002) also argue that the educational community lacks a shared language for describing aspects of teaching and that video has a particular role to play here. For example, key phrases such as 'problem-solving' or 'language experience' often mean different things to different teachers. Videotapes of lessons therefore offer the possibility of pinning down aspects of classroom experience so that the teacher has a clearer frame of reference and can therefore be more specific about their own actions and intentions. Video extracts also offer the possibility of co-constructing knowledge through interpretation (see Mann et al., 2019 for more examples from the Video in Language Teacher Education project[11]).

4. Conclusion

In this article we have argued that in order to ensure that CPD is effective and valued, it should be systematic, collaborative, innovative, reflective, and digital. For each dimension, we have given several concrete examples to illustrate the kind of CPD that we are arguing it is necessary to promote. Our decision to include more than one option under each dimension is key to the ethos of this and subsequent chapters. Flexibility over the tools and platforms used for CPD and the way in which CPD is organised and carried out allows for it to be tailored to the specific local, national, or international contexts in which it is happening, and thus to facilitate the kind of up-close professional understanding that it is fundamentally aiming to foster. We have reiterated the idea that when possible, teachers should be given the choice over the way they engage in CPD, and stated that it should be a collective enterprise that is supported by schools and educational systems. When done in this way, we believe that teachers are more likely to have positive perceptions of CPD and that it will therefore have

---

11. https://vilte.warwick.ac.uk/

a greater chance of becoming an ongoing process rather than a periodic event. This, in turn, will increase the likelihood of CPD having a sustained impact on the teachers themselves, the learners they work with, and the organisations in which they work.

5. Key resources

The British Council has lots of CPD publications, resources, and links (including their influential CPD framework – https://www.teachingenglish.org.uk/).

Simon Borg maintains a blog which is full of relevant links and comments to issues in CPD (http://simon-borg.co.uk/).

University of Warwick maintains two CPD resources with links, videos, and publications (https://warwick.ac.uk/fac/soc/al/research/vilte/resources/ – https://vilte.warwick.ac.uk/).

References

Ahmed, E., Nordin, Z., Shah, S., & Channa, M. (2018). Peer observation: a professional learning tool for English language teachers in an EFL institute. *World Journal Of Education*, *8*(2), 73-87. https://doi.org/10.5430/wje.v8n2p73

Al-Habsi, T., Al-Busaidi, S., & Al-Issa, A. (2021). Integrating technology in English language teaching through a community of practice in the Sultanate of Oman: implications for policy implementation. *Educational Research For Policy And Practice*. https://doi.org/10.1007/s10671-021-09291-z

Allier-Gagneur, Z., McBurnie, C., Chuang, R., & Haßler, B. (2020, May). *Characteristics of effective teacher education in low-and middle-income countries. What are they and what role can EdTech play*. EdTech Hub. https://docs.edtechhub.org/lib/R9VVKUH5

Ally, M., Grimus, M., & Ebner, M. (2014). Preparing teachers for a mobile world, to improve access to education. *PROSPECTS*, *44*(1), 43-59. https://doi.org/10.1007/s11125-014-9293-2

Argyris, C., & Schön, D. (1980). *Inner contradictions of rigorous research*. Academic Press.

Atkinson, D. J., & Bolt, S. (2010). Using teaching observations to reflect upon and improve teaching practice in higher education. *Journal of the Scholarship of Teaching and Learning, 10*(3), 1-19.

Bailey, K., & Springer, S. (2013). Reflective teaching as innovation. In K. Hyland & L. Wong (Eds), *Innovation and change in English language education* (pp. 106-122). Routledge.

Bates, C., & Morgan, D. (2018). Seven elements of effective professional development. *The Reading Teacher, 71*(5), 623-626. https://doi.org/10.1002/trtr.1674

Bolitho, R., & A., Padwad. (2013). *Continuing professional development: lessons from India*. British Council.

Boon, A. (2005). Is there anybody out there. *Essential Teacher, 2*(2), 38-41.

Borg, S. (2015a). *Contemporary perspectives on continuing professional development*. British Council. https://www.britishcouncil.in/sites/default/files/contemporary_perspectives_on_cpd.pdf

Borg, S. (2015b). *Teacher cognition and language education: research and practice*. Bloomsbury Publishing.

Borg, S., Lightfoot, A., & Gholkar, R. (2020). *Professional development through teacher activity groups*. https://www.britishcouncil.ro/sites/default/files/teachingenglish_-_professional_development_through_teacher_activity_groups.pdf

British Council. (2016). *Teaching for success*. https://www.britishcouncil.org/sites/default/files/teaching_for_success_brochure.pdf

British Council. (2019). *Continuing professional development (CPD) framework for teachers. Teaching for success* [online]. British Council. https://www.teachingenglish.org.uk/sites/teacheng/files/CPD%20framework%20for%20teachers_WEB.PDF

Broad, K., & Evans, M. (2006). *A review of literature on professional development content and delivery modes for experienced teachers*. Canadian Ministry of Education.

Canagarajah, A. S. (2005). (Ed.). *Reclaiming the local in language policy and practice*. Routledge. https://doi.org/10.4324/9781410611840

Carroll, C., & O'Loughlin, D. (2013). Peer observation of teaching: enhancing academic engagement for new participants. *Innovations in Education and Teaching International, 51*(4), 446-456. https://doi.org/10.1080/14703297.2013.778067

Cordingley, P., Higgins, S., Greany, T., Buckler, N., Coles-Jordan, D., Crisp, B., Saunders, L. A., & Coe, R. (2015). *Developing great teaching: lessons from the international reviews into effective professional development. Project Report*. Teacher Development Trust.

Cosh, J. (1999). Peer observation: a reflective model. *ELT Journal, 53*(1), 22-27. https://doi.org/10.1093/elt/53.1.22

Cuesta, A., Batlle, J., González, V., & Pujolà, J.-T. (2022). Approaches to the development of pre-service language teachers' e-portfolios. In G. Schwab, M. Oesterle & A. Whelan (Eds), *Promoting professionalism, innovation and transnational collaboration: a new approach to foreign language teacher education* (pp. 191-212). Research-publishing.net. https://doi.org/10.14705/rpnet.2022.57.1388

Darling-Hammond, L. (2010). Teacher education and the American future. *Journal of teacher education, 61*(1-2), 35-47. https://doi.org/10.1177/0022487109348024

Day, C. (1993). Reflection: a necessary but not sufficient condition for professional development. *British educational research journal, 19*(1), 83-93.

Day, C. (1999). *Developing teachers: the challenges of lifelong learning.* Falmer Press.

Day, C., & Leitch, R. (2007). The continuing professional development of teachers: issues of coherence, cohesion and effectiveness. In D. Reynolds & C. Teddlie (Eds), *International handbook of school effectiveness and improvement* (pp. 707-726). Springer.

De Vries, S., van de Grift, W. J., & Jansen, E. P. (2014). How teachers' beliefs about learning and teaching relate to their continuing professional development. *Teachers and Teaching, 20*(3), 338-357. https://doi.org/10.1080/13540602.2013.848521

Desimone, L. M. (2011). A primer on effective professional development. *Phi delta kappan, 92*(6), 68-71. https://doi.org/10.1177/003172171109200616

Dick, L. (2013). Top tips: a model for participant-led, shared learning. In J. Edge & S. Mann (Eds), *Innovations in pre-service education and training for English language teachers.* British Council.

Donnelly, R. (2007). Perceived impact of peer observation of teaching in higher education. *International Journal of Teaching and Learning in Higher Education, 19*(2), 117-129.

Edge, J. (1992). *Cooperative development.* Longman.

Edge, J. (2002). *Continuing cooperative development: a discourse framework for individuals as colleagues.* University of Michigan Press. https://doi.org/10.3998/mpub.8915

Edge, J. (2006). Computer-mediated cooperative development: non-judgemental discourse in online environments. *Language Teaching Research, 10*(2), 205-227. https://doi.org/10.1191/1362168806lr192oa

Edge, J., & Attia, M. (2014). Cooperative development: a non-judgemental approach to individual development and increased collegiality. *Actas de las VI y VII jornadas didácticas del instituto cervantes de mánchester*, 65-73.

Edge, J., & Mann, S. (2013). (Eds). *Innovations in pre-service education and training for English language teachers.* British Council.

Edge, J., & Mann, S. (2014). Innovation in the provision of pre-service education andtraining for English language teachers: issues and concerns. In G. Pickering & P. Gunashekar (Eds), *Innovation in English language teacher education.* British Council. https://www.teachingenglish.org.uk/sites/teacheng/files/pub_Tec14%20Papers%20Final%20online.pdf

Edge, J., & K. Richards (1993). (Eds). *Teachers develop teachers research.* Heinemann.

Evans, L. (2002). What is teacher development? *Oxford review of education, 28*(1), 123-137. https://doi.org/10.1080/03054980120113670

Farrell, T. S. (2016). Anniversary article: the practices of encouraging TESOL teachers to engage in reflective practice: an appraisal of recent research contributions. *Language Teaching Research, 20*(2), 223-247. https://doi.org/10.1177/1362168815617335

Farrell, T. (2019). Reflective practice in L2 teacher education. In S. Walsh & S. Mann (Eds), *The Routledge handbook of English language teacher education* (pp. 38-67). Routledge. https://doi.org/10.4324/9781315659824-5

Firestone, A. R., Cruz, R. A., & Rodl, J. E. (2020). Teacher study groups: an integrative literature synthesis. *Review of Educational Research, 90*(5), 675-709. https://doi.org/10.3102/0034654320938128

Forte, A. M., & Flores, M. A. (2014). Teacher collaboration and professional development in the workplace: a study of Portuguese teachers. *European Journal of Teacher Education, 37*(1), 91-105. https://doi.org/10.1080/02619768.2013.763791

Freeman, D. (1982). Observing teachers: three approaches to in-service training and development. *TESOL Quarterly, 16*(1), 21-28. https://doi.org/10.2307/3586560

Freeman, D. (2002). The hidden side of the work: teacher knowledge and learning to teach. *Language teaching, 35*(1), 1-13. https://doi.org/10.1017/S0261444801001720

Gaible, E., & Burns, M. (2005). *Using technology to train teachers: appropriate uses of ICT for teacher professional development in developing countries.* infoDev. https://www.infodev.org/infodev-files/resource/InfodevDocuments_13.pdf

Gosling, D. (2002). *Models of peer observation of teaching.* Paper for LTSN Generic Centre.

Gosling, D. (2015). Collaborative peer-supported review of teaching. *Professional Learning and Development in Schools and Higher Education, 9,* 13-31.

Gulzar, N., & Barrett, H. C. (2019). Implementing ePortfolios in teacher education: research, issues and strategies. In G. Hall (Ed.), *The Routledge handbook of English language teacher education* (pp. 488-506). Routledge. https://doi.org/10.4324/9781315659824-38

Hadfield, J. (1992). *Classroom dynamics.* Oxford University Press.

Hamilton, E. (2013). His ideas are in my head: peer-to-peer teacher observations as professional development. *Professional Development in Education, 39*(1), 42-64.

Hammersley-Fletcher, L., & Orsmond, P. (2005). Reflecting on reflective practices within peer observation. *Studies in Higher Education, 30*(2), 213- 224.

Hayes, D. (2014). *Innovations in the continuing professional development of English language teachers.* British Council.

Hayes, D. (2019). Continuing professional development/continuous professional learning for English language teachers. In S. Walsh & S. Mann (Eds), *The Routledge handbook of English language teacher education* (pp. 155-168). Routledge. https://doi.org/10.4324/9781315659824-14

Henrichsen, L. E. (1989). *Diffusion of innovations in English language teaching: the ELEC effort in Japan, 1956–1968.* Greenwood Press.

Hiebert, J., & Hollingsworth, H. (2002). Learning from international studies of teaching: the TIMSS-R video study. *2002-Providing World-Class School Education, 5.*

Hobbs, V. (2007). Faking it or hating it: can reflective practice be forced? *Reflective practice, 8*(3), 405-417. https://doi.org/10.1080/14623940701425063

Holliday, A. (1994). *Appropriate methodology and social context.* Cambridge University Press.

James, P. (2001). *Teachers in action.: tasks for in-service language teacher education and development.* Cambridge University Press.

Joyce, B. R., & Showers, B. (2002). *Student achievement through staff development* (3rd ed.). Association for Supervision and Curriculum Development.

Kane, R., Sandetto, S., & Heath, C. (2002). Telling half the story: a critical review of research on the teaching beliefs and practices of university academics. *Review of Educational Research, 72,* 177-228. https://doi.org/10.3102/00346543072002177

Kaymakamoglu, S. E. (2018). Teachers' beliefs, perceived practice and actual classroom practice in relation to traditional (teacher-centered) and constructivist (learner-centered) teaching (note 1). *Journal of Education and Learning, 7*(1), 29-37.

Kumaravadivelu, B. (2001). Toward a postmethod pedagogy. *TESOL Quarterly, 35*(4), 537-560. https://doi.org/10.2307/3588427

Kurtoğlu-Hooton, N. (2013). Providing 'the spark' for reflection from a digital platform. In J. Edge & S. Mann (Eds), *Innovations in pre-service education and training for English language teachers* (pp. 17-32). British Council.

Lamb, M. (1995). The consequences of INSET. *ELT Journal, 49*(1), 72-80.

Lamb, M., & Wyatt, M. (2019). Teacher motivation: the missing ingredient in teacher education. In S. Walsh & S. Mann (Eds), *The Routledge handbook of English language teacher education* (pp. 522-535). Routledge. https://doi.org/10.4324/9781315659824-41

Lee, I. (2007). Preparing pre-service English teachers for reflective practice. *ELT Journal, 61*(4), 321-329. https://doi.org/10.1093/elt/ccm022

Lightfoot, A. (2019). ICT and English language teacher education. In S. Walsh & S. Mann (Eds), *The Routledge handbook of English language teacher education* (pp. 52-67). Routledge. https://doi.org/10.4324/9781315659824-6

Lofthouse, R., & Birmingham, P. (2010). The camera in the classroom: video-recording as a tool for professional development of student teachers. *Teacher Education Advancement Network Journal, 1*(2). https://eprints.ncl.ac.uk/167882

Madzgalj, V., & Kandybovich, S. (2018) *Continuing professional development for vocational teachers and principals in Montenegro.* https://www.etf.europa.eu/en/publications-and-resources/publications/continuing-professional-development-vocational-teachers-9

Maley, A. (2016). More research is needed–a mantra too far. *Humanising Language Teaching, 18*(3).

Mann, S. (2002). Talking ourselves into understanding. In K. E. Johnson & P. R. Golombek (Eds), *Teachers' narrative inquiry as professional development* (pp.195-209). Cambridge University Press.

Mann, S. (2005). The language teacher's development. *Language Teaching, 38*(3), 103-118.

Mann, S. (2013). Kaizen and appropriate methodology: innovation in the provision of pre-service education and training for English language teachers. In S. Velikova, Z. Markova & T. Harakchiyska (Eds), *Openness and connectedness: exploring the landscape of English language teaching in the modern world.* 22nd Annual International Conference of BETA-IATEFL. https://www.beta-iatefl.org/wp-content/uploads/2013/10/Newsletter_September-October-2013.pdf

Mann, S. (2021). *Understanding the effectiveness of professional development opportunities for teachers delivered remotely.* British Council. https://www.teachingenglish.org.uk/sites/teacheng/files/Effectiveness_remotely_delivered_professional_development_teachers.pdf

Mann, S., Davidson, A., Davis, M., Gakonga, J., Gamero, M., Harrison, T., & Mosavian, P. (2019). Video in language teacher education. *ELT Research Papers.* https://www.teachingenglish.org.uk/sites/teacheng/files/J201%20ELT%20Video%20in%20language%20teacher%20education%20FINAL_Web.pdf

Mann, S., & Edge, J. (2013). Innovation as action new-in-context – an introduction to the PRESETT collection. In J. Edge & S. Mann (Eds), *Innovations in pre-service education and training for English language teachers* (pp. 5-13). British Council.

Mann, S., & Walsh, S. (2017). *Reflective practice in English language teaching* (1st ed.). Routledge. https://doi.org/10.4324/9781315733395-1

Masats, D., & Dooly, M. (2011). Rethinking the use of video in teacher education: a holistic approach. *Teaching and Teacher Education, 27*(7), 1151-1162. https://doi.org/10.1016/j.tate.2011.04.004

McAleavy, T., Hall-Chen, A., Horrocks, S., & Riggall, A. (2018). *Technology-supported professional development for teachers: lessons from developing countries.* Education Development Trust (UK).

Moon, J. A. (2001). *Short courses and workshops: improving the impact of learning, training and professional development.* Kogan Page.

Motteram, G., Adi, A., N'goran, M., & Dawson, S. (2021). *TATE project*. https://tateproject.wordpress.com/about/

Motteram, G., & Dawson, S. (2019). *Resilience and language teacher development in challenging contexts: supporting teachers through social media.* British Council.

Motteram, G., Dawson, S., & Al-Masri, N. (2020). *WhatsApp* supported language teacher development: a case study in the Zataari refugee camp. *Education and Information Technologies, 25*, 5731-5751. https://doi.org/10.1007/s10639-020-10233-0

Oesterle, M., & Schwab, G. (2022). Developing a framework of CPD for the context of foreign language teaching. In G. Schwab, M. Oesterle & A. Whelan (Eds), *Promoting professionalism, innovation and transnational collaboration: a new approach to foreign language teacher education* (pp. 45-79). Research-publishing.net. https://doi.org/10.14705/rpnet.2022.57.1383

Orlova, N. (2009). Video recording as a stimulus for reflection in pre-service EFL teacher training. *English Teaching Forum, 2*, 30-35.

Orr, D., Westbrook, J., Pryor, J., Durrani, N., Sebba, J., & Adu-Yeboah, C. (2013). *What are the impacts and cost effectiveness of strategies to improve performance of untrained and under-trained teachers in the classroom in developing countries? A systematic review.* EPPICentre, University of London.

P'Rayan, A. (2013). Peer observation of teaching: a tool for professional development. *English for Specific Purposes World, 14*(39), 45-54.

Peachey, N. (2016). *Thinking critically through digital media.* PeacheyPublications Ltd.

Peachey, N. (2017). *Digital tools for teachers.* PeacheyPublications. Com.

Prabhu, N. (1990). There is no best method – why? *TESOL Quarterly, 24*(2), 161-176. https://doi.org/10.2307/3586897

Rich, P., Recesso, A., Allexsaht-Snider, M., & Hannafin, M. J. (2007). *The use of video-based evidence to analyze, act on, and adapt preservice teacher practice.* American educational research association American Educational Research Association.

Richards, K. (2003). *Qualitative inquiry in TESOL.* Springer.

Richards, J., C., & Farrell, T., S. C. (2005). *Professional development for language teachers.* Cambridge University Press. https://doi.org/10.1017/CBO9780511667237

Samb, M. (2013). Formative assessment for a pedagogy of success. In J. Edge & S. Mann (Eds), *Innovations in pre-service education and training for English language teachers.* British Council.

Schwab, G, (2020). Introduction: classroom observation revisited. In F. Lenz, M. Frobenius & R. Klattenberg (Eds), *Classroom observation: researching interaction in English language teaching* (pp. 9-29). Peter Lang.

Seedhouse, P. (2021). *Video enhanced observation for language teaching* (1st ed). Bloomsbury Publishing. https://doi.org/10.5040/9781350085060

Showers, B., & Joyce, B. (1996). The evolution of peer coaching. *Educational leadership, 53*, 12-16.

Tang, E., Lee, J. C., & Chun, C. (2012). Development of teaching beliefs and the focus of change in the process of pre-service ESL teacher education. *Australian Journal of Teacher Education, 37*(5), 90-107. https://doi.org/10.14221/ajte.2012v37n5.8

Timperley, H., Wilson, A., Barrar, H., & Fung, I. (2008). *Teacher professional learning and development: best evidence synthesis iteration (BES).* New Zealand Ministry of Education.

Tripp, T. R. (2009). *Understanding the use of video analysis tools to facilitate reflection among pre-service teachers.* Unpublished Master's Thesis, Brigham Young University.

Wallace, M. J., & Bau, T. H. (1991). *Training foreign language teachers: a reflective approach.* Cambridge University Press.

Walsh, S. (2002). Construction or obstruction: teacher talk and learner involvement in the EFL classroom. *Language teaching research, 6*(1), 3-23.

Walsh, S. (2019). SETTVEO: evidence-based reflection and teacher development. *Teaching English ELT Research Papers, 19*, 1-24.

Walsh, S., & Mann, S. (2015). Doing reflective practice: a data-led way forward. *Elt Journal, 69*(4), 351-362. https://doi.org/10.1093/elt/ccv018

Walsh, S., & Mann, S. (2019). *The Routledge handbook of English language teacher education*. Routledge.

Wang, W., & Day, C. (2001, February 27 – March 3). *Issues and concerns about classroom observation: teachers' perspectives* [Conference Presentation]. Annual Meeting of the Teachers of English to Speakers of Other Languages (TESOL), St. Louis, MO.

Webb, K. (2020). Peer observation for development: if you don't have the right ingredients, you can't cook the dish. *ELTED, 23*, 48-60.

Webb, K., Mann, S., & Aqili-Shafie, K., (2022). *Using computer-mediated cooperative development in a virtual reflective environment among English language teachers*. Springer.

Wedell, M. (2009). *Planning for educational change: putting people and their contexts first*. Bloomsbury.

Wenger, E. (2011). *Communities of practice: a brief introduction.* https://scholarsbank.uoregon.edu/xmlui/bitstream/handle/1794/11736/A%20brief%20introduction%20to%20CoP.pdf

Weston, D., Hindley, B., & Cunningham, M. (2019). *A culture of improvement: reviewing the research on teacher working conditions*. https://tdtrust.org/coi/

Wright, T., & Bolitho, R. (2007). *Trainer development.* Lulu.com.

Wu, C., & Kao, H. (2008). Streaming video in peer assessment to support training pre-service teachers. *Educational Technology & Society, 11*(1), 45-55.

Wyatt, M., & Dikilitaş, K. (2016). English language teachers becoming more efficacious through research engagement at their Turkish university. *Educational Action Research, 24*(4), 550-570. https://doi.org/10.1080/09650792.2015.1076731

2 Developing a framework of CPD for the context of foreign language teaching

Mareike Oesterle[1] and Götz Schwab[2]

1. Introduction

"When learning is at the centre of the teaching enterprise we would assume that the continuing professional development of teachers would be a priority of both education system and teachers alike" (Sachs, 2007, p. 1).

Figure 1. proPIC handbook QR Code

Based on large-scale surveys, it has become evident that the teacher has a major impact on the learning processes and outcomes of the pupils (Hattie, 2009). Transnationally, the impact of the teacher has been widely acknowledged (Day, 2017; European Council, 2009; Lortie, 1975). Many authors suggest that

---

1. University of Education Ludwigsburg, Ludwigsburg, Germany; mareike.oesterle@gmx.de; https://orcid.org/0000-0002-9458-7927

2. University of Education Ludwigsburg, Ludwigsburg, Germany; goetz.schwab@ph-ludwigsburg.de; https://orcid.org/0000-0003-0939-3325

How to cite: Oesterle, M., & Schwab, G. (2022). Developing a framework of CPD for the context of foreign language teaching. In G. Schwab, M. Oesterle & A. Whelan (Eds), *Promoting professionalism, innovation and transnational collaboration: a new approach to foreign language teacher education* (pp. 45-79). Research-publishing.net. https://doi.org/10.14705/rpnet.2022.57.1383

Continuing Professional Development (CPD) is a process that takes place within a particular context and that is most effective when related to the daily activities of teachers and learners (Fullan, 2007; Richards & Farrell, 2005). It is considered a long-term process and that teachers learn over time. CPD is therefore seen as an essential process of a teacher's career to gain a lifelong learning perspective and to be able to adapt to the fast changes in society (European Commission, 2021b; Nitsche, 2014). Looking at relevant literature in the field of teacher education, one finds many definitions and interpretations of the term CPD. Especially in recent years, CPD and related terms such as *on-going teacher development*, *continuous learning*, or just *professional development*, have frequently been used as buzzwords or as referring to Kelchtermans (2004, p. 217) so-called 'container concepts' in teacher education (see also Mann & Webb, 2022, Chapter 1 this volume). Yet, what exactly lies behind these terms and what does CPD look like when put in practice?

In the context of the proPIC project, we combined a variety of theoretical perspectives and approaches to develop a CPD framework for English language teacher education. This framework serves as a theoretical basis for the proPIC study programme (Hoinke & Clausen, 2022, Chapter 3 this volume) and was created in the form of a multimodal online handbook (scan QR code). In the course of the proPIC project, the CPD framework – or at least major parts of it – were introduced three times to three cohorts of students of foreign language teacher education at five different partner institutions across Europe.

The final version consists of diverse digital documents and other external online resources. It can be described as a multimodal catalogue in the form of a working document, including concrete suggestions on how to embed it in foreign language teacher education. This catalogue combines the following elements:

- the conceptualising of CPD in the context of foreign and second language learning and teaching at university level;

- the discourse on a professional identity of foreign and second language teacher educators;

- didactic comments comprising a selection of innovative strategies, activities, and methods in order to promote CPD in the context of foreign and second language learning and teaching at university level; and

- the promotion and integration of transnational, multilingual networks not only among the teacher educators, but also at a student level with the help of mobile apps like Slack or Google Docs.

The aim of this chapter is to outline the overall structure, as well as individual elements of the CPD framework (see Figure 2) developed in the course of the proPIC project. To illustrate our concept, we will introduce five sessions of it in more detail.

Figure 2. Overview CPD framework

```
• session 1: What is CPD?                Module I.B
• session 2: CPD as language teachers
• session 3: reflective practices and tools
• session 4: dialogic reflection
• session 5: practitioner research
• session 6: challenges for CPD
• develop your research project
```

We have identified each section of this chapter according to the sessions of the framework. All sessions are comprised of theoretical perspectives and approaches, as well as didactic comments that illustrate some of the practice-oriented examples being called *cases* and a number of interactive and/or individual tasks. These comments further entail some results developed by the participating students during the sessions. Based on this information, we will introduce and discuss the feedback received from the participating students, as well as evaluative data from the project partners that was collected in the course of the project. In the final section, we will conclude with suggestions for improvement and further implementation in other or similar contexts.

Chapter 2

1.1. Didactic comments

Most of the sessions begin with a stimulating question or answer, which then commences an individual or collective task. This introductory phase can serve as either repetitive, motivating, preparative, or cumulative (Wahl, 2006, p. 121 ff.). We further include multimodal elements to introduce the different sessions, e.g. short video clips or excerpts from research studies.

In between the theoretical inputs, the students are asked to engage in a variety of interactive tasks. Either in the context of those tasks or in connection to the theoretical inputs, they are further introduced to a variety of practical *cases*. One case shows for, instance, how in-service teachers practise dialogic reflection. With these cases, we plan to promote evidence-based and content-specific interactions. We consider a case to be a diverse, multi-perspective, and multimodal representation of practical examples as a key to a controversial exchange between students. Throughout the sessions, we further make use of a variety of methods and didactic approaches. Some examples will be described in the following sections.

Figure 3. Students working collaboratively on their e-portfolio[3]

To facilitate an active and multi-perspective discourse between the students, the whole framework is based on collaborative teaching and learning. In order to

---

3. Republished from http://www.propiceuropa.com/best-practice-examples.html

engage in processes of CPD in their later work life, we consider it crucial that pre-service teachers get the chance to voice their own ideas and opinions freely. Moreover, we believe that the use of content-specific and professional language needs to be practised and used more often to be ultimately finally internalised.

As the nature of the study programme (see Hoinke & Clausen, 2022, Chapter 3 this volume) is highly research-oriented, we believe it is central to include research findings, some sort of *evidence* in the content of the CPD framework. Thus, the prospective teachers are given a variety of problem-oriented assignments which are connected to any kind of data (e.g. interview excerpts, video clips, audio sequences). Since the beginning of the last century, Dewey (1997) describes reflection as follows:

> "[r]eflection thus implies that something is believed in (or disbelieved in), not on its own direct account, but through something else which stands as witness, evidence, proof, voucher, warrant; that is, as ground of belief" (p. 8).

In his work, he stresses the importance of including evidence in the process of reflection. As we aim at promoting CPD among future language teachers, we think it is necessary to implement data-led reflection beginning in pre-service teacher programmes. Teachers need to learn how to reflect effectively in order to engage in processes of professional development throughout their work life. The importance of data-led reflection is also stressed by Mann and Walsh (2017) who state that "data-led discussions of practice are a means of promoting deep (as opposed to surface) reflection" (p. 29).

Especially due to the COVID-19 pandemic, the use of mobile technologies and innovative teaching and learning methods have become inevitable. However, even before the pandemic, digital learning had become crucial and necessary for creating successful teaching and learning environments. In 2010, Burden stresses the importance of supporting teachers and teacher educators "to understand and embrace the processes of change" (p. 148), particularly in regard to teaching about and with digital technologies. Thus, promoting digital competences and skills of pre- and in-service teachers has become a crucial element of their on-going professional development (European Commission, 2021a). In the proPIC project, the integration of mobile technologies therefore became another major element of the CPD framework that was developed. It comprises a variety of digital tools and multimodal resources that proved to be beneficial and that we consider helpful for professional learning and development.

Yet, we would like to emphasise that we do not only intend to promote teaching and learning *with* but also *about* mobile technologies. The practical application as well as the critical dialogue are at the centre of this framework. In the course of each session, we intend to create *spaces* where the students try out and use a range of different mobile technologies and create innovative digital outputs against the background of their future profession. Thus, next to providing a theoretical basis of CPD in foreign and second language learning and teaching, we included a variety of context-specific innovative methods and approaches using digital tools (e.g. interactive e-books, video papers, individual and collaborative e-portfolios, film productions or best-practice examples of educational apps, and innovative tools).

2. Session 1: What is CPD?

The authors Day and Sachs (2005) describe CPD as "all the activities in which teachers engage during the course of a career which are designed to enhance their work" (p. 3). This rather short definition goes along with Day's (1999) earlier work, in which he claims that this process is never completed and should take place throughout the whole academic lifespan of a teacher. He describes CPD as the following:

> "[professional development] is the process by which, alone and with others, teachers review, renew and extend their commitment as change agents to the moral purposes of teaching; and by which they acquire and develop critically the knowledge, skills and emotional intelligence essential to good professional thinking, planning and practice with

children, young people and colleagues through each phase of their teaching lives" (Day, 1999, p. 4).

Both Day (1999) and Sachs (2007) emphasise the active engagement of teachers as an essential step towards CPD. Moreover, the two authors claim that change is central to the teaching profession. Teachers must act as change agents and actively respond to change, which requires flexibility and openness (Day, 1999; Sachs, 2007). Just like other professionals, teachers "need to update their skill and knowledge base" (Sachs, 2007, p. 9). As such, CPD comprises the individual engagement with this topic. Most important, however, is the interactionist character of CPD (Kelchtermans, 2007). In order to be efficient, CPD must be an "open and trusting dialogue about teaching and learning with colleagues and outside facilitators" (Sachs, 2007, p. 16).

In contrast to Day and Sachs (2005) who deal with the professional development of teachers in general and address various contexts, Mann and Walsh (2017) look into the CPD of English language teachers. Focusing on *reflective practices*, they argue that professional development is about developing a distinct 'mindset', a professional habit or attitude to constantly strive to learn and develop.

From a political viewpoint, CPD is seen as essential to improvements in the teaching and learning quality. It is thus increasingly supported through a variety of activities such as, for example, training courses or (online) workshops. However, one issue is that these activities are often rather managerial. According to Day and Sachs (2005), this so-called "managerial professionalism" (p. 7) leaves no room for teachers to become actively involved in and take control of their own CPD. They merely act as consumers. Instead, Day and Sachs (2005) call for a "democratic professionalism" (p. 7). This form emphasises dialogic and collaborative formats. It further insists that professional development should be profession-driven and contextual.

Important CPD activities for teachers include updating their knowledge and skills, reflective activities, and collaboration among colleagues (Leliveld, Van Tartwijk, Verloop, & Bolk, 2008). That is, updating activities provides a basic grounding for reflection and collaboration (Cheetham & Chivers, 2001); reflective activities in turn appear essential for professional growth (Eraut, 1994; Schön, 1983). What further activities can a teacher's development include? The British Council (2017) has provided a variety of ideas which are summarised below:

- talk, discuss, and collaborate with colleagues;
- participate in a face-to-face, online, or blended workshop or course;
- participate in seminars and conferences;
- read professional magazines, journals, and books;
- watch 'professional' videos;
- experiment with new resources and ideas in the classroom;
- keep a reflective CPD diary or journal; and
- carry out small-scale classroom-based research.

A final comment on these activities: although these ideas might seem too far-fetched for a single teacher, they could serve as a blueprint for further discussions on what steps should be taken in regard to one's individual CPD.

At the beginning of the first session, the students are asked the following question and given the following task:

> *What does CPD include and mean to you as a future language teacher?*
>
> Please – in teams – write down 15-20 words that come to your mind reading this question. Cut them out and make a 'concept' with them. Explain your concept to another team and vice versa. Please video-record this explanation and share it on your e-portfolio.

With this task, we intend to encourage the students to verbalise their thoughts and experiences. This is based on the assumption of Mann and Walsh (2017) that "professional development occurs through talk, especially talk between peers who jointly create understandings of complex phenomena" (p. 252). It is our intention to activate the students' previous knowledge, and to motivate and engage them in collaborative learning. Through this task, the students become acquainted with other perspectives and opinions. They can resolve possible disputes or misunderstandings and externalise their knowledge, as well as their professional experiences.

Figure 4. The concept map of a group of students[4]

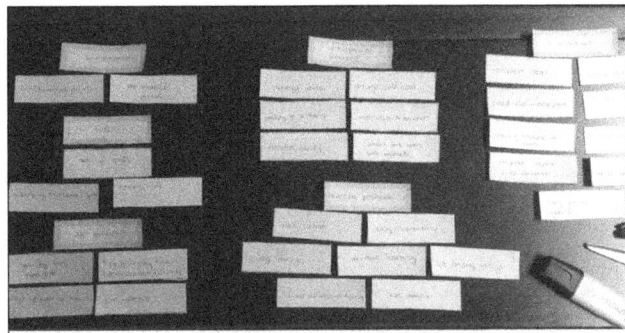

Creative task

In this activity we reflected about Continuing Professional Development (CPD). In a first step we collected some general ideas and terms that we related to this method. We then shared our thoughts with the group and sorted them in different categories. In a final step we added a headline for each of these categories and highlighted them.

To illustrate the theoretical input given in this session, several practical cases are presented. One *case* in this session gives an example of CPD. The school uses VEO to support the teachers in their own CPD. The students are then asked to discuss and to further describe whether they have already come across facets of CPD in their own studies. Another *case* shows two video examples of data-led CPD, using video to reflect on teaching and learning (TeachingChannel, 2018a, 2018b). To give an example of collaborative CPD, two videos are included.

---
4. Republished from https://sites.google.com/view/our-ph-portfolio/in-class-activities?authuser=0

The first is made by Teachers TV/UK Department of Education (Teachers TV/ UK Department of Education, 2008); the second video is called 'Teachers Lab: Making Professional Development Collaborative' (Edutopia, 2017). Both show how CPD can take place at school and identify school leaders as critical when it comes to implementing CPD effectively. This viewpoint is also supported by Mann and Walsh (2017) who describe leadership as one key consideration when planning effective CPD.

3. Session 2: CPD as language teachers

Although the importance of the CPD of teachers has increased during the last 30 years, it has mainly been dealt with in educational studies. Within the field of literature, there is a lack of theoretical perspectives and empirical research on CPD in subject-specific contexts that can be applied, for example, in the field of language learning and teaching (Allwright, 1999; Borko, 2004; Crandall & Christison, 2016; Freeman & Johnson, 1998). These fields are often limited to their own traditions (see Richards & Farrell, 2005).

Further, the integration and combination of innovative and subject-specific ways of teaching and learning using mobile technologies or establishing professional networks have not yet become an integral part of the CPD of teachers. Many are still struggling with effective pedagogical approaches in the context of this new learning and teaching culture (Burden & Kearney, 2016; Estapa, Pinnow, & Chval, 2016; McLoughlin & Lee, 2009).

In addition to the above-mentioned characteristics of CPD, there are two aspects that we think are crucial concerning the development of (future) language teachers.

3.1. Multilingual and intercultural learning

Due to an increasing motility, there is a general expanse of multilingual classrooms, not only in the EU, but also beyond. However, looking at the

European Context, the number of students speaking a different mother tongue has gone up significantly: "in the EU as a whole, just under 10% of all students learn in a language other than their mother tongue" (European Commission, 2021c). In 2013, only about 5% of students spoke a different language at home than at school (cf. European Commission, 2015). We argue that language teachers in particular need to become aware of this linguistic diversity and actively design classrooms that promote multilingual and intercultural learning. In line with the European Centre for Modern Languages of the Council of Europe[5] (ECML, 2021), we believe that (future) language teachers must take a holistic approach to language teaching and learning. The integration of transnational and multilingual networks therefore becomes crucial to foster motivation, intercultural learning, communicative skills, competence and performance, and further professional development (Davies, 2007; Laakkonen, 2011). Professional networks that go beyond one's own institutional or national context can further promote the exchange of best-practice examples. This can lead to an authentic collection of effective possibilities for learning and teaching a foreign and second language from which everyone could benefit.

3.2. Didactic comments

The second session starts with a short brainstorming phase. The students are asked how language teachers in particular can enhance their CPD and to discuss these aspects in regard to their own context(s). The students are further asked to record this discussion and upload it to their e-portfolio (see Figure 5).

Figure 5. A podcast created by three students from the University of Education Karlsruhe and the QR Code to open it

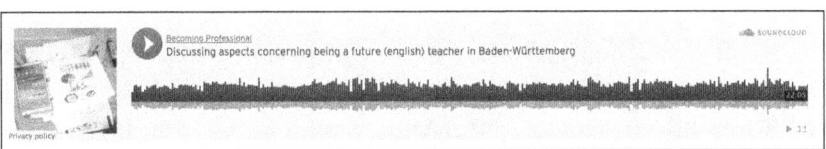

---

5. https://www.ecml.at/

Figure 6. A video clip produced by three international students talking about CPD in regard to their own context[6]

There have been striking commonalities among the participating students from all partner institutions, most of them emphasising the following aspects:

- engage in formal professional learning opportunities (e.g. specific teacher training courses);
- read academic literature;
- observe colleagues/be observed and give/receive feedback;
- collaborate with colleagues;
- get to know your students and their needs (e.g. collect their feedback);
- reflect on your teaching; and

---

6. Republished from https://sites.google.com/view/our-ph-portfolio/in-class-activities?authuser=0

- go abroad from time to time.

We noted that what the students believe could enhance language teachers' CPD and can, to a certain degree, be applied to teachers of any subject or discipline (i.e. to communicate with other teachers; read research articles; attend workshops and trainings; reflect). The answers also reflect the general challenge that some authors describe (Blömeke, 2001; Gerlach, 2020), which is to extract subject-specific elements of CPD.

Figure 7. A Padlet created as part of the CPD framework

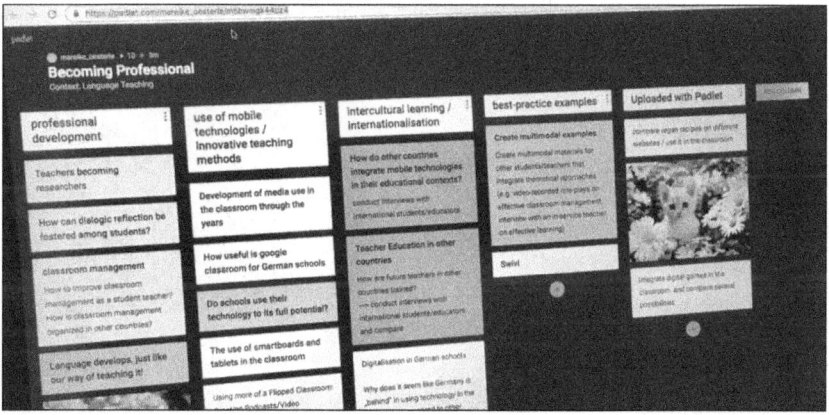

A practical *case* from these sessions presents two vignettes taken from Mann and Walsh (2017). These vignettes contain written feedback and illustrate reflective practices in the context of language teacher education. The students are asked to read the vignettes and to note aspects that they find effective, questionable, or critical, and to discuss them in teams.

In the proPIC project, English was used as a *lingua franca*, which brought an added value to the project as partners and students were able to improve their language skills. However, the focus did not lay on a particular language that is learned and taught, but rather on how a foreign language is learned and taught at different institutions in general. By enhancing intercultural understanding and

Chapter 2

multilingualism in foreign language teacher education (e.g. through the study week, Schwab & Oesterle, 2022, Chapter 4 this volume), the project met the needs of a changing and diverse society. It emphasises the need for language teachers to not only encourage their students "to draw upon all of their linguistic and cultural resources and experiences in order to fully participate in social and educational contexts, achieving mutual understanding, gaining access to knowledge and in turn further developing their linguistic and cultural repertoire" (Council of Europe, 2018, p. 157), but also to practise what they preach and to engage in intercultural experiences whenever possible.

Figure 8. A Flipgrid created to promote transnational collaboration

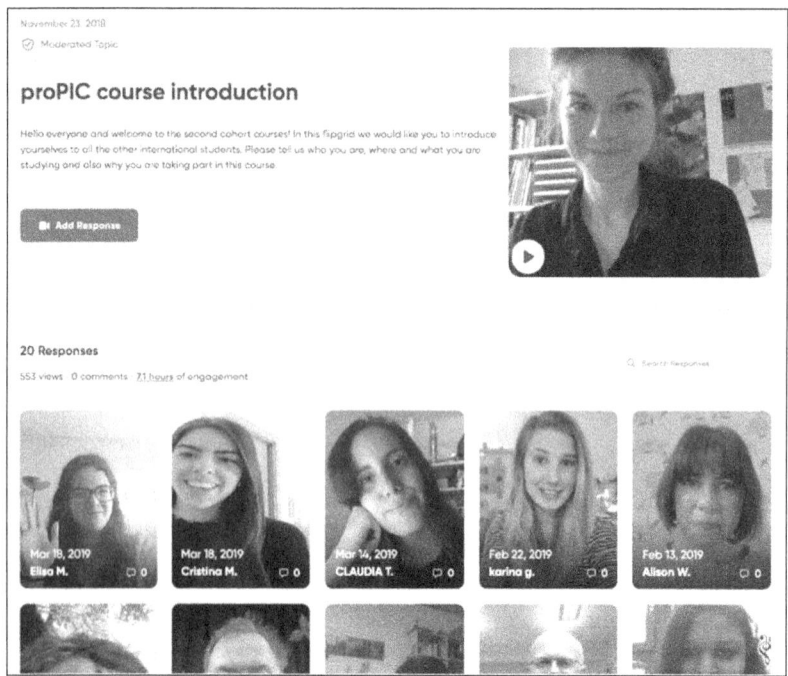

To initiate transnational collaboration before the study week and as part of the CPD framework, all students were asked to take part in a number of tasks and activities together with students from the other partner institutions. These

activities included, for example, getting in touch with other students on Slack, which was used as a main communication platform in the course of the project. Another platform which we used to engage the students in transnational collaboration was Flipgrid (see Figure 8 above).

4. Sessions 3-5: reflective practice

The importance for teachers to reflect on how they work has widely been acknowledged in regard to their professional development. Reflection has become a key competence in pre-service teacher education, as well as in in-service teacher training (Holdsworth, 2021; Loughran, 2002; Mann & Walsh, 2017). Despite this acknowledgement, however, the concept of reflective practice is still not clear and agreed upon as it carries a range of diverse meanings and understandings (Holdsworth, 2021). According to Beauchamp (2015), it seems that "[e]ven those who promote it do not completely understand the term" (p. 123).

In our framework, we have introduced a number of definitions to approach the rather complex concept of reflection, inspired by Dewey (1997) who described it as 'hesitation' or 'a state of perplexity' which is an essential first step towards "turning one's head" (p. 9), i.e. identifying a problem or asking a question that can then lead into an act of search or investigation.

Further, Mann and Walsh (2017) present four major principles that are relevant to reflective practice. Based on Vygotsky's socio-cultural theory, Mann and Walsh (2017) highlight the crucial role that **social interaction** plays in regard to CPD: "understanding and knowledge are 'publicly derived' but 'privately internalized'" (p. 11). In order to learn and develop, teachers need to interact with others. Thus "learning takes place through our participation in multiple social practices, practices which are formed through pursuing any kind of enterprise over time" (Farnsworth, Kleanthous, & Wenger-Trayner, 2016, p. 3). Knowledge and new experiences need dialogue and discussion – they need to be verbalised – to be understood and reflected: "[e]ssentially, through dialogue, professional development is mediated by language; new understandings emerge through conversations with other professionals, through experience and reflection on that experience" (Mann & Walsh, 2017, p. 12).

Another major principle of reflective practice, according to Mann and Walsh (2017), is the use of **data-led accounts**. These accounts are necessary to "provide the kind of evidence which promotes understanding of reflection. Data-led accounts help us acquire the close-up understandings of our professional practice" (Mann & Walsh, 2017, p. 17). This data can vary from audio and video recordings to journal extracts and/or feedback from students or colleagues. According to the authors, this process is mediated through certain tools and techniques: "[d]evelopment may be assisted by **scaffolding**" (p. 11).

Furthermore, Mann and Walsh (2017) claim that "[t]hrough discussion, dialogue and reflection, new understandings are **appropriated**" (p. 12). This last principle is supported by Farnsworth et al. (2016), who state: "[i]f a really important part of learning is the shaping of an identity, then one key implication for education is that you cannot give people knowledge without inviting them into an identity for which this knowledge represents a meaningful way of being" (p. 8). It is crucial that teachers internalise new knowledge and understand it as a part of their own professional identity.

In line with the work of Mann and Walsh (2017), we believe that reflection always needs to be put into practice. As reflective practice is a complex concept, it should be understood as a holistic approach to professional development, not as a single method or tool (Farrell, 2008). However, reflective practice needs to be scaffolded through tools and activities, as well as supported through some sort of evidence and reflective talk.

4.1. Reflective tools

Based on several authors (Farrell, 2008; Mann & Walsh, 2017), this session further introduces a number of reflective tools to promote and engage in reflective practice (Table 1).

Table 1. Reflective Tools

Written reflection	Spoken reflection
• Diaries, journals, and portfolios	• Dialogic reflection (e.g. conversations with colleagues)
• Folder systems (Google Drive, Dropbox)	• Voice memos, voice apps
• Checklists, forms	• Video recordings
• e-portfolios (e.g. OneNote, blogs, iBook Author)	

As a special focus lies on the integration of digital tools, it was our aim to give the participating students the opportunity to try out a range of different online tools and applications. One example is presented in Figure 9 where a group of students used WhatsApp to create a theory-based interview scenario talking about 'Teachers as Researchers', which they then uploaded on their e-portfolio.

Figure 9. Using WhatsApp to present an interview scenario on 'Teachers as Researchers'[7]

4.2. Dialogic reflection

Talking to and collaborating with others are often key elements of reflective processes, allowing

> "new understandings to emerge, current practices to be questioned and alternatives to be explored. The very act of talking[ing] through a recent

---

7. Republished from http://www.propiceuropa.com/best-practice-examples.html

experience, e.g. a segment of one's teaching, facilitates reflection and may ultimately result in changes to practise" (Mann & Walsh, 2017, p. 189).

As already indicated, the importance of collaboration is stressed in the literature, based on the assumption that knowledge and learning are embedded in social contexts and experiences and promoted through interactive, reflective exchanges. Even though there may be opportunities for individual reflection, research suggests that most effective CPD occurs through meaningful interaction (Clement & Vandenberghe, 2000). There is a growing awareness of the potential of teacher collaboration for encouraging teacher learning (Westheimer, 2008). Fraser, Kennedy, Reid, and McKinney (2007) suggest that CPD based on collaborative enquiry most likely leads to transformational educational practices. The key conditions for effective collaborative learning include "shared purpose and vision, an explicit focus on learning (as opposed to merely doing), and mutual trust and respect: purpose, focus and relationships" (Kennedy, 2011, p. 4). McLoughlin and Lee (2009) criticise the fact that collaboration and professional networks have not yet become an integral part of the CPD of teachers and teacher educators. In the area of pre-service teaching and teacher education for prospective language teachers, research points to the importance of transnational, multilingual networks in fostering motivation, intercultural learning, communicative skills, competence, and performance (Laakkonen, 2011). Here, the exchange of best-practice examples can lead to an authentic collection of effective affordances of learning and teaching a foreign and second language in higher education. Research shows, however, that teacher education is still nationally oriented and overly dependent on national policies, which restricts transnational cooperation (Goetz, Jaritz, & Oser, 2011; Jaritz, 2011).

4.3. Practitioner research

Key to successful reflection is the integration of more concrete and data-led accounts (Mann & Walsh, 2017). Mann (2005), for example, describes practitioner research as a "desirable option for development" (p. 108) with the intention to solve a problem and enhance professional practices, thus being guided by a specific question or doubt. Action research is a specific form of practitioner research, referring to a combination of action and research; using each to inform the other, to observe, plan, implement, and reflect on these effects (Burns, 2009).

4.4. Didactic comments

The third session is introduced by a short TED Talk[8] from Bill Gates, speaking about the importance for teachers to receive feedback in order to reflect on their professional practices and improve them. His talk is motivated by the general lack of systematic feedback that teachers receive in the course of their careers, worldwide. Gates believes that the system must be changed, and that feedback needs to become an integral part of pre-service teacher education, as well as of in-service teacher training.

To draw the attention to the context of the participating students, the discussion afterwards is guided by two questions.

- How would you describe the ways in which teachers are supported professionally in your own country?

- Why do you think feedback and reflection are important for teachers?

After having been introduced to the concept of reflective practice, the students are asked to take a look at two examples of a teaching journal. Based on this, the students talk about their own experiences regarding the documentation of their reflections. This discussion is led by the question of how the students have reflected so far in their studies and/or practical internships. A short brainstorming activity is conducted before the discussion, using a Padlet to collect ideas. Some of these results (taken from student Cohorts 1 and 2) are presented in Figure 10 below.

---

8. https://www.youtube.com/watch?v=81Ub0SMxZQo&t=1s

Figure 10. Student feedback collected through a Padlet

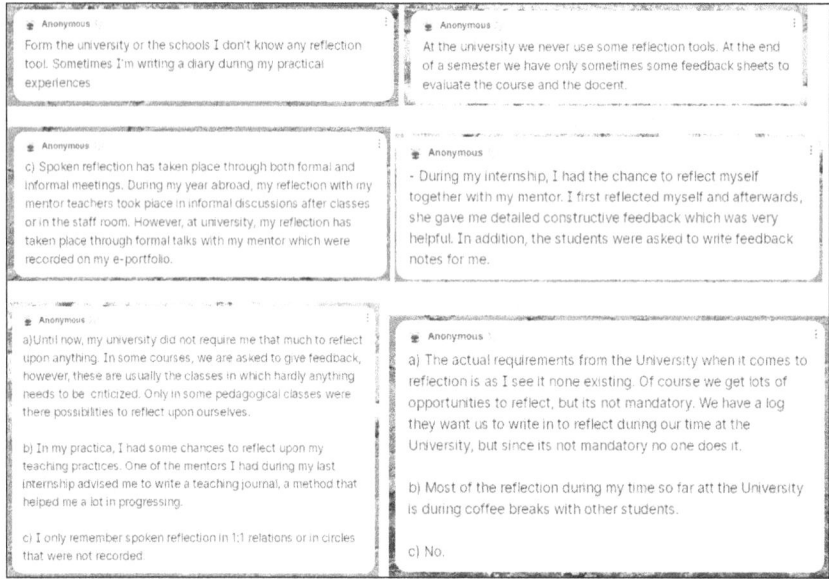

These examples illustrate the diversity and ambiguity among (international) student teachers when it comes to reflection put into practice. Some report that they have not been introduced to any reflective tools in their studies so far, and others have worked with numerous instruments to promote reflective practice (e.g. e-portfolios, feedback sheets). Moreover, the data suggest that there is a clear gap between practice and theory, i.e. practical internships and theory-driven courses at university. Many students consider the reflective discussions and feedback sessions during their internships as helpful and beneficial, although they are seldom/rarely being documented. It can also be noted that only a few students mentioned collecting evidence, for example video recordings, which they then used as a basis for their reflections.

A special focus lay on using video as a tool for reflection and data collection, as it is regarded by many as an effective instrument to document, analyse, and reflect on one's professional practices and teaching experiences (Farrell, 2008; Mann, Crichton, & Edmett, 2020; Schwab & Oesterle, 2021; Seidel,

Blomberg, & Stürmer, 2010). In line with Mann and Walsh (2017), we believe that digital video is a central tool to develop spoken and data-led reflective processes. Advocating for the use of digital video, the students are therefore introduced to a variety of video tools that can be used to either (1) record and document evidence to promote a data-led reflection afterwards, or (2) stimulate collaborative reflection through the use of video. In the course of the project, three tools were introduced and used.

- **VEO** (https://veo.co.uk/)

VEO was created by Paul Miller and Jon Haines in 2014 with the intention to develop "a system which was easy to use, flexible and readily available, to enable the sharing of good practice within, and from, the classroom" (Miller & Haines, 2021, p. 21). The app presents a new approach to use digital video as a stimulator for collaborative reflection and development. While recording, certain moments can be tagged using a predefined tag set. Afterwards, the tagged video can be used as evidence to engage in a professional dialogue. Through VEO, students or colleagues can quickly jump through the tags they have set. Moreover, they can upload and share their video on the VEO platform (for more on VEO see Seedhouse, 2021).

- **Flipgrid** (https://info.flipgrid.com/)

The Flipgrid platform is used many times during the project. As part of the CPD framework it was used to promote discussions and collect feedback. Flipgrid is only a basic version for video discussions. After starting a grid and introducing a topic or asking a question, others record a short video in which they comment on the topic or reply to the question. Others can then continue the process and comment or provide feedback on each video (Figure 11).

- **Swivl Robot** (https://www.swivl.com/)

In the course of the project, the Swivl Robot was used as a research instrument to analyse the meta level of the project and the meetings of the project partners

(Oesterle, Schwab, Hoffmann, & Baldwin, 2020). Moreover, the robot was introduced to the participating students as a tool for collecting evidence and reflecting collaboratively. A Swivl is an innovative tool that rotates and tracks the teacher/speaker automatically, being tethered to an iPad and connected to a Swivl Marker that captures audio throughout the room. After recording a lesson, the students are able to upload and share the video to the Swivl platform and comment on different moments either jointly or individually (Figure 12).

Figure 11. Using Flipgrid to engourage video discussions

Figure 12. Using Swivl to comment on video sequences

5. Feedback and evaluation

This section leads us into some feedback that was collected from the participating students, as well as evaluative data retrieved from the project partners on the CPD framework. Some of the data used in this chapter are also referred to in Schwab and Oesterle (2022, Chapter 4 this volume) which presents the proPIC study week. However, in this chapter, the following data are relevant (Table 2).

Table 2. Data overview

Participating students	Project partners
• 61 e-portfolios containing tasks and activities	• 2:40 hours of audio-recorded feedback during partner meetings
• 23 online surveys giving feedback on the framework	• 11 answers in final project evaluation on CPD framework
• 2 Padlets collecting feedback on the different sessions	

5.1. Participating students

Looking at the data collected throughout the proPIC project, we identified three themes that occurred when analysing the feedback of the students that took part:

- praising the use of mobile technologies;
- becoming more aware of their own context; and
- connecting the use of mobile technologies and reflective practice to learn and develop.

5.1.1. Praising the use of mobile technologies

The following examples show that the students paid much more attention to *how* the content was delivered than to *what* kind of content it was.

> "It was great that we got to know so many different ways of using media tools" (online survey, anonymous student, May 2019).

Chapter 2

> "I really liked that we learned so much about new technologies and possibilities how to use them in the classroom and for our future teaching. I really liked some of the tools and applications, and I'm sure I will use them" (online survey, anonymous student, May 2019).

> "I liked that we could be creative, work independently and try out digital tools" (online survey, anonymous student, April 2020).

> "In the future, I will definitely try to implement more digital media in the classroom and continue to get to know more tools and apps" (online survey, anonymous student, April 2020).

Based on the data collected in the proPIC project, we believe it is essential to integrate the use of mobile technologies among future teachers as early as possible. We observed that the students valued the 'space' we gave them to test and try out a range of digital tools:

> "I learned quite a lot about using technology for teaching and reflecting in school. It was very useful to get to know new ICT tools for collaborative and interactive work" (online survey, anonymous student, April 2020).

These extracts emphasise and praise the variety of digital tools, mobile technologies, and innovative formats that were introduced, and, above all, could be tried out. The focus lay much more on the didactic setting and tools than on the theoretical content.

5.1.2. Becoming more aware of their own context

Our data further suggests that the students became more aware of their own context.

> "At university we normally have to reflect our studies and work by writing a non-digital portfolio with a certain topic like pedagogical approaches or psychological processes. During the internships the

conversation with the mentors is the most important instrument for me. I got to know so many reflective tools in this course. Before, we were used to filling in observation sheets" (Padlet, anonymous student, February 2019).

"Before, I've been reading books about reflection and been writing in my logbook. Now, I started an e-portfolio and so far, I really enjoy it and understand the benefits of keeping a portfolio where I can keep track of my development" (Padlet, anonymous student, March 2020).

"In general, I feel that peers (and sometimes teachers) are often afraid to give feedback because they feel like they're criticising the other person. Thus, we have to move away from criticism (in a negative way) and move on to feedback, thereby understanding that it is supposed to help us become better teachers/professionals" (Padlet, anonymous student, March 2020).

This was supported by the transnational character of the framework which promoted a constant alternation between 'otherness' and 'sharedness', scaffolding collaborative and individual reflective processes.

5.1.3. Connecting the use of mobile technologies and reflective practice to learn and develop

Crucial for us was that although many students emphasised the use of mobile technologies, there were also a number of students who connected this with their own learning. These students critically reflected on their own role as a future teacher in regard to their students' learning when it comes to digital skills. They also stressed the role that digital tools can play in regard to reflective practice.

"I will take with be the use of creative apps which allow the students to interact with each other and 'control' their knowledge and for me definitely make use of the e-portfolio for my own reflective practice" (online survey, anonymous student, April 2020).

"I was totally new to the concept of CPD and I am now also more aware of the fact that I'm myself responsible to always offer my students access to the newest technology" (online survey, anonymous student, May 2019).

"To always stay up-to-date on new technologies and to try to use it more often in a way that it improves one's own learning and that of my future pupils" (online survey, anonymous student, May 2019).

"Especially e-portfolios are a good way of learning – if you have enough time to work on it" (online survey, anonymous student, April 2020).

5.2. Project partners

The evaluative data received from the project partners highlights three major issues:

- commonly used materials should be developed together;
- terminology should have been discussed and agreed upon before; and
- the great potential of multimodal digital content should be recognised.

5.2.1. Commonly used materials should be developed together

As the CPD framework was the project output that the University of Education Karlsruhe was leading, the other partners were not overly involved in its production. Our findings indicate that this made the delivery of the framework more difficult for them.

"Should have been developed more in transnational teams […]" (final partner evaluation, anonymous, July 2020).

"Difficult to implement when not involved in the production" (final partner evaluation, anonymous, July 2020).

Although the first sessions had been video-recorded so it could just have been shown to the students, the feedback of the partners hints that learning and teaching materials that are supposed to be integrated in different courses across European institutions should be developed collaboratively with all actors involved. Otherwise, the implementation of such resources might not include all perspectives and possibly not fit into each course structure (for more on this issue see also Whelan & Seedhouse, 2022, Chapter 6 this volume on assessment).

5.2.2. Terminology should have been discussed and agreed upon before

> "I still have the feeling that everybody has a different understanding of what a portfolio is, even though we did the last meeting, we talked about it, but conceptually I think they understand something completely different" (partner 12, partner interview, 2019).

Here, one partner describes that after two years the differences have become even more visible. This was an issue that many partners reported. In order to deliver the CPD framework to the participating students most effectively, all partners need to agree upon a shared understanding in regard to relevant terms, such as reflection, professional learning, or e-portfolio, beforehand. Thus, the terminology and different concepts, often highly complex and culturally or institutionally rooted, were a challenging issue, especially when English as a *lingua franca* or international language is involved.

5.2.3. Great potential of multimodal digital content should be recognised

In general, all partners reported that the multimodal digital format of the CPD framework was highly effective.

> "Crucial, also for my own development, was to learn more about how to use new technologies in my own teaching" (final partner evaluation, anonymous, July 2020).

"For me, learning about new technology packages and how young teachers employ them was most beneficial" (final partner evaluation, anonymous, July 2020).

"I have learned how enriching mobile technologies can be for transnational collaboration and reflective practice. I think the way we teach must change" (final partner evaluation, anonymous, July 2020).

Also, the possibility to only take easy bits and pieces for one's own teaching was described positively. The innovative format of the framework that included theory, practice, and research combined with a variety of interactive tasks and activities may have helped in this case. Based on the partner evaluations, the CPD framework had a great impact on fostering digital literacy, as well as raising the awareness of new and innovative approaches to teaching and learning in language teacher education.

6. Conclusion

In this chapter we have illustrated how CPD can be put into practice in the context of foreign language teacher education. After outlining the overall structure of the CPD framework developed in the proPIC project, we introduced five sessions in detail. Throughout the different sections, we highlighted the importance of promoting reflective practice among prospective language teachers in order for them to develop professionally. Yet, we also critically discussed the concept of reflective practice in our context and its conceptual and terminological ambiguity and intricacy. In line with the literature, the results of the interactive tasks and activities of the CPD framework indicate that there is no common agreement on what exactly reflective practice comprises, not among the teacher educators nor among the participating students. Nevertheless, most consider reflection to be highly relevant for their professional learning and development.

What lessons have we learned from developing and testing this framework? Based on the data collected throughout the project, our findings indicate three major issues that we believe are relevant for creating a teaching and learning scenario that scaffolds reflective practice and – at least to some extent – puts CPD into practice.

6.1. Develop a shared understanding

Mann and Walsh (2017) point out that reflective practice "is often described in ways that are elusive, general and vague" (p. 5), which is supported by Holdsworth (2021) who illustrates the importance of arriving at a shared understanding of the concept of 'reflective practice'. This need is also stressed by Farrell (2008) who states: "[w]e need a common language and understanding about what these terms mean before we can encourage TESOL teachers to engage in reflective practice" (p. 15). Thus, we make a strong argument for systematically developing a clear consensus and shared understanding in regard to the terminology of CPD in order to put it into practice.

6.2. Systematically put CPD into practice

After developing a common understanding, approaches and methods have to be explored and possibly developed, for example, how 'reflective practice' can not only be deployed, but also how it can be taught to future teachers so that it can have an impact on their CPD.

Systematic practice postulates research that informs it. The fact that many teachers and teacher educators believe that CPD is relevant and also think they are reflective and critical but cannot actually explain what they do or how they teach it calls for systematic research in this field (Holdsworth, 2021). Further research needs to be conducted to gain insights into how much substance lies behind the term CPD and how it can be put into practice.

CPD also includes becoming part of a learning community and focuses on systematically sharing expertise and experience with other professionals, which cannot be developed by teachers themselves on the job but needs to be initiated and promoted beginning in teacher education (OECD, 2009, p. 49). Support can be crucial in making CPD successful. From the very beginning of their careers, future teachers need to be empowered by their institution and their teacher educators to become reflective agents of their own development.

6.3. Change the way we teach

Last but not least, we would like to advocate one statement collected in this project: We believe that in order to put CPD successfully into practice, a major issue is to change the way we teach and train future teachers.

We believe that CPD can empower teachers and teacher educators to help them become reflective agents of their own development. Our data indicates that scenarios in which reflection can or should take place need to be more digital, multimodal, interconnected, and collaborative, and in the context of foreign language teacher education, also more transnational.

References

Allwright, D. (1999). Three major processes of teacher development and the appropriate design criteria for developing and using them. In B. Johnston & S. Irujo (Eds), *Research and practice in language teacher education: voices from the field* (pp. 115-133). CARLA.

Beauchamp, C. (2015). Reflection in teacher education: issues emerging from a review of current literature. *Reflective Practice, 16*(1), 123-141. https://doi.org/10.1080/14623943.2014.982525

Blömeke, S. (2001). Erwerb professioneller Kompetenz in der Lehrerausbildung und die Aufgabe der Zentren für Lehrerbildung. Folgerungen aus einer Theorie universitärer Lehrerausbildung. In N. Seibert (Ed.), *Probleme der Lehrerbildung. Analysen, Positionen, Lösungsversuche* (pp. 131-162). Klinkhardt.

Borko, H. (2004). Professional development and teacher learning: mapping the terrain. *Educational Researcher, 33*(8), 3-15. https://doi.org/10.3102/0013189X033008003

British Council. (2017). *Frameworks of continuing professional development.* https://www.britishcouncil.in/teach/continuing-professional-development

Burden, K. (2010). Conceptualising teachers' professional learning with Web 2.0. *Campus-Wide Information Systems, 27*(3), 148-161. https://doi.org/10.1108/10650741011054456

Burden, K., & Kearney, M. (2016). A snapshot of teacher educators' mobile learning practices. *Proceedings of the International Mobile Learning Festival 2016.* http://mttep.weebly.com/uploads/5/6/0/9/56091311/a_snapshot_of_teacher_educators%E2%80%99_mobile_learning_practices_final_version.pdf

Burns, A. (2009). Action research in second language teacher education. In A. Burns & J. C. Richards (Eds), *The Cambridge guide to research in language teaching and learning* (pp. 289-297). Cambridge University Press.

Cheetham, G., & Chivers, G. (2001). How professionals learn in practice: an investigation of informal learning amongst people working in professions. *Journal of European Industrial Training, 25*(5), 247-292. https://doi.org/10.1108/03090590110395870

Clement, M., & Vandenberghe, R. (2000). Teachers' professional development: a solitary or collegial (ad)venture? *Teaching and Teacher Education, 16*(1), 81-101. https://doi.org/10.1016/S0742-051X(99)00051-7

Council of Europe. (2018). *Common European framework of reference for languages: learning, teaching, assessment companion volume with new descriptors.* https://rm.coe.int/cefr-companion-volume-with-newdescriptors-2018/1680787989

Crandall, J., & Christison, M. A. (2016). (Eds). *Teacher education and professional development in TESOL. Global perspectives.* Routledge. https://doi.org/10.4324/9781315641263

Davies, A. (2007). *An introduction to applied linguistics: from practice to theory.* Edinburgh University Press. https://doi.org/10.1515/9780748633562

Day, C. (1999). *Developing teachers. The challenges of lifelong learning.* Routledge.

Day, C. (2017). *Teachers' worlds and work. Understanding complexity, building quality.* Routledge. https://doi.org/10.4324/9781315170091

Day, C., & Sachs, J. (2005). *International handbook of the continuing professional development of teachers.* Open University Press.

Dewey, J. (1997). *How we think.* Dover Publications.

ECML. (2021). *Using ICT in support of language teaching and learning.* European Centre for Modern Languages of the Council of Europe. https://www.ecml.at/TrainingConsultancy/ICT-REV/tabid/1725/language/en-GB/Default.aspx

Edutopia. (2017). *Teacher labs: making professional development collaborative* [Video]. YouTube. https://www.youtube.com/watch?v=gf5KcyHGhRA

Eraut, M. (1994). *Developing professional knowledge and competence.* Falmer Press.

Estapa, A., Pinnow, J. R., & Chval, K. B. (2016). Video as a professional development tool to support novice teachers as they learn to teach English language learners. *The New Educator, 12*(1), 85-104. https://doi.org/10.1080/1547688X.2015.1113350

European Commission. (2015). *Strengthening teaching in Europe: new evidence from teachers compiled by Eurydice and CRELL, June 2015.* http://ed.europa.eu/education/library/policy/teaching-profession-practices.en.pdf

European Commission. (2021a). *Digital education action plan.* https://ec.europa.eu/education/education-in-the-eu/digital-education-action-plan_en

European Commission. (2021b). *European education area.* https://ec.europa.eu/education/education-in-the-eu/european-education-area_en

European Commission. (2021c). *Multilingual classrooms.* https://ec.europa.eu/education/policies/multilingualism/multilingual-classrooms_en

European Council. (2009). Council conclusions on the professional development of teachers and school leaders. *Official Journal of the European Union, C*(203), 6-9.

Farnsworth, V., Kleanthous, I., & Wenger-Trayner, E. (2016). Communities of practice as a social theory of learning: a conversation with Etienne Wenger. *British Journal of Educational Studies, 64*(2), 139-160. https://doi.org/10.1080/00071005.2015.1133799

Farrell, T. S. (2008). *Novice language teachers: insights and perspectives for the first year.* Equinox Publishing.

Fraser, C., Kennedy, A., Reid, L., & McKinney, S. (2007). Teachers' continuing professional development: contested concepts, understandings and models. *Journal of In-Service Education, 33*(2), 153-169. https://doi.org/10.1080/13674580701292913

Freeman, D., & Johnson, K. E. (1998). Reconceptualizing the knowledge-base of language teacher education. *TESOL Quarterly, 32*(3), 397-417. https://doi.org/10.2307/3588114

Fullan, M. (2007). *The new meaning of educational change.* Teachers College Press.

Gerlach, D. (2020). *Zur Professionalität der Professionlisierenden. Was machen Lehrerbilder*innen im fremdsprachendidaktischen Vorbereitungsdienst?* Narr Francke Attempto Verlag.

Goetz, T., Jaritz, G., & Oser, F. (2011). (Eds). *Pains and gains of international mobility in teacher education.* Sense Publishers. https://doi.org/10.1007/978-94-6091-496-6

Hattie, J. (2009). *Visible learning: a synthesis of over 800 meta-study analyses relating to achievement.* Routledge.

Hoinke, U., & Clausen, K. (2022). Getting curious and gaining knowledge through transnational collaboration in foreign language teacher education. In G. Schwab, M. Oesterle & A. Whelan (Eds), *Promoting professionalism, innovation and transnational collaboration: a new approach to foreign language teacher education* (pp. 83-106). Research-publishing.net. https://doi.org/10.14705/rpnet.2022.57.1384

Holdsworth, P. (2021). Being a reflective teacher educator. Professionalism or pipe dream? In A. Swennen & E. White (Eds), *Being a teacher educator. Research-informed methods for improving practice* (pp. 10-26). Routledge. https://doi.org/10.4324/9781003055457-2

Jaritz, G. (2011). Developing a culture of (inter)national mobility in initial teacher training: expectations, limitations and ways forward. In T. Goetz, G. Jaritz & F. Oser (Eds), *Pains and gains of international mobility in teacher education* (pp. 7-24). Sense Publishers.

Kelchtermans, G. (2004). CPD for professional renewal: moving beyond knowledge for practice. In C. Day & J. Sachs (Eds), *International handbook on the continuing professional development of teachers* (pp. 217-237). Open University Press.

Kelchtermans, G. (2007). Chapter 2: Teachers' self-understanding in times of performativity. In L. F. Deretchin & C. J. Craig (Eds), *International research on the impact of accountability systems. Teacher education yearbook XV* (pp. 13-30). Rowman & Littlefield Education.

Kennedy, A (2011). Collaborative continuing professional development (CPD) for teachers in Scotland: aspirations, opportunities and barriers. *European Journal of Teacher Education, 34*(1), 25-41. https://doi.org/10.1080/02619768.2010.534980

Laakkonen, I. (2011). Personal learning environment in higher education language courses: an informal and learner-centred approach. In S. Thouësny & L. Bradley (Eds), *Second language teaching and learning with technology: views of emergent researchers* (pp. 9-28). Research-publishing.net. https://doi.org/10.14705/rpnet.2011.000004

Leliveld, M. J., Van Tartwijk, J., Verloop, N., & Bolk, J. (2008, June). *Characteristics of effective professional development: a research in the medical faculty.* Paper presented at the Onderwijs Research Dagen 'Licht op Leren', Eindhoven.

Lortie, D. C. (1975). *Schoolteacher. A sociological study.* The University of Chicago Press.

Loughran, J. J. (2002). Effective reflective practice: in search of meaning in learning about teaching. *Journal of Teacher Education, 53*(1), 33-43. https://doi.org/10.1177/0022487102053001004

Mann, S. (2005). The language teacher's development. *Language Teaching, 38*(3), 103-118. https://doi.org/10.1017/S0261444805002867

Mann, S., Crichton, R., & Edmett, A. (2020). Evaluating the role of video in supporting reflection beyond INSET. *System, 90*. https://doi.org/10.1016/j.system.2019.102195

Mann, S., & Walsh, S. (2017). *Reflective practice in English language teaching. Research-based principles and practices*. Routledge. https://doi.org/10.4324/9781315733395

Mann, S., & Webb, K. (2022). Continuing professional development: key themes in supporting the development of professional practice. In G. Schwab, M. Oesterle & A. Whelan (Eds), Promoting professionalism, innovation and transnational collaboration: a new approach to foreign language teacher education (pp. 15-44). Research-publishing.net. https://doi.org/10.14705/rpnet.2022.57.1382

McLoughlin, C., & Lee, M. J. W. (2009). Personalised learning spaces and self-regulated learning: global examples of effective pedagogy. In R. Atkinson & C. McBeath (Eds), *Same places, different spaces* (pp. 639-645). ASCILITE.

Miller, P., & Haines, J. (2021). From teaching to learning: the development of the VEO App. In P. Seedhouse (Ed.), *Video enhanced observation for language teaching. Reflection and professional development* (pp. 21-38). Bloomsbury Academic.

Nitsche, K. (2014). *UNI-Klassen. Reflexion und Feedback über Unterricht in Videolabors an Schulen*. Published doctoral dissertation. Ludwigs-Maximilians-Universität, München, Germany. https://edoc.ub.uni-muenchen.de/16637/1/Nitsche_Kai.pdf

OECD. (2009). Chapter 3. The professional development of teachers. In OECD (Eds), *Creating effective teaching and learning environments. First results from TALIS* (pp. 49-86). https://www.oecd.org/education/school/43023606.pdf

Oesterle, M., Schwab, G., Hoffmann, S., & Baldwin, R. (2020). The potentials of a transient transnational community for teacher educators' professional learning and development. *European Journal of Education Studies, 7*(8), 117-147.

Richards, J. C., & Farrell, T. S. C. (2005). *Professional development for language teachers*. Cambridge University Press. https://doi.org/10.1017/CBO9780511667237

Sachs, J. (2007, January). *Learning to improve or improving learning: the dilemma of teacher continuing professional development*. Paper presented at the International Congress for School Effectiveness and Improvement Conference, Slovenia.

Schön, D. A. (1983). *The reflective practitioner: how professionals think in action*. Basic Books.

Schwab, G., & Oesterle, M. (2021). Integrating VEO in foreign language teacher education in Germany. In P. Seedhouse (Ed.), *Video enhanced observation for language teaching. Reflection and professional development* (pp. 65-82). Bloomsbury Academic.

Schwab, G., & Oesterle, M. (2022). The proPIC study weeks: experiencing transnational exchange. In G. Schwab, M. Oesterle & A. Whelan (Eds), *Promoting professionalism, innovation and transnational collaboration: a new approach to foreign language teacher education* (pp. 107-130). Research-publishing.net. https://doi.org/10.14705/rpnet.2022.57.1385

Seedhouse, P. (2021). (Ed.). *Video enhanced observation for language teaching. Reflection and professional development.* Bloomsbury Academic. https://doi.org/10.5040/9781350085060

Seidel, T., Blomberg, G., & Stürmer, K. (2010). Observer – Validierung eines videobasierten Instruments zur Erfassung der professionellen Wahrnehmung von Unterricht. Projekt OBSERVE. In E. Klieme, D. Leutner & M. Kenk (Eds), *Kompetenzmodellierung. Zwischenbilanz des DFG-Schwerpunktprogramms und Perspektiven des Forschungsansatzes* (56th supplement to Zeitschrift für Pädagogik) (pp. 296-306). Beltz.

Teachers TV/UK Department of Education. (2008). *CPD leaders, collaborative professional development* [Video]. Big Heart Media. https://search.alexanderstreet.com/view/work/bibliographic_entity%7Cvideo_work%7C1783934/cpd-leaders-collaborative-professional-development

TeachingChannel. (2018a). *Using video to reflect on teaching and learning. A classroom strategy* [Video]. Teaching Channel. https://www.teachingchannel.org/video/use-video-to-improve-teaching-ousd

TeachingChannel. (2018b). *Using video to improve practice: do it yourself!* [Video]. Teaching Channel. https://www.teachingchannel.org/video/improve-teaching-with-video

Wahl, D. (2006). *Lernumgebungen erfolgreich gestalten. Vom trägen Wissen zum kompetenten Handeln. 2. Auflage mit Methodensammlung.* Klinkhardt.

Westheimer, J. (2008). Chapter 41. Learning among colleagues: teacher community and the shared enterprise of education. In M. Cochran-Smith, S. Feiman-Nemser & J. McIntyre (Eds), *Handbook of research on teacher education.* Association of Teacher Educators.

Whelan, A., & Seedhouse, P. (2022). Developing an innovative and collaborative assessment framework for proPIC Europa. In G. Schwab, M. Oesterle & A. Whelan (Eds), *Promoting professionalism, innovation and transnational collaboration: a new approach to foreign language teacher education* (pp. 147-189). Research-publishing.net. https://doi.org/10.14705/rpnet.2022.57.1387

Part 2.

3 Getting curious and gaining knowledge through transnational collaboration in foreign language teacher education

Ulrich Hoinkes[1] and Kyra Clausen[2]

1. Introduction

The claim to strive for greater internationalisation in the fields of academic education not only corresponds to the pressures of an increasingly globalised world but is also a response to the ever-growing challenges of cultural diversity that exist within one's own country. For students, however, the geographical space relevant to their education is usually constituted not by the nation state but by an educationally autonomous entity of subordinate size. This is especially true in states such as Germany, where the federal system is constitutive of public education. However, every territory with educational sovereignty is in constant contact with national and international educational concepts which – depending on the topic – have a concrete relevance for its own educational structure. This interplay can be well seen, for example, in the appreciation of social multilingualism and its consideration in school policy. The field of foreign language teacher training is a prime example in this respect in its interweaving with overarching educational concepts. For teachers and students, the importance of individual multilingualism is revealed in their dealings with people from a wide variety of migrant backgrounds, in different places on journeys, and in many professional fields around the world. Therefore, it is

---

1. Christian-Albrechts-Universität zu Kiel, Kiel, Germany; hoinkes@romanistik.uni-kiel.de; https://orcid.org/0000-0001-5781-7722

2. Christian-Albrechts-Universität zu Kiel, Kiel, Germany; kclausen@romanistik.uni-kiel.de; https://orcid.org/0000-0002-3617-9503

How to cite: Hoinkes, U., & Clausen, K. (2022). Getting curious and gaining knowledge through transnational collaboration in foreign language teacher education. In G. Schwab, M. Oesterle & A. Whelan (Eds), *Promoting professionalism, innovation and transnational collaboration: a new approach to foreign language teacher education* (pp. 83-106). Research-publishing.net. https://doi.org/10.14705/rpnet.2022.57.1384

particularly effective for prospective teachers to experience the benefits and function of foreign language skills in an international context from the very beginning and to incorporate these experiences into their teaching skills. In this sense, the internationalisation of foreign language teacher education is an essential element of professionalisation that broadens teachers' subject didactic horizons, enables them to experience the social significance of foreign language learning in a transnational perspective, strengthens motivation to acquire communicative competences in several languages, and clarifies the special status of regional and migrant languages alongside the use of national languages. Thus, it is of great value for prospective language teachers in one country to recognise the role that French, Spanish, English, or German play as foreign languages in other countries and to be aware of the different situations of social multilingualism. It is important to recognise that a couple of well-defined factors significantly influence the way foreign languages are taught and learned in other places.

2. Transculturality as a theoretical background

The increasing internationalisation of the teaching profession requires that contact with other countries and nations takes place from a pedagogical perspective. In this context, the concept of transculturality is of particular importance and has a formative effect on forms of intercultural learning and professional development. Fundamentally, the aspect of transculturality must be distinguished from the experience of intercultural learning: the modern understanding of cultural reality and its experience defines itself as 'transcultural' and not as 'intercultural'. In the 1990's, Wolfgang Welsch consciously coined the term 'transculturality' as the antithesis to that of 'interculturality', because the latter threatened to fossilise in the notion of a specific cultural determination of identity in each case – connected with the distinction between self-culture and foreign culture – as well as in cultural thinking in separate clusters. Nevertheless, it remains justified to ascribe so much modernity to today's understanding of intercultural learning that the continued use of the term in foreign language didactics seems sensible (Heimböckel & Weinberg, 2014)[3].

What makes 'transculturality' indispensable as an analytical concept, however, is made clear by three "essential determining moments" (Welsch, 1999, p. 197ff.):

- the inner differentiation and complexity of modern cultures, which thus usually appear as inhomogeneous;

- the external networking of cultures, especially across national borders; and

- a form of hybridisation, by which is essentially meant the interweaving of the most diverse cultures anywhere in the world.

The connection between transculturality and internationality is represented in Welsch's (1999) definition in particular by the aspect of networking, on which he states the following:

> "[c]ultures today are extremely interconnected and entangled with each other. Lifestyles no longer end at the borders of national cultures, but go beyond these, are found in the same way in other cultures. The way of life for an economist, an academic or a journalist is no longer German or French, but rather European or global in tone. The new forms of entanglement are a consequence of migratory processes, as well as of worldwide material and immaterial communication systems and economic interdependencies and dependencies. It is here, of course, that questions of power come in" (p. 197).

---

[3]. The concept of intercultural learning is held onto especially in Europe, both in subject didactic research and in educational policy. The discussion has been going on for more than three decades and has led to a great variety of definitional approaches. Our concept of cultural learning fits into a line of interpretation that emphasises the subjective experience of cultural diversity and sees the change of perspective as essential. From a pedagogical point of view, we agree with the following statement: "the idea of this learning process is that the student should learn to tolerate diversity between people and cultures, to look sensitively at members of other cultural groups and, through discovering and learning about the foreign, to perceive and treat his or her own culture from a different, new perspective" (Walkowska, 2018, p. 193, own translation).

In this sense, the goal of internationalisation in teacher education is based on the concept of transculturality, which seeks to discover what connects rather than what divides individual identity formation and culture shaping with the characteristics of cultural interpenetration and cultural commonalities. Moreover, the concept of transculturality seems ideally suited to recognise and use the aspect of cultural diversity as a constructive experience in any living and educational space (Wulf, 2020).

3. The proPIC project as a positive experience of internationalisation in higher education

The proPIC project was an Erasmus+ funded project, being part of the worldwide initiatives for more internationalisation in higher education (cf. the summarising and informative presentation by De Wit & Altbach, 2020). In practice, proPIC adopted the concept of transnational collaboration as far as it applies to the education sector. The defining moments of this concept decisive for proPIC were the following[4].

- Partnership: friendly ties and commitment to the other (at proPIC, five universities from four European countries worked together[5]).

- Common concern: fixation on problem areas of supranational relevance (at proPIC, among other things, the use of digital media in education, see below).

- Integration: strengthening interaction to achieve an overarching goal (at proPIC, promoting transculturality and intercultural learning, see above).

---

[4]. A systematic review of transnational collaboration in higher education can be found in Caniglia et al. (2017).

[5]. In detail, the following institutions were involved: University of Education Karlsruhe (Germany), Kiel University (Germany), University of Borås (Sweden), University of Barcelona (Catalonia, Spain), and Newcastle University (England, Great Britain).

- Cooperation: mutual coordination of measures, structural development to increase efficiency (more information on this in the course of this article).

- Professionalism: development of a self-reflective attitude as an individual approach to one's Continuing Professional Development (more information on CPD can be found in Mann & Webb, 2022 and Oesterle & Schwab, 2022, Chapters 1 and 2, this volume).

The course of the proPIC project clearly showed that a practice-oriented exchange of foreign language teachers beyond the subject boundaries in the narrower sense proves its worth. To the extent that dealing with transculturality and social multilingualism is at the forefront of such an exchange, teaching and learning can no longer be solely about optimising the structural teaching of individual foreign languages. Particularly in international educational contexts, it is very much possible to focus on the specific dimensions and realities associated with the acquisition of communicative competence in a second or third language and to sharpen the focus on how students can be supported in acquiring this competence. Attention to the very different conditions that exist in schools and universities in other countries with regard to foreign language learning may also create a better awareness of the value and possibilities of including first languages. Finally, the function of English as a global language of communication is also grasped in a more differentiated way when it is understood from the perspective of English teaching in different countries[6].

Empirical studies on the diverse intercultural learning processes promoted in the proPIC project as well as on the gain in foreign language didactic competences are still pending[7]. However, based on students' statements in surveys and feedback questionnaires, as a positive outcome of proPIC, we can support the thesis that every effort towards transnational collaboration makes a valuable contribution to the professional development of teacher candidates. It is not only in Germany

---

6. On some of the main problems associated with internationalisation in higher education, see Makhmudov (2020), Smith (2010), and Crăciun and Orosz (2018).

7. Cf. on this desideratum with reference to Eastern Europe Onishchuk et al. (2020) as an example.

that the training of foreign language teachers, which is limited to the respective federal state, carries the danger of a fixation on the curricular framework and teaching practice in one's own country, making it difficult to focus on the diversity of multilingual experiences and the diversity of the use of 'foreign languages' in different parts of the world. Ultimately, this shortcoming leads to a significant limitation of the possible change of perspective on the value of multilingualism outside the cultural and educational horizon given solely by the particular place of education. Of course, within the framework of educational institutions, there are several mechanisms to get out of the isolation or narrowness of one's own cultural consideration. However, in this endeavour, the effort of transnational collaboration contributes efficiently and sustainably in any case to give teacher education a decisive *kick* in this direction. It also shows a way to constructively use forms of internationalisation 'at home' in the educational process alongside the experiences of otherness abroad. It probably even represents a decisive key to permanently anchoring a transcultural awareness of foreign language teachers in their professional practice.

4. The special challenge of internationalisation and mobility in teacher education

The desideratum of internationalising teacher education is not new and has already led to a number of measures of cooperation between various countries (cf. a comparative study of Leutwyler, Popov, & Wolhuter, 2017). These are pilot initiatives to promote the cross-border mobility of student teachers – partly on the basis of special study programmes – whose results can be meta-analytically evaluated. This evaluation of already existing experiences – especially on the basis of feedback studies – was an important basis for the concrete design of the study programme of proPIC as an essential component of this project with the aim of profound professionalisation through transnational collaboration.

In a recent Germany-wide study on the mobility of students of various subjects, Krämer and Springob find that, overall, teacher trainees are no less mobile than students of other subjects. According to this, 60% of foreign language students spend some time of their education abroad (Krämer & Springob, 2019, p. 197f.). However, Ahlgrimm et al. point out that the framework conditions for stays abroad in teacher education are often unfavourable due to the study structure and the lack of recognition of externally earned credits (Ahlgrimm, Westphal, Wallert, & Heck, 2019, p. 221f.). In a meta-analysis of 33 international studies on the effects of international mobility of student teachers, Kercher and Schifferings summarise that intercultural learning, self-reflection, and strengthening of professional self-confidence are cited as positive areas of impact. They also note that even a short stay leads to positive effects (Kercher & Schifferings, 2019, p. 250ff.). Leutwyler (2014) points out that

> "teaching-specific benefit increases when (pre-service or in-service) teachers are involved in occupational activities (either as a participant or as an observer), provided they have the opportunity to teach at least some units in the foreign context themselves, or if they have the opportunity to observe daily school routines and discuss what they have observed with local counterparts" (p. 113).

Furthermore, a comprehensive structural embedding of the stay abroad in the home study programme is of particular importance; for example, its adequate preparation, an individual support programme (coaching, supervision) during the stay, and the evaluation phase (debriefing, wrap-ups) after the return (Leutwyler, 2014). Of course, this requirement is very difficult to realise when there is no firm bilateral cooperation between the respective training institutions.

Cushner (2009) emphasises the importance of "carefully structured, international field experiences" (p. 158f.) and points out in this context that the stay abroad should ideally include a brief immersion in the new and different cultural environment. He also emphasises that an accompanied critical self-reflection of one's own and the foreign culture is an indispensable prerequisite for the success of any transnational study programme. This component can be at least partially integrated into local training programmes with the help of a teaching module on intercultural learning. However, it also depends on the general educational level of the students in this respect.

Before we present our specific proPIC programme, we would like to call attention to another important consideration. The approach of proPIC goes beyond the general desire for a transnational component in the studies of students of different subjects. ProPIC does not primarily aim to promote the internationalisation of teacher education by creating offers in the sense of exchange programmes. Rather, the aim is to call for an area of the curriculum in which a form of transnational cooperation is clearly structured, which corresponds to the competence orientation of the professional field, uses the digital possibilities more creatively than before for professional training, and creates a collective expert awareness on a level that may be transdisciplinary but is nevertheless strictly related to the professional field. This extended training offer is primarily foreign language didactic and can also take place at training locations abroad where the foreign language studied by the trainees in their home country is not represented as a school subject. Following these objectives, the proPIC team has developed an adaptable study programme which, in the sense of an extended transcultural experience during foreign language studies, contributes to strengthening the CPD of the trainees at an early stage.

5. The proPIC study programme as a concrete proposal for transnational collaboration

The guiding principle of the ProPIC project is to enable both trainee teachers and teacher educators to actively engage in lifelong learning processes in terms of CPD and to cooperatively establish a professional ethos of self-reflection, innovation, and transculturality in foreign and second language learning and teaching. Three main objectives, previously identified in the funding application, guided the development of the study programme, as below.

- Research orientation: through a variety of problem-based assignments and their own research project, participants link the theoretical framework (CPD) to their personal experiences, while continuously documenting, reflecting, and sharing their progress, experiences, and results through the use of mobile technologies.

- Transnational collaboration: promoting intercultural understanding and multilingualism in relation to the needs of a changing and diverse society. Participants share their traditions and methods in teaching and learning a foreign language and build intercultural and transnational networks.

- Mobile technologies: mobile technologies are seen as tools for creative development and application of theory in practice. Participants practise the use of new technologies to enrich teaching, enhance learning experiences, enable virtual mobility, and create new opportunities for research. Further specific objectives are set in relation to different groups, which can be reviewed in the final report[8] on the developed study programme.

ProPIC has developed and continuously improved the programme over a period of three years, above all by constructively taking into account local conditions and feedback from participants as far as we were able. In its final form, it looks like the following.

Figure 1. The research-oriented, transnational study programme

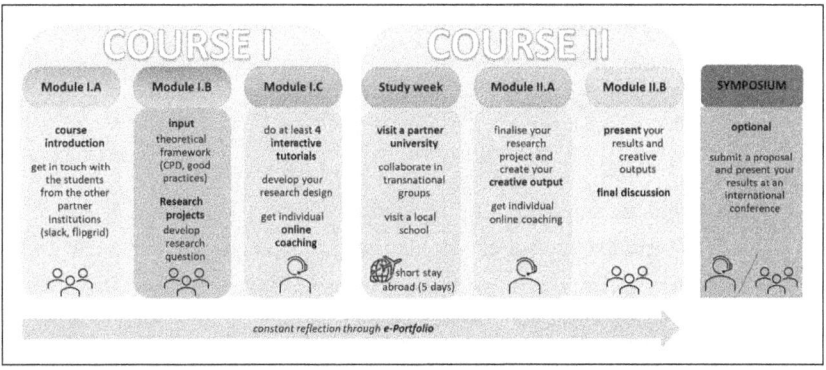

8. http://www.propiceuropa.com/uploads/1/0/8/0/108097905/propic_io3_final_report.pdf

The programme consists of two courses (Course 1 and 2) with three modules (Module 1.1, 1.2, 1.3) in the first course and two modules (Module 2.1, 2.2) and a study week (a short five-day stay at a partner university) in the second course. Module 1.1 contains an introductory overview, and Module 1.2 consists of an input phase (including CPD as a framework) and the development of individual research projects. Module 1.3 focuses on individual work on interactive tutorials and research projects embedded in online coaching, Module 2.1 promotes individual development of creative outputs embedded in online coaching, and Module 2.2 includes the presentation of results and a final discussion. A final conference at the end of the project allows participants to present their results to an international audience. Twelve prospective teachers per course and organisation were able to participate, for a total maximum of 60 students per cohort. The project credited the programme with between eight and ten ECTS points, depending on the local circumstances of the partner universities. After the first cohort, two possible model scenarios were developed on how the programme could be implemented: in an integrated model, the courses were incorporated into an existing degree programme, with the study week being an additional module for some students. In a separate model, the study programme was implemented as a new course, with the study week being a compulsory part of the course.

Students who participated in the project according to one of the models gave consistently positive feedback on their experience, especially with regard to their active participation in the study week. One student gave the following feedback.

> "I found the inputs during the study week very useful because that the discussion and exercises we had gave me a new point of view and it was also useful to discuss my own ideas with similar peers" (first cohort 2018, Respondent #20, SurveyMonkey).

However, this encouragement is matched by the major task of implementing the study programme in other institutional contexts beyond the current phase of proPIC. Such an undertaking depends on the will of those responsible locally, the willingness to adapt the respective training curriculum, and, of course, the financial possibilities, especially to support student travel.

The fact that there are two delivery models (the integration and the separation model) makes it easier for the cooperation partners to adapt the study programme to their local needs and conditions. The partner institutions decide individually on the format of the sessions, which can take place either face-to-face or online. In doing so, the different circumstances of the institutions as well as the possibilities to also conduct the study programme by means of online sessions are taken into account. Basically, it is evident that flexibility in planning and concretisation is an elementary criterion for successful implementation. Due to the very different timetables and curricula, it was difficult for proPIC to recruit many students for the first cohort. According to the teacher trainers, many were interested in participating in the study programme but did not have enough time and capacity to go abroad for five days in between. Following the evaluation of the first cohort we limited the amount of work in the courses (e.g. by reducing the number of activities) as students stated that, for example:

> "The days were a bit long so you were completely exhausted at the end of the day" (first cohort 2018, Respondent #20, SurveyMonkey).

> "Not so many activities, because it's better to focus on less activities than doing a lot of them but in a superficial way" (first cohort 2018, Respondent #27, SurveyMonkey).

The different education systems pose a great challenge for the project participants to find suitable dates for the implementation of the programme. In addition to the regular semester and examination times, other points of conflict have to be explored, such as the so-called practical semester at the university in teacher training in Germany. This is accompanied by the question of the workload resulting from additional travel. These experiences coincide with Ahlgrimm et al.'s (2019) indication that the often complex study structure combined with the required time commitment can be a hindrance.

Based on the evaluations of students and partners within the first cohort, the study week was reported to have had the greatest impact so far, as it made them aware of the importance of cooperating internationally and how helpful and inspiring it is to get other perspectives on learning and teaching (for further details see also Schwab & Oesterle, 2022, Chapter 4 this volume). This result is in line with the meta-analysis by Kercher and Schifferings (2019), according to which even short stays can have a positive effect. However, the experiences of the first cohort also showed the critical condition of too little or too unbalanced participation (e.g. in a study week with six Germans in Barcelona but no one from England or Sweden)[9].

Another challenge is the allocation of study-relevant ECTS points to the respective degree programme at the students' home university. Here, a different allocation of points can have a negative impact on the atmosphere or the acceptance of the entire programme. Students from the second Karlsruhe year, for example, criticised the workload in relation to the credit points received. Above all, the presentation of many new technologies was very time-consuming. At Newcastle University, on the other hand, student participation in the proPIC project was voluntary, so students did not receive credit points for their studies if they took part. According to Ahlgrimm et al. (2019), insufficient recognition as a course credit leads student teachers to refrain from studying abroad. It can also be assumed that a different allocation of points has an effect on the motivation and performance of the project participants when working together.

Finally, it should also be noted that the success of a project like ProPIC depends heavily on the coordination and willingness of the project partners. On the one hand, staff fluctuations lead to new perspectives in the project, but on the other hand, they can also inhibit the process, as the continuous joint collection and

---

9. For details on critical feedback from the participants, see Schwab and Oesterle (2022, Chapter 4 this volume). Complaints included too few activities for group cohesion, days that were too long and exhausting, and a lack of time to carry out their own research projects. In response to this, the proPIC team created a guideline for the conception and implementation of a study week with adaptations to the study programme. These experiences show the particular relevance of a sensible group composition, the implementation of team-building measures, and clearly communicated guidelines on work assignments and workload.

processing of experiences are particularly valuable. In the context of ProPIC, international teams have proven their worth in partner meetings on specific topics and in planning social activities to foster a sense of togetherness among the individual project partners. Coordinators need a high level of commitment, problem-solving skills, and management strategies.

All optimisation strategies ultimately depend on the respective commitment of the individual partners, with whom they jointly agree on the ideas of transculturality and intercultural learning. As teacher educators, they serve as role models for internationalisation, research orientation, and digitalisation.

6. The role of digital tools and activities in transnational collaboration

The 'i' in proPIC stands for innovation and points to the consistent use of digital and mobile technologies in education, especially as preparation for later use in the teaching profession. In the context of this contribution, we will endeavour to present the innovative use of these technologies as an essential component of transnational cooperation and to illustrate their value. Our focus is on both the collaboration of international student learning groups and the technologically supported processes of collaboration among project partners as team-based research and organisation. Based on the survey after the first study week, the focus of our presentation will be on our experiences with the use and interaction of the digital tools and activities within proPIC. In doing so, we will also refer to the empirical results of relevant research.

Two now relatively widespread methods of digital support for learning were explicitly defined as the outputs of the project: interactive tutorials and e-portfolios. Both are discussed in more detail in separate contributions in this volume (see Baldwin & Ruhtenberg, 2022, and Cuesta, Batlle, González, & Pujolà, 2022, Chapters 5 and 7 this volume). At this point, we will only address the question of how these two products can influence certain forms of transnational cooperation.

Chapter 3

Interactive tutorials are usually understood to be supportive learning scenarios that take place online and use personal knowledge exchange as a measure to increase individual learning progress. In contrast, the concept of interactive tutorials in proPIC is primarily digital (though not necessarily online) and to a large extent oriented towards forms of autonomous learning. As a media reference and product orientation, the focus is on the iBook and its use in transnational learning groups. Tool-based interactive tutorials, as represented by the iBook, are fundamentally aimed at multimodally supported knowledge acquisition (Kuleshow, 2008). Their conception and creation require, on the one hand, professional expertise, but also a high degree of media competence and didactic understanding. An essential moment in our creation of iBooks was the determination of use and user group. At the same time, it should be ensured that they make the learning material accessible to the widest possible circle of students. To achieve this last goal, it was necessary to use English as the vehicle language. A concrete difficulty was that the specific level of prior knowledge of the learners could not be assessed and taken into account, although it is possible in principle to design tool-based interactive tutorials in a differentiated way for example. With a selection of different learning paths and speeds taking into account the prior knowledge and experience of the learners, this proved to be utopian in the context of the concrete project work simply because of the effort involved.

The interactive tutorials iBooks of proPIC[10] were created by the teams of the individual project partners according to their respective expertise. The principle of international cooperation could only be realised to some extent at this point, namely by means of a cooperative evaluation of all partners involved. However, it must be taken into account that the tutorials were created as a quintessence of the particular focus at the individual educational institutions and are intended to create self-learning opportunities for students, so that interested parties from different national educational systems can gain expert access to this central educational content. Transnational cooperation is thus guaranteed here in the broadest sense by the fact that forms of autonomous learning are

---

10. http://www.propiceuropa.com/io4-interactive-tutorials.html

also consciously placed in a meaningful international context. In addition, in the course of producing the tutorials, peer reviewing among the partners also provides an occasion for transnational academic exchange and helps to promote further developments.

However, with a view to the given scope of the interactive tutorials, more incentives for collaborative work could also be created. On the one hand, the added value of the respective topic, for example, digital tools (Interactive tutorial 6, see Ruhtenberg, Baldwin, & Oesterle, 2020), for special forms of collaboration is discussed in the individual tutorials. On the other hand, elements to promote factual collaboration among the participants would also be conceivable as a supplement. For example, a constructive proposal would be to design exercises that must be carried out compulsorily with a project participant from another university. However, such conditions would increase the organisational effort. In particular, it could prove difficult for a student to cooperate with a fellow student from another country in completing certain tasks due to different semester times or non-synchronised learning phases of autonomous learning. Therefore, the framework conditions for such individual cooperation in the transnational learning scenarios could certainly be further improved.

The e-portfolio has gained importance in recent years, especially in the field of foreign language teaching and learning (Shulman, 1998; Stefani, Mason, & Pegler, 2007). Its tasks are diverse and range from the functions of a learning diary to documentation tools and collections of tasks. It is not only used by learners in the school environment, but also in the overarching training phases of trainee teachers, preferably in the practical parts. In the latter case, the e-portfolio as a digital collection tool offers a variety of possibilities for media presentation and storage of very different products, both individual and collected in class (Alexioua & Paraskeva, 2010). The possibility of reviewing also offers insights into one's own and others' learning processes and opportunities for professional reflection, which is promoted as a core competence for future teachers.

Chapter 3

Within the framework of proPIC, the e-portfolio has proven its special importance as a reflection tool[11]. In the first cohort, only individual e-portfolios were created; from the second cohort onwards, joint portfolios were possible. Thus, some students also embedded in their portfolios jointly created materials from the study week, such as their film made during a workshop at Kiel University[12]. It is striking that in such cases only students from the same university have joined forces. It would therefore be a sensible task for the project partners from the different countries to encourage the participants to cooperate across countries in creating their e-portfolios.

Ultimately, the organisational effort and the importance of the e-portfolio as an assessment basis for the students should be taken into account. Without a doubt, e-portfolios have a much greater potential for transnational cooperation than was used in the framework of proPIC (see also Cuesta et al., 2022, Chapter 7 this volume). The online format would allow students to create and edit contributions asynchronously, independent of location, which the cooperation partner could in turn view and comment on. Further testing of these possibilities seems appropriate. It should also be noted that the project partners themselves have created a joint teacher training portfolio[13]. The project coordinator in Karlsruhe was responsible for the design and compilation of the contributions, but the embedded material was produced in an organised form through international cooperation. This shows that a joint transnational e-portfolio is certainly conceivable.

In the following, we will look at two groups of digital tools and activities that have played an important role in proPIC, interactive tutorials, and e-portfolios. One serves to realise efficient communicative settings and the other is intended to support the learning process of the participants.

---

11. http://www.propiceuropa.com/students.html

12. https://sites.google.com/view/propic-kiel/home/2nd-day-in-project?authuser=0

13. http://www.propiceuropa.com/teacher-educators.html

The proPIC project has also used various tools for different communicative purposes. The project partners have regularly communicated digitally, both asynchronously – mostly by email, but occasionally via Slack – and synchronously via the now commonly known web conferences. Interestingly, neither traditional phone calls nor data-based spontaneous calls have played a major role in communication. All documents, presentations, photos, etc. were uploaded to a shared cloud folder and could be viewed by all project partners. In text documents with shared access, it was thus possible to work together with others. For their part, the students also networked with the communication tool Slack, on which special information and exchange channels (e.g. for study week) were set up in advance. The special communication structure of Slack, which also enables private chats and group chats, suggests that the students no longer resorted to WhatsApp or comparable media beyond that. In addition, from the second cohort onwards, participants were asked to upload a self-introduction as a video on Flipgrid before the start of the study week so that everyone could get to know each other in advance. During the study week itself, a web conference scheduled by the organisers was held with all participants from the second cohort onwards. Although most of the students first had to familiarise themselves with the communication tools used, they ultimately found their use to be a good basis for joint work and with their help quickly developed uncomplicated ways of working together while overcoming the distance. Various tools were also used to convey the specific learning content. For the joint generation of ideas, these were mainly Padlet and Mindmeister. Padlet was also used as a feedback tool (see Figure 2 below).

For scientific exchange, a public document in Google Docs was set up as a file for research topics and literature references[14]. The basic idea was that students with similar research interests could get in touch with each other. This opportunity was ultimately not used as some students did not share their projects. It can thus be stated that the collaborative potential of the tools used in the learning context within the framework of proPIC was mainly used in

---

14. https://docs.google.com/document/d/1WNkkZJ5MiY0yCEzlszxVQjr-ykVn-oH5Byz6Ic6MUQ0/edit

Courses 1 and 2 at the home universities. The decisive factor for this was the respective familiarity of the lecturers with these media in their everyday teaching.

Figure 2. Extract of a Padlet used as feedback tool at CAU during the first cohort

> **padlet**   padlet.com/isabelmurillo/1gf3chv7t0gc
>
> ## Comments and suggestions
> Thank you for helping us improve ProPIC!
> ISABEL MWILSTER   AUG 01, 2018 12:39PM
>
> **Day 4**
> I can't believe that we've already finished the 4th day! Day to day I even more like our group and the friendly, respectful atmosphere during the week. The activity in which we organized this mind map and used one of these new tools we've talked about yesterday I liked definitely the most. I was surprised how easy it works and what a good method to work together it is. I really try to implement some tools like this in my teaching and I'm sure that students will love it.
>
> **Day 4**
> Yes! This is today's winner. I absolutely agree. But while planning the activity I was kind of afraid. Brainstorming is a
>
> The exercise of today I liked the most was definitely the mind mapping about possible upcoming challenges for us as future language teachers. I think we came up with many aspects and the collaboration helped to think about other aspects you weren't conscious about before. I am sure the mind map will be useful for my future reflection process, because it offers us many small pieces to think about in regard to lesson planning. I would also agree that the last video about action research may not have been necessary to treat, because we had been speaking about it in detail before. All in all, I am really thankful that you shared many personal information with us which was totally encouraging and without the great dynamic within the team may not have been possible. I am looking forward for tomorrow and I am kind of sad that it's our last day of the course

So far, we have discussed the use of digital tools and activities in the context of transnational collaboration from the point of view of their practical affordances. However, we have seen in the past COVID-19 times that this is far from sufficient. A meaningful digitalisation of teaching must also ensure and support the social community of learning groups and their respective form of virtual collaboration in an appropriate way. While the good infrastructure of proPIC enabled participants to have a positive learning experience within a community, other initiatives that are less well secured in terms of material and structure run the risk of degenerating into poorly organised distance learning with a lack of contact among learners. This danger is countered by team-based and product-oriented learning tasks, which can be very well harmonised with the use of digitally based forms of learning.

A fruitful contribution to the digital development of our transnational training format was the integration of self-made video productions within the framework of the proPIC project, with which CAU already has many years of experience in foreign language teacher training. The Viducation project has been used at CAU since 2013 and is dedicated to the idea of filmmaking by students as part of curricular training, especially for the teaching profession[15]. The success of the project lies in the creative use of a form of media expression that is familiar to students both passively and actively – e.g. through the everyday use of tools such as Youtube, Vimeo, Instagram, or TikTok. As a partner university, Kiel has therefore stressed the importance of including educational videos and their self-production by students as a topic in proPIC from the very beginning. On the one hand, this has led to the creation and use of a corresponding interactive tutorial; on the other hand, it has also shaped the design of the proPIC courses in Kiel for the preparation and follow-up of the study week. The workshops were a special highlight on video production during the Kiel study weeks[16] and the videos created by the participants themselves[17].

The innovative character of this activity lay above all in the conceptual expansion of the educational video away from the pure explanatory video to a broad spectrum of alternative genres, which – partly in combination – represent a completely new form of inspiration for learning processes. The students also used this innovative potential of filmmaking in proPIC with joy and creativity:

> "we had a lot of fun. […] It's been really interesting to make this video, we were four girls from different countries. We all have the same opinion about that self-produced videos is a didactic potential, but we needed our time to agree on how to put it on an image" (Participant of the second cohort 2019, collected through the e-portfolio).

---

15. Link to the project presentation of 'Viducation' on the 'Good Teaching Blog' of Kiel University; https://viducation.net/
16. Link to the workshop slides on 'Viducation' at the Kiel study weeks.
17. https://youtu.be/bNBrb6Q6ZaI

During the first study week, four incoming students had the task of making a documentary video[18] that offers a lot of space for interpretative accents and reflections on the learning processes experienced. These small film productions were one (and by no means the only) example within the framework of proPIC that offered the clear advantage of experiencing digitally based learning activities in internationally composed small groups as a community, while creating a small project in transnational collaboration. The mere fact that the specifics of the experienced learning scenarios and joint learning activities on site were perceived as 'different' from the perspective of the specific national realities of teacher education and provided food for thought for one's own professionalisation can and must be considered a success. Furthermore, it should be mentioned that the finished product of the self-made short film can be used in many different and sustainable ways for further forms of transnational collaboration.

7. Concluding reflections

We have titled this paper 'getting curious and gaining knowledge', and in the end we can draw a positive conclusion: the new learning experience in teacher education initiated by proPIC was an enrichment for teachers and learners and associated with a clear increase in knowledge for all involved. At the same time, we have found that transnational collaboration is very demanding in practical implementation. The framework of the study programme developed by proPIC gave us the opportunity to prove the practicality of the concept and to show not only that it can work, but also how it can work and what can be done to improve it. Thinking beyond proPIC, we would perhaps identify the organisational and financial burden (especially for the students) as the biggest problem with a lasting impact. The financial protection provided by an Erasmus+ project offered an exceptionally protected space here. In this context, it was very encouraging to learn that important focal points of foreign

---

18. https://youtu.be/A5LmB4LGI0Q

language didactics, such as intercultural learning and digitalisation, could be strengthened within the framework of transnational collaboration and that the use of new technologies proved to be particularly efficient in this context. In the cooperation of different institutions with different expertise, there was also a good opportunity for the students to realise research-oriented learning. In this sense, the concept of internationalisation provides essential impulses for more curiosity, motivation, inquisitiveness, commitment, competence development, and communication skills. And last but not least, important learning and knowledge contents are addressed which, in a positive sense, go beyond the basic subject didactic knowledge of the foreign language learners and lead them to reflect critically on their (later) professional activities in a sustainable way. All in all, transnational collaboration as part of a study programme thus makes an important contribution to CPD for student teachers.

References

Ahlgrimm, F., Westphal, A., Wallert, A., & Heck, S. (2019). Weshalb Studierende (nicht) ins Ausland gehen. Prädikatoren für Mobilität im Lehramtsstudium. In C. Falkenhagen, N. Grimm & L. Volkmann (Eds), *Internationalisierung des Lehramtsstudiums. Modelle, Konzepte, Erfahrungen* (pp. 211-233). Ferdinand Schöningh. https://doi.org/10.30965/9783657728459_014

Alexioua, A., & Paraskeva, F. (2010). Enhancing self-regulated learning skills through the implementation of an e-portfolio tool. *Procedia Social and Behavioral Sciences, 2*(2010), 3048-3054. https://doi.org/10.1016/j.sbspro.2010.03.463

Baldwin, R., & Ruhtenberg, T. (2022). Student reactions to using interactive tutorials as part of the proPIC study programme. In G. Schwab, M. Oesterle & A. Whelan (Eds), *Promoting professionalism, innovation and transnational collaboration: a new approach to foreign language teacher education* (pp. 131-145). Research-publishing.net. https://doi.org/10.14705/rpnet.2022.57.1386

Caniglia, G., Luederitz, C., Groß, M., Muhr, M., John, B., Withycombe Keeler, L., von Wehrden, H., Laubichler, M., Wiek, A., & Lang, D. (2017). Transnational collaboration for sustainability in higher education: lessons from a systematic review. *Journal of Cleaner Production, 168*(1), 764-779. https://doi.org/10.1016/j.jclepro.2017.07.256

Crăciun, D., & Orosz, K. (2018). *Benefits and costs of transnational collaborative partnerships in higher education: executive summary*. EENEE Analytical Report 36. https://data.europa.eu/doi/10.2766/395704

Cuesta, A., Batlle, J., González, V., & Pujolà, J.-T. (2022). Approaches to the development of pre-service language teachers' e-portfolios. In G. Schwab, M. Oesterle & A. Whelan (Eds), Promoting professionalism, innovation and transnational collaboration: a new approach to foreign language teacher education (pp. 191-212). Research-publishing.net. https://doi.org/10.14705/rpnet.2022.57.1388

Cushner, K. (2009). The role of study abroad in preparing globally responsible teachers. In R. Lewin (Ed.), *The handbook of practice and research in study abroad: higher education and the quest for global citizenship issues* (pp. 151-169). Taylor & Francis Group. https://doi.org/10.4324/9780203876640

De Wit, H., & Altbach, P. G. (2020). Internationalization in higher education: global trends and recommendations for its future. *Policy Reviews in Higher Education, 5*(1), 28-46. https://doi.org/10.1080/23322969.2020.1820898

Heimböckel, D., & Weinberg, M. (2014). Interkulturalität als Projekt. *Zeitschrift für interkulturelle Germanistik, 5*, 119-144. https://doi.org/10.14361/zig-2014-0211

Kercher, J., & Schifferings, M. (2019). Auslandsmobilität von Lehramtsstudierenden in Deutschland. Ein Überblick zur Datenlage und zu praktischen Umsetzungsbeispielen. In C. Falkenhagen, N. Grimm & L. Volkmann (Eds), *Internationalisierung des Lehramtsstudiums. Modelle, Konzepte, Erfahrungen* (pp. 235-261). Ferdinand Schöningh. https://doi.org/10.30965/9783657728459_015

Krämer, A., & Springob, J. (2019). Mobilität von Lehramtsstudierenden - Desiderat in Lehre und Forschung. Beispiele der Umsetzung an der Universität zu Köln. In C. Falkenhagen, N. Grimm & L. Volkmann (Eds), *Internationalisierung des Lehramtsstudiums. Modelle, Konzepte, Erfahrungen* (pp. 193-207). Ferdinand Schöningh. https://doi.org/10.30965/9783657728459_013

Kuleshow, G. (2008). Web-enhanced vs. traditional approach for a science course. In T. Hansson (Ed.), *Handbook of research on digital information technologies. innovations, methods, and ethical issues* (pp. 102-116). Information Science Reference. https://doi.org/10.4018/978-1-59904-970-0

Leutwyler, B. (2014). Between myths and facts. The contribution of exchange experiences to the professional development of teachers. *Journal of Curriculum and Teaching, 3*(2), 106-117. https://doi.org/10.5430/jct.v3n2p106

Leutwyler, B., Popov, N., & Wolhuter, C. (2017, June). *The internationalization of teacher education: different contexts, similar challenges* [Conference presentation]. Annual International Conference of the Bulgarian Comparative Education Society (BCES) (15th) and the International Partner Conference of the International Research Centre (IRC), Borovets, Bulgaria. https://www.academia.edu/37616581/The_Internationalization_of_ Teacher_Education_Different_Contexts_Similar_Challenges

Makhmudov, K. (2020). Ways of forming intercultural communication in foreign language teaching. *Science and Education, 1*(4), 84-89.

Mann, S., & Webb, K. (2022). Continuing professional development: key themes in supporting the development of professional practice. In G. Schwab, M. Oesterle & A. Whelan (Eds), Promoting professionalism, innovation and transnational collaboration: a new approach to foreign language teacher education (pp. 15-44). Research-publishing.net. https://doi.org/10.14705/rpnet.2022.57.1382

Oesterle, M., & Schwab, G. (2022). Developing a framework of CPD for the context of foreign language teaching. In G. Schwab, M. Oesterle & A. Whelan (Eds), Promoting professionalism, innovation and transnational collaboration: a new approach to foreign language teacher education (pp. 45-79). Research-publishing.net. https://doi.org/10.14705/rpnet.2022.57.1383

Onishchuk, I., Ikonnikova, M., Antonenko, T., Kharchenko, I., Shestakova, S., Kuzmenko, N., & Maksymchuk, B. (2020). Characteristics of foreign language education in foreign countries and ways of applying foreign experience in pedagogical universities of Ukraine. *Revista Romaneasca pentru Educatie Multidimensionala, 12*(3), 45-65. https://doi.org/10.18662/rrem/12.3/308

Ruhtenberg, T., Baldwin, R., & Oesterle, M. (2020). proPIC Interactive tutorial 6□. Innovative digital tools and methods [iBook]. iTunes. https://books.apple.com/us/book/propic-interactive-tutorial-6/id1525356644?ls=1

Schwab, G., & Oesterle, M. (2022). The proPIC study weeks: experiencing transnational exchange. In G. Schwab, M. Oesterle & A. Whelan (Eds), Promoting professionalism, innovation and transnational collaboration: a new approach to foreign language teacher education (pp. 107-130). Research-publishing.net. https://doi.org/10.14705/rpnet.2022.57.1385

Shulman, L. (1998). Teacher portfolios: a theoretical activity. In N. Lyons (Ed.), *With portfolio in hand: validating the new teacher professionalism* (pp. 23-37). Teachers College Press.

Smith, K. (2010). Assuring quality in transnational higher education: a matter of collaboration or control? *Studies in Higher Education, 35*(7), 793-806. https://doi.org/10.1080/03075070903340559

Stefani, L., Mason, R., & Pegler, C. (2007). *The educational potential of e-portfolios: supporting personal development and reflective learning.* Routledge. https://doi.org/10.4324/9780203961292

Walkowska, K. (2018). Interkulturelles Lernen und Lehren im Fremdsprachenunterricht – warum, wozu und wie? *Forum Filologiczne Ateneum, 1*(6), 187-202. https://doi.org/10.36575/2353-2912/1(6)2018.187

Welsch, W. (1999). Transculturality - the puzzling form of cultures today. In M. Featherstone & S. Lash (Eds), *Spaces of culture: city, nation, world* (pp. 194-213). Sage.

Wulf, C. (2020). Transkulturalität. *Bildungsforschung, 1*, 1-13. https://doi.org/10.25656/01:19316

# 4. The proPIC study weeks: experiencing transnational exchange

Götz Schwab[1] and Mareike Oesterle[2]

1. Introduction

A core element of the proPIC project is the development and implementation of the so-called study weeks: a five day face-to-face stay abroad at one of the partner institutions in which all the participating students took part. In this chapter, we present and discuss the results and impact of these events which took place twice during the project[3]. In order to do so, we have included the overall framework of the events, as well as assorted materials developed by the project partners to present the scope of the various study weeks. Additionally, an overview of relevant literature dealing with the concept of short stays abroad in teacher education programmes will be provided.

To discuss the impact of two cohorts of exchange students, we use a rich body of collected data of the project partners and students, as well as some fieldwork data (e.g. video- and audio-recordings) that were gathered during the study week and analysed afterwards. The chapter will conclude with recommendations for conducting similar activities in collaboration with international partners.

---

1. University of Education Ludwigsburg, Ludwigsburg, Germany; goetz.schwab@ph-ludwigsburg.de; https://orcid.org/0000-0003-0939-3325

2. University of Education Ludwigsburg, Ludwigsburg, Germany; mareike.oesterle@gmx.de; https://orcid.org/0000-0002-9458-7927

3. Unfortunately, a third study week had to be cancelled on short notice due to the outbreak of the COVID-19 pandemic.

How to cite: Schwab, G., & Oesterle, M. (2022). The proPIC study weeks: experiencing transnational exchange. In G. Schwab, M. Oesterle & A. Whelan (Eds), *Promoting professionalism, innovation and transnational collaboration: a new approach to foreign language teacher education* (pp. 107-130). Research-publishing.net. https://doi.org/10.14705/rpnet.2022.57.1385

2. Literature review

Especially for future language teachers, a certain amount of time spent abroad is much more than the icing on the cake of one's studies. Obviously, it is not a new idea to provide opportunities for studying at a foreign university when becoming a foreign language (FL) teacher (Bruce, 1991; Heuer & Klippel, 1987). Thus, it has already been implemented in many study programmes across the globe, and also the European Commission is heavily promoting this notion when they state that "spending time abroad to study and learn should become the norm" (European Commission, 2018b, p. 21). Nonetheless, the global pandemic showed us how difficult this can get, especially with regard to longer stays.

For a number of reasons, it looks like an important educational aim to give students the opportunity to attend institutions abroad: next to improving one's linguistic competences in a natural and (more) authentic environment of the target language – even if it is 'just' used as a lingua franca – gaining inter- and transcultural competence is usually considered the greatest asset in going abroad (Boye, 2016; for a general perspective on teacher education see e.g. Marx & Moss, 2011). In addition, personal growth seems to be a key feature of such endeavours (Dwyer & Peters, 2004). Furthermore, student mobility can help to elevate one's professional perspectives in teacher education (Bruce, 1991). Additionally, it can raise awareness of global issues (Jaritz, 2011), which are important in today's diverse, multicultural, and multilingual classroom settings (Stewart, 2008). Finally, international mobility is intended to strengthen the identity of European citizenship (European Commission, 2018a).

Interestingly enough, this understanding is not just promoted by teacher educators or other professionals in the field, but by students alike. In a survey conducted by the European Commission (2018b), it turned out that more than 90% of the participating young people between the ages of 15 and 30 "consider it important to have an experience abroad" (p. 3) and almost 50% of them considered it to be "very important" (p. 4). However, other studies indicate that, in particular, the field of education still remains quite locally, if not nationally oriented (Goetz, Jaritz, & Oser, 2011; Jaritz, 2011), which can be related to the fact that teacher education policy is still overly dependent on national policy makers and often lacks a global perspective.

It is obvious that international endeavours such as virtual exchanges or short study abroad programmes cannot fully compensate for an extended stay abroad of one or two semesters. They are more likely to be seen as an option for those who are not able to spend a longer time away from home due to personal or financial reasons (Dooly & O'Dowd, 2012; Kessler, Haim, & Schwab, forthcoming), or as an add-on to existing agreements (Waldman, Harel, & Schwab, 2019). Nonetheless, we have also seen in another of our projects, 'Extended Telecollaboration Practice', that these short term engagements can be a trigger for further activities abroad (Waldman et al., 2019).

Summing up, we agree with Marx and Moss (2011) when they state that "[t]eacher education study abroad programs can be powerful vehicles in teacher educators' efforts to prepare preservice teachers for work with culturally diverse students, providing a unique opportunity for them to learn how to 'mind the culture gap' that can exist in school contexts" (p. 45). In this line, the study week abroad became key to our study programme.

3. The outline of the study weeks

3.1. How were the study weeks organised?

The study week is a central component of the proPIC project (see Figure 1). As part of the overall study programme (see Hoinke & Clausen, 2022, Chapter 3 this volume), prospective teachers visited one of the other four European partner institutions where they worked and studied together with international students from the other participating universities. All study weeks took place at the same time as this turned out to be the only way of handling the sheer amount of differences among students and lecturers and their national constraints with regard to workload or examinations. The study weeks were (almost) completely funded by the project grant.

Figure 1. Overview of the proPIC study programme[4]

COURSE I				COURSE II			final conference (July 2020)
Module I.A	Module I.B	Module I.C	Study week	Module II.A	Module II.B		
course introduction	input theoretical framework (CPD, working with cases)	work with the *interactive tutorials*	visit a partner university	finalise your research project and create your creative outputs	present your results and creative outputs		optional submit a proposal and present your results at an international conference
get in touch with the students from the other partner institutions (social media, MOODLE)	research project develop your own research question	elaborate your research design get individual online-coachings	collaborate in transnational groups elaborate work with *interactive tutorials* visit a local school	get individual coaching	final discussion		
	start your ePortfolio						
f-2-f / online	f-2-f / online	online	5-Tage-Aufenthalt	online	f-2-f		f-2-f
constant reflection through *ePortfolios*							

3.2. Who took part in the study weeks and who hosted them?

All participants of the study weeks were prospective foreign and second language teachers and therefore students already enrolled in one of the partner universities' study programmes[5] (graduates and undergraduates). Students had to apply for these trips in advance as there were only a limited number of spots available. The events were hosted by the project partners and usually conducted by two local partners. In Germany, Study Week 2 was hosted by the University of Kiel (CAU) and conducted by both partners from Germany: Kiel and Karlsruhe. Where possible, a number of teacher trainers were given the opportunity to teach in one the study weeks at a different institution in order to broaden their own professional development in the field of internationalisation[6].

---

4. http://www.propiceuropa.com/uploads/1/0/8/0/108097905/propic_io1_online_handbook_2020.pdf

5. This is important for their health insurance status.

6. Based on the very positive feedback of both lecturers and students, we intended to extend this idea in our third cohort which then had to be cancelled due to the pandemic.

In total, 30 students took part in the first study week and 44 in the second study week.

The following graph (Figure 2) shows how students – here: those attending Karlsruhe University of Education (PHKA) – were to be distributed equally among the other four institutions during the study week.

Figure 2. Distribution of students during Study Week 1 sent by PHKA[7]

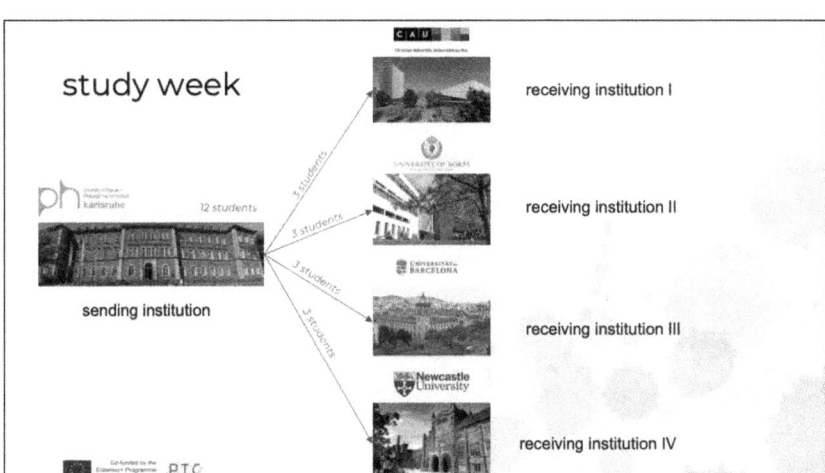

As not all of the 12 students were able to go abroad, the number of students from Karlsruhe dropped to nine. This also happened at other institutions. It transpired that some students were more reluctant (or afraid?) to go abroad than others and that organisational and more subjective challenges for such a trip ('Can I afford the extra costs?'; 'Will the accommodation provided be suitable for me?'; 'I only want to go to xy') formed an obstacle so that we could not send as many students as we wanted to and as our budget would have allowed us to do.

---

7. proPIC Europa (2020). Study Week; http://www.propiceuropa.com/study-week.html

Chapter 4

3.3. What was the main content and what were the main activities of the study weeks?

All study week events were given a special focus in line with the expertise of the host institution. Continuous Professional Development (CPD), however, was an overarching topic all partners dealt with. The accompanying material on CPD was developed in advance by one partner and then presented during the study week. In addition, all partners included social activities and at a certain point all groups met online on Zoom for a brief welcome session.

The following image depicts a typical schedule of such a study week (Figure 3).

Figure 3. Programme for Study Week 2 (University of Barcelona, UB)[8]

STUDY WEEK AGENDA

Monday (6th)	Tuesday (7th)	Wednesday (8th)	Thursday (9th)	Friday (10th)
9.00-9.30 Study week opening: introductory session	10.30-11.30 Digital communicative strategies in the elaboration of an e-portfolio (Joan-Tomàs Pujolà)	9.00-10.00 Introductory workshop on the use of VEO for lesson observation (Jaume Batlle)	9.00-9.30 Presentation session: mobile tasks (Preparation)	9.00-11.00 Show & Tell: our e-portfolios (Azahara Cuesta y Joan-Tomàs Pujolà)
9.30-11.00 1 image and 1000 words: Reflective introductory activity (Azahara Cuesta)		10.30-12.30 Lesson observation (UB-Vanesa Torquero y Cristina Castillo)	9.30-11.30 Presentation session: mobile tasks (Azahara Cuesta y Joan-Tomàs Pujolà)	11.00-12.00 Study week evaluation
BREAK	BREAK			12.00-12.30 Certificates, Farewell cava and deadline for handing in extra cost original copies of tickets and invoices
11.30-13.30 Elaborating a Starting Point on a snapshot of digital competences with Digcompedu (Azahara Cuesta)	11.45-13.45 Active Learning, mobile learning (Joan-Tomàs Pujolà)	12.30- 13.00 Uploading video	BREAK	
		13.00-13.30 LUNCH	12.00 -13.00 EPORTFOLIO TIME: Improving your e-portfolio	12.30 Study week closing
13.30-14.30 LUNCH	13.45-15.00 LUNCH	13.30-15.30 Shared reflection with VEO (Jaume Batlle)	13.00-13.30 LUNCH	
14.30-16.00: Catalan survivor toolkit: A first day lesson in catalan language (Jaume Batlle)	15.00-16.00 Designing a "mobile" communicative task	15.30-16.00 EPORTFOLIO TIME: Individual work on the personal e-portfolio	13.30 -15.30 Cultural visit: Laberint d'Horta	
	16.00-16.30-Skype PROPIC partners			
16.00-17.00 EPORTFOLIO TIME: Individual work on the personal e-portfolio	16.30-17.30 EPORTFOLIO TIME: Individual work on the personal e-portfolio	21.30 Social Event: Dinner La Cervesería de Gràcia	16.00-17.00: Use of ICTS in Secondary education. (Maria del Mar Rosso Febrer)	

As can be seen in this outline, the Spanish partner focused in particular on e-portfolios as a substantial aspect of professional development and reflection

---

8. http://www.propiceuropa.com/uploads/1/0/8/0/108097905/propic_p4_stud_week_ii_schedule.pdf

for future language teachers. As this is also a core feature of the university's FL teacher education programme, it tied in very well with the objectives of the project. Of course, other students involved in the project also worked on e-portfolios as part of their professional development though less intensively than the groups in Spain (for more details on the use of e-portfolios in general see also Cuesta, Batlle, González, & Pujolà, 2022, Chapter 7 this volume).

Though based on a similar framework, each partner had a different focal aspect they dealt with. In Kiel, students worked intensively on video production (cf. Whelan & Baldwin, 2022, Chapter 11 this volume). In Newcastle, the main focus of the students' work involved the VEO (Video Enhanced Observation) and Linguacuisine app. The Swedish partners approached the notion of professional development from a slightly broader angle as they dealt with an array of digital and mobile devices, a topic that turned out to be more than beneficial for both students and lecturers just a few months later when the pandemic broke out. In Karlsruhe, we took a specific look at the use of iBooks and their potential use in the (foreign) language classroom (more on these topics in Baldwin & Ruhtenberg, 2022, Chapter 5 this volume).

Most of the content of the study week programme remained the same all through the project period. However, some minor adjustments had to be made, especially after the first cohort. This was related to the sheer amount of activities offered by some partners. At the beginning, ambitious schedules were put up to provide students a comprehensive insight into the different focal points, together with a wide array of educational and social activities. It soon turned out that students needed more time to work on their individual and group projects, as well as to digest the new environment. By limiting the amount of work in the courses (e.g. reducing the number of activities), we managed to get more students involved in the second and (planned) third cohort (which unfortunately could not take place due to the restrictions caused by the pandemic).

During the study week, student teachers visited local schools, got to know teachers and the education system of the respective countries, documented their learning in a personal e-portfolio, developed a research project, and took part in social and cultural activities. Most importantly, the participants had the opportunity to meet and collaborate with international students and professionals with different expertise and cultural backgrounds (Figure 4).

Figure 4. proPIC Europa video – Study Week 2

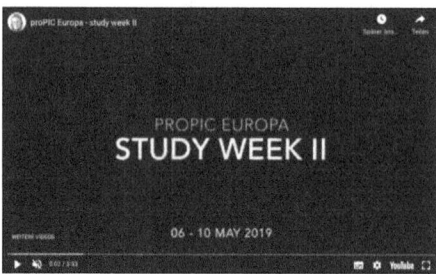

In addition to that, participating students were introduced to a wide range of mobile technologies that they could use for their own teaching and learning. Among the tools included here were such popular apps as Kahoot, Flipgrid, Padlet, or Nearpod, but also more specific tools such as the classroom observation app VEO (Schwab & Oesterle, 2021), the Linguacuisine app (Seedhouse, Heslop, & Kharrufa, 2019), and different tools for video production. As the project was conducted pre-COVID-19, we were pleasantly surprised to see many of these tools used afterwards during numerous online-teaching sessions in higher education programmes and at schools.

Additionally, students were given the opportunity to work on small projects with students coming from the other partner institutions, exchange their experiences and their traditions and methodologies of learning and teaching a foreign and second language, and build intercultural and transnational networks.

4. Evaluation of Study Weeks 1 and 2

As our programme was specifically tailored to the needs of future language teachers, we dedicate the main body of this section to the feedback given by the participating students. Nonetheless, the teacher educators' comments on their work with the students is considered here as well.

4.1. Student evaluation

Beyond doubt, the study weeks and their impact on the participants can be considered as one of if not the most crucial element of the proPIC project. In order to receive a comprehensive picture of what those participating students perceived during their stays at one of the partner institutions, we conducted a number of evaluative activities. Among them were (1) an online survey, (2) collections of written reflections as provided in a Padlet, as well as (3) Flipgrid video feedback by individuals or in pairs. The data will be presented in the following.

The main instrument used to evaluate the two study weeks was an online survey (SurveyMonkey) which all participating students had to fill in at the end of the week. In the following, we showcase the main results of it graphically as well as with sample comments by the participating students. In the latter part, we also include data from data sources (2) and (3).

4.2. Student surveys

The survey comprised ten items (Q1-10) and included multiple choice questions (e.g. 'Please select the institution you come from') as well as six open-ended questions. The latter ones will mainly be referred to in the next section. Here, a summary of the overall judgement of the students is given.

When looking at the overall feedback of both study weeks, especially with regard to how useful students considered them (Q8), a number of indicators become obvious: in both cases, the most positive category is 'interaction with teacher educators/lecturers' (100% and 94%).

In Cohort 1, this was followed by 'fun' (84%), 'clarity of presented input' (76%) and 'effectiveness of presented input', 'technical support', and

Chapter 4

'supporting international collaboration' (72% all). Cohort 2 gave high marks to 'cooperation with international students' and 'fun' (both 84%), and 'clarity of presentation' (76%). Only one student in each cohort made use of the option 'poor' for any of the categories. Interestingly, a lot of students named 'school visits' as a highlight of the study week in other evaluations (Flipgrid video/ Padlet), though only 68% and even 40% indicated this activity as 'very good' in the survey on the usefulness of the activities. It seems as if the social aspects of working or being together with others were perceived as very beneficial, which becomes even more enlightening when looking at it from a post-COVID-19 angle.

Figure 5 and Figure 6 provide an overview of all the aspects asked about.

Figure 5. Study Week 1 – overall feedback

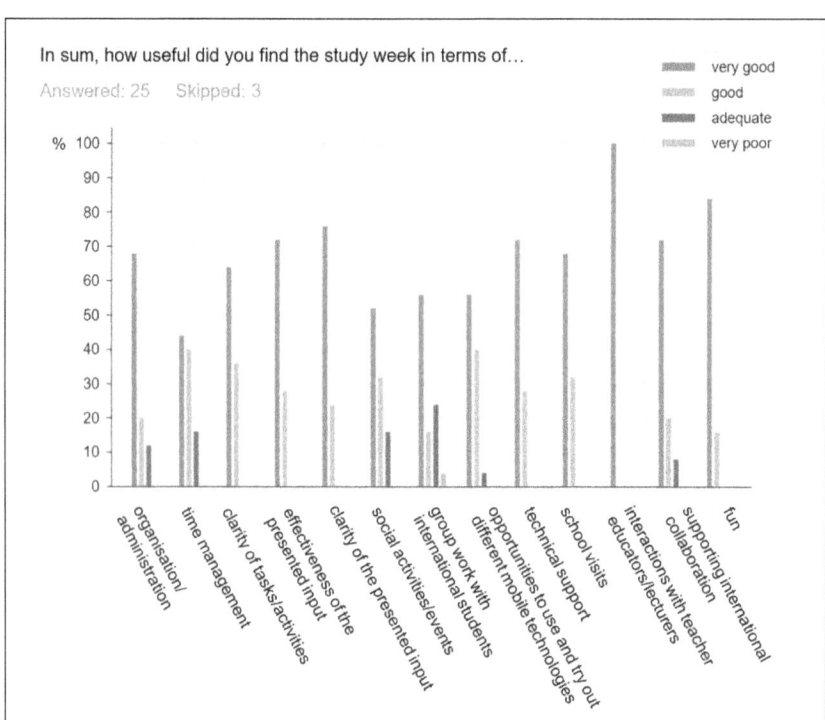

Figure 6. Study Week 2 – overall feedback

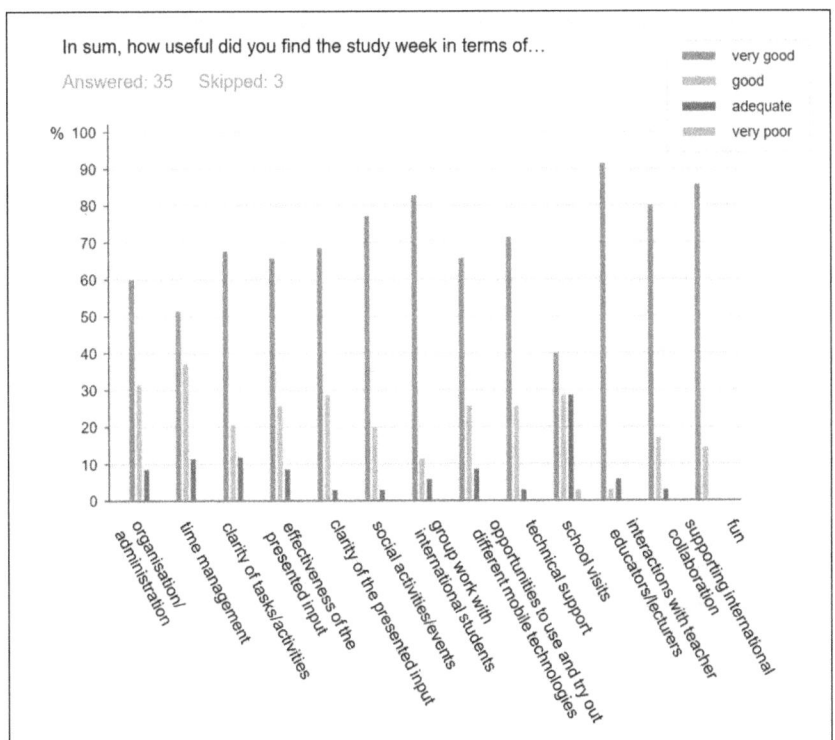

As we show below, students seem to judge some of the activities differently when using other reflection tools and formats such as Padlet (written) or Flipgrid (video). As all the evaluations were conducted during the study week, this seems to have other reasons. It might be that questions were not posed exactly the same way, e.g. 'How useful did you find the study week' (survey) versus 'What did you like the most about the study week' (Flipgrid). Thus, the feedback on the various aspects of the study week differed quite a bit.

Most surprisingly, the school visits did not get such an overwhelmingly positive review by either cohort, as this was expressed by individual students, especially in the video feedback.

Chapter 4

A further point of interest for us was how useful students considered digital tools and mobile technologies presented during the study weeks. A great majority perceived this part of the study week as very positive (88%/86%) whereas all the others deemed it 'somewhat useful'.

When looking at the comments from the students, it becomes obvious that there is still a great need for more emphasis on the topic of digitisation in teacher education.

4.3. Student voices

All of the surveys conducted provided room for individual written feedback. Additionally, students were given the opportunity to record their feedback on video – in teams or on their own. Consequentially, a number of key features emerged from the comments. The most salient were: (1) school visits, (2) use of digital tools and mobile technologies, (3) collaboration, (4) one's own individual and professional development, as well as (5) reflections on the study week. This section will finish with (6) some general feedback, together with (7) recommendations students gave to improve the concept of a study week abroad.

4.4. School visits

As mentioned above, school visits were referred to in the video feedbacks in a more positive way than in the survey.

> "This project provided me the chance to visit some German schools, some local schools. This is a really good experience" (SWII_Repondent No. 4_Flipgrid).

> "I think the classroom observations gave me the most, actually. It was so fun to see how lessons are done in other countries" (SWII_ Respondent No. 5_Flipgrid).

In the feedback on Study Week 1, this perception was described as below.

> "If I talk about an activity that I considered especially useful, I have to say the school visit and all that this implied" (SWI_anonymous_Padlet).

> "For me the school visits was what I was looking forward to the most I think they also got me a lot to reflect about" (SWI_Respondent #3).

Still, students occasionally referred to some aspects that could be improved, in particular with regard to the organisation of the different school trips in the participating countries.

> "Nevertheless I think it would have been good to separate our proPIC group and watch different classes or even different schools" (SWII_Respondent #10).

> "The school trip could be improved so as for us to stay there for four hours and observe and also reflect upon it deeply or complete an activity in which you have to think about the pros and the cons of the class and also what you'd have changed" (SWII_Respondent #13).

All in all, most students asked for 'more school visits', often in combination with a request for an extension of the study week(s).

4.4.1. Use of digital tools and mobile technologies

Fostering digital competences among future teachers has become a common goal in teacher training programmes all across the globe (e.g. European Commission, 2021). Nonetheless, there is still a wide gap between what policy makers intend and higher education institutions actually offer. In order to narrow this gap somehow, digitalisation and mobile technologies became a major part of our programme, including during the study weeks. Obviously, students appreciated this.

> "Glad to have been part of this project, and I have learned a lot about many technologies and tools that I can use both in the future as a teacher, and in my studies" (SWII_Respondent #25).

Chapter 4

Although each partner could use different apps and mobile devices, the core of the mobile technology is described by a student who went to the CAU during the second study week.

> "We have worked with e-portfolios, mentimeter, socrative, video editing software (iMovie and Movie Maker), Splice, Padlet, Google sites, Plickers, etc. [...]. We also completed our own e-portfolio using wix, wordpress, etc" (SWII_Respondent #23).

On the whole, the feedback on this part was fairly positive and may be summarised with the following quotation:

> "For me, this one week experience outcome is worth a full course on teaching technologies" (SWII_Resondent #7).

Even if this might be considered an exaggeration, it clearly tells us something about the state of digitalisation in European teacher training programmes.

4.4.2. Collaboration

A core feature of proPIC was to bring together prospective teachers from different countries and backgrounds, an aspect which met with overwhelming approval:

> "To meet the other students and talk about learning was the best part" (SWII_Respondent unknown).

This aspect was also referred to in the written account of a student using a Padlet for her evaluation:

> "I have never imagined that proPic could be so beneficial in so many ways (I absolutely encourage people to do it!). I have learnt a lot with the interviews, courses and conferences, but I believe that the best thing above all was meeting you [=other participants of the week]" (SWI_anonymous_Padlet).

This might include working with international teacher educators too, who certainly provided an additional twist to the notion of collaboration and motivation in one's professional and personal development.

4.4.3. Individual and professional development

With proPIC we intended to empower prospective teachers in their profession by giving a better understanding of what CPD is or could be (see also Mann & Webb, 2022 Chapter 1 and Oesterle & Schwab, 2022 Chapter 2, this volume).

> "proPIC has already been one of the most intense study experiences I've had and it has enabled me to work on many aspects of my professionality as well as personality" (SWII_Respondent #18).

> "For my professional development, I can say that I have really and, but not fully, grown as a future teacher" (SWII_Respondent #9).

4.4.4. Reflection

Professional development to a great extent relies on reflection processes (see also Mann & Webb, 2022 Chapter 1 and Oesterle & Schwab, 2022 Chapter 2, this volume). In line with this notion, all participants had to regularly reflect upon their activities, either in their e-portfolios or in our course and study week feedback.

> "The most enriching experience was the reflection in the end after having held a lesson with and for the others and doing a videopaper based reflection. It was useful not only to see our process but also the ones of the others" (SWII_Respondent #18).

> "E-portfolio. A blog with everything we did and my reflections about it. It is a good way to remember what I was thinking about things to see how that changes, also a good way to share my experiences with others to have a deeper discussion about it and develop skills for my future profession" (SWII_Respondent #22).

4.4.5. Overall judgement by student

Wrapping up this section, we would like to provide written feedback from one student summing up their experience during a study week abroad:

> "I think what I've learned here [during the study week] and in Kiel will have a big impact on my future way of teaching and reflecting" (SWII_Respondent #11).

4.4.6. Suggestions for improvement

Even if a number of students were more than satisfied with the study week ('it was perfect'/'It was great! I wouldn't change anything'), we still asked students what needed to be changed or improved, especially as the programmes offered at the various institutions differed in some ways. One main theme was that students came with different expectations and background knowledge. This diversity made things more complicated and challenging not only for the lecturers, but also for the students who suggested the following.

> "Have the same preparation before the week, so everyone here has got the same knowledge (the tutorials). It had made a better discussion, it felt now that people didn't know things about the digital benefits, which made it hard to discuss things in the level I expected" (SWII_Respondent #22).

> "every university should do the same beforehand […]. Same prerequisites (some were primary school teacher trainers, others were secondary)" (SWII_Respondent #35).

Often the study week was not directly linked to the study programme at home and students had difficulties in connecting their individual research projects to what was offered abroad. Regarding the organisation and logistics, students thus recommend a few important aspects be taken into consideration when planning a study week.

> "General: better organisation and clarification towards the aim of the project; prerequisites should be all the same, only secondary school teachers" (SWII_Respondent #34).

> "The only problem we experienced during the study week was that not all universities were on the same page in regards of the tasks to be completed" (SWII_Respondent #36).

Additional suggestions mentioned were as below.

> "Providing more opportunities for participants to use various technologies regarding L2 teaching" (SWII_Respondent #38).

> "In my opinion, I would like to have the opportunity to use the apps that were introduced" (SWII_Respondent #26).

Or in an even more specific way:

> "I would focus more on video editing, different softwares and how to use them. Maybe a video-related project that assembles all of the study week could be great, so that there is some thread that connects all the different workshops, school visits and activities we have had" (SWII_Respondent #23).

Teacher education has just begun to foster these aspects of the curriculum in an appropriate manner and one course or study week is by no means sufficient. There is certainly still a long way to go before digital and online devices become as self-evident and natural as textbooks and vocabulary tests.

4.5. Teacher educator evaluation

Although we consider students' feedback on the study week as pivotal to a final judgement and possible starting point for improvement which was or should have been taken into consideration, we also asked all participating lecturers to share their impressions. This again was done in various ways, such as video feedback (Flipgrid), a joint teacher educator e-portfolio, or written comments for the final evaluation of the project. When being part of such a project, one would certainly expect a large amount of enthusiasm and motivation on the part of the lecturers. Looking back at the two study weeks we were able to conduct, it turned out that this was undoubtedly the case even if almost all of them admitted that it was an 'exhausting' week and experience. Some referred to it as the 'highlight' of the project.

> "It was great to see students from different European universities come together to discuss learning and teaching from their perspectives and thereby enriching each other" (final report).

Enthusiasm among students was observed across the cohorts and courses. Their work attitudes and eagerness were mentioned together with the intensive collaboration among participants from different social, ethnic, and institutional backgrounds.

> "The most beneficial was the opportunity for our students to have a rich intercultural experience, to live with students with similar concerns, to work together in reflection, to begin to develop their teaching competence together with other future teachers" (final report).

In a similar vein, another lecturer stated the following when asked for the most beneficial aspects of the week:

> "Definitely border-crossing exchange of experience between students, insight into local teacher training practices and school life, and the joint exploration of learning paths that make students in different European countries good teachers" (final report).

During the study weeks, lecturers tried to offer a wide variety of input in order to foster their students' digital skills and professional development.

> "The participants were able to pick up and adapt new ideas" (final report).

> "The possibility of the students developing their own CPD through the activities we prepared" (final report).

Nevertheless, some of lecturers realised that their own enthusiasm and motivation in planning went well beyond what could be expected from students in such a time, which was also in line with comments collected from some students who noted that the workload during the study week was sometimes too much:

> "A week before the study week I was amazed and proud of the diverse activities planned, but we just could not do all of them. This is something to consider when planning the second study week. I will leave more time and space to my students" (Study Week 1, written reflection).

With regard to their own profession, lecturers underscored the fact that this was not just a 'unique experience' with 'intensive cooperation' (Flipgrid), but also a great opportunity to learn from each other. This was even more the case when teacher trainers from different institutions could join or work together during the study week, e.g. by providing additional lectures, planning activities together with national hosts, or just supporting students in their research activities during the stay. However, this option was possible just once, when two teams were put together in Cohort 2 to save on personal resources. In order to foster this idea of international collaboration, though, lecturers were given the opportunity to join project partners during the regular part of the study programme before or after the study week (see also Hoinke & Clausen, 2022, Chapter 4 on the study programme, this volume).

Finally, the study week provided an intensive exchange between lecturers and visiting students so that relationships could be developed, and learning became twofold, i.e. students learned from lecturers and the other way around.

5. Discussion

Based on the online survey on the study week, as well as on the data collected through the e-portfolios, written reflections, and video feedbacks, it can be stated that the study week was reported to have the greatest impact on all participants, students, and teacher trainers alike. Students reported that taking part in it made them realise how important it is to experience 'otherness' in order to reflect better on one's own context. The notion of CPD, therefore, became a more important and settled part of their mind set. In particular, students perceived it to be helpful and inspiring to experience other perspectives on learning and teaching an FL. Interestingly, the participating teacher trainers reported that they felt that the returning students were much more motivated and thus put a lot of effort into their research projects.

The study week abroad was not only a key component of the whole study programme of the project, it was certainly the most important and popular part of it, as indicated by the student and lecturer feedback presented above. To us, this evokes an important consideration in light of the COVID-19 pandemic. Although students had been in touch with each other before and after the study week via Slack, email, or other social media and a distinct familiarity with digital tools could be seen among all participants, the impact of direct face-to-face interaction cannot be overstated. The close encounter of students in international collaboration cannot simply be replaced by virtual exchange, even if this has become more and more important (Waldman et al., 2019).

6. Conclusion: recommendations and checklist

ProPIC was planned pre-COVID-19 and conducted during the COVID-19 pandemic. Looking back at our attempt to combine student mobility and international collaboration, we need to see it through the lens of the developments triggered by the pandemic. This means that a student week may combine hybrid elements or can be conducted in different phases – on-campus and on-screen.

Still, a physical exchange remains the most important part and as such should be planned in-depth. In line with these considerations, we decided not to offer a replacement for the last and final stay abroad in 2020.

All in all, for us, the main important points of consideration are:

- the course programmes in which the study week is embedded should have the same or similar conditions, content, and objectives;

- the content, activities, schedule, and outputs of the study weeks should be similar at each partner institution and clear from the start;

- at least one school visit at each partner institution is recommended; if possible, two visits should be integrated;

- the recruitment of students should be planned thoroughly and long in advance;

- cooperation between local and international lecturers, as well as the integration of local students, is recommended; and

- thorough planning and organisation (timetable, finances, etc.) is crucial with regard to a successful and satisfying outcome.

In addition to these recommendations we have provided a checklist[9] for international study weeks based on our experiences.

---

9. https://www.europarl.europa.eu/RegData/etudes/STUD/2021/652237/IPOL_STU(2021)652237_EN.pdf

Chapter 4

References

Baldwin, R., & Ruhtenberg, T. (2022). Student reactions to using interactive tutorials as part of the proPIC study programme. In G. Schwab, M. Oesterle & A. Whelan (Eds), *Promoting professionalism, innovation and transnational collaboration: a new approach to foreign language teacher education* (pp. 131-145). Research-publishing.net. https://doi.org/10.14705/rpnet.2022.57.1386

Boye, S. (2016). *Intercultural communicative competence and short stays abroad: perceptions of development (Münchener Arbeiten zur Fremdsprachen-Forschung)*. Waxmann.

Bruce, M. (1991). Internationalizing teacher education. *British Journal of Educational Studies, 39*(2), 163-172. https://doi.org/10.1080/00071005.1991.9973882

Cuesta, A., Batlle, J., González, V., & Pujolà, J.-T. (2022). Approaches to the development of pre-service language teachers' e-portfolios. In G. Schwab, M. Oesterle & A. Whelan (Eds), *Promoting professionalism, innovation and transnational collaboration: a new approach to foreign language teacher education* (pp. 191-212). Research-publishing.net. https://doi.org/10.14705/rpnet.2022.57.1388

Dooly, M., & O'Dowd, R. (2012). *Researching online foreign language interaction and exchange: theories, methods and challenges. Telecollaboration in Education. Volume 3*. Peter Lang.

Dwyer, M. M., & Peters, C. K. (2004). The benefits of study abroad. *Transitions abroad, 37*(5), 56-58. https://www.transitionsabroad.com/publications/magazine/0403/benefits_study_abroad.shtml

European Commission. (2018a). *A Clean Planet for all. A European strategic long-term vision for a prosperous, modern, competitive and climate neutral economy.* https://euagenda.eu/publications/a-clean-planet-for-all-a-european-long-term-strategic-vision-for-a-prosperous-modern-competitive-and-climate-neutral-economy

European Commission. (2018b). *Making the European education area a reality: state of affairs, challenges and prospects.* https://www.europarl.europa.eu/RegData/etudes/STUD/2021/652237/IPOL_STU(2021)652237_EN.pdf

European Commission. (2021). *European education area*. https://ec.europa.eu/education/education-in-the-eu/european-education-area_en

Goetz, T., Jaritz, G., & Oser, F. (2011). (Eds.). *Pains and gains of international mobility in teacher education.* Sense Publishers. https://doi.org/10.1007/978-94-6091-496-6

Heuer, H., & Klippel, F. (1987). *Englischmethodik: Problemfelder, Unterrichtswirklichkeit und Handlungsempfehlungen*. Cornelsen.

Hoinke, U., & Clausen, K. (2022). Getting curious and gaining knowledge through transnational collaboration in foreign language teacher education. In G. Schwab, M. Oesterle & A. Whelan (Eds), *Promoting professionalism, innovation and transnational collaboration: a new approach to foreign language teacher education* (pp.83-106). Research-publishing.net. https://doi.org/10.14705/rpnet.2022.57.1384

Jaritz, G. (2011). Developing a culture of (inter)national mobility in initial teacher training: expectations, limitations and ways forward. In T. Goetz, G. Jaritz & F. Oser (Eds), *Pains and gains of international mobility in teacher education* (pp. 7-24). Sense Publishers. https://doi.org/10.1007/978-94-6091-496-6_1

Kessler, J.-U., Haim, O., & Schwab, G. (forthcoming). Telecollaboration in the education of TESOL teachers. *TESOL Online Encyclopedia*.

Mann, S., & Webb, K. (2022). Continuing professional development: key themes in supporting the development of professional practice. In G. Schwab, M. Oesterle & A. Whelan (Eds), *Promoting professionalism, innovation and transnational collaboration: a new approach to foreign language teacher education* (pp. 15-44). Research-publishing.net. https://doi.org/10.14705/rpnet.2022.57.1382

Marx, H., & Moss, D. M. (2011). Please mind the culture gap: intercultural development during a teacher education study abroad program. *Journal of teacher education*, *62*(1), 35-47. https://doi.org/10.1177/0022487110381998

Oesterle, M., & Schwab, G. (2022). Developing a framework of CPD for the context of foreign language teaching. In G. Schwab, M. Oesterle & A. Whelan (Eds), Promoting professionalism, innovation and transnational collaboration: a new approach to foreign language teacher education (pp. 45-79). Research-publishing.net. https://doi.org/10.14705/rpnet.2022.57.1383

Schwab, G., & Oesterle, M. (2021). Integrating VEO in foreign language teacher education in Germany. In P. Seedhouse (Ed.), *Video enhanced observation for language teaching: reflection and professional development* (pp. 65-81). Bloomsbury. https://doi.org/10.5040/9781350085060.ch-5

Seedhouse, P., Heslop, P., & Kharrufa, A. (2019). The Linguacuisine app: learning languages and cultures while cooking. *Babel The Language Magazine*, *28*, 24-29. https://cloud.3dissue.com/18743/41457/106040/babelno28/index.html

Stewart, Y. (2008). *Mainstreaming the European dimension into teacher education in England – enabling and disabling factors.* http://www.pef.uni-lj.si/tepe2008/papers/Stewart.pdf

Waldman, T., Harel, E., & Schwab, G. (2019). Extended telecollaboration practice in teacher education: towards pluricultural and plurilingual proficiency. *European Journal of Language Policy, 11*(2), 167-185. https://doi.org/10.3828/ejlp.2019.11

Whelan, A., & Baldwin, R. (2022). Impact beyond the project: exploring engagement in proPIC Europa and potential lasting impact on teaching studies and professional development. In G. Schwab, M. Oesterle & A. Whelan (Eds), *Promoting professionalism, innovation and transnational collaboration: a new approach to foreign language teacher education* (pp. 243-252). Research-publishing.net. https://doi.org/10.14705/rpnet.2022.57.1392

5. Student reactions to using interactive tutorials as part of the proPIC study programme

Richard Baldwin[1] and Tobias Ruhtenberg[2]

1. Introduction

In this chapter, we outline the use of interactive textbooks or tutorials in the form of iBooks that were developed as a major output of the proPIC project. All of these iBooks can also be retrieved on the accompanying project website[3]. Interactive textbooks or tutorials are documents, software, or other media digitally created for the purpose of (interactively) presenting any kind of content and can further comprise a wide variety of tasks for the reader. This chapter focuses on so-called iBooks, a distinct form of e-books available exclusively for the Mac Operating System (OS – by Apple).

Generally, an e-book can be defined as an "electronic book, containing a body of text and images suitable for distributing electronically and displaying on-screen in a manner similar to a printed book" (Attwell, 2022, n.p). In contrast, iBooks published with iBooks Author are usually more advanced digitally published texts which often include multimodal content such as embedded videos, images, interactive links, and sound files. The application supports the use of different multimodal content and third-party widgets. Those additional small applications can help the writer of an iBook to make the publication more flexible and interactive. The iBooks Author application is not available from Apple anymore.

---

1. Högskolan i Borås, Borås, Sweden; richard.baldwin@hb.se

2. Högskolan i Borås, Borås, Sweden; tobias.ruhtenberg@hb.se; https://orcid.org/0000-0001-9693-7305

3. http://www.propiceuropa.com/

How to cite: Baldwin, R., & Ruhtenberg, T. (2022). Student reactions to using interactive tutorials as part of the proPIC study programme. In G. Schwab, M. Oesterle & A. Whelan (Eds), *Promoting professionalism, innovation and transnational collaboration: a new approach to foreign language teacher education* (pp. 131-145). Research-publishing.net. https://doi.org/10.14705/rpnet.2022.57.1386

Chapter 5

The company is now only supporting the software Pages, where you can find some of the features in iBooks Author.

After providing some background information on the project and e-books in a wider context, this chapter focuses on illustrating and exemplifying the iBooks that were created in the proPIC project. Moreover, it presents and discusses some of the student reactions to using the eight iBooks, as well as subsequent practical implications of using such digital tools effectively in teacher education.

2. The context: the proPIC project

The tutorials that are central in this chapter were developed as part of the proPIC project and were one element of an adaptable and innovative study programme[4] for language teacher education, which was developed by the project partners. It is designed to be integrated in different international curricula in higher education systems in the field of language teacher education and beyond. The study programme is described in more detail by Hoinkes and Clausen (2022, Chapter 2 of this edited volume).

The study programme includes a theoretical framework of Continuing Professional Development (CPD) in the context of language teacher education. This framework is presented in the form of an interactive online handbook (see Mann & Webb, 2022, Chapter 1 this volume). The handbook includes theory and practice examples, which are supported by a range of interactive and research-oriented tasks, integrating the use of digital tools and applications.

In addition, eight interactive tutorials in the form of interactive electronic books (iBooks) were created, using the application iBooks Author. These iBooks promote the use of mobile technologies and digital methods in foreign language learning, the application of various research methods and instruments, as well as reflective practices. They were developed and designed collaboratively by the

---

4. http://www.propiceuropa.com/io3-study-programme.html

project partners and were modified during the project-based feedback from other partners as well as student evaluations.

3. Using e-books in language teacher education

In a rapidly changing world, teaching professions require an increasingly broad and more sophisticated set of competences than in the past. The growth in the number of digital devices and applications as well as the need to help students become digitally competent requires educators to develop their own digital competence in order to meet these challenges. These needs are no less important in the area of second language teaching and learning. There is a widespread gap between student needs and current teacher levels of competence. The challenge is to reduce this disparity. According to Kırkgöz (2014), "[a]cknowledging that teacher candidates should be encouraged to experience and be empowered by developing their technology skills to produce instructional materials is a challenge, but one which is essential for teacher educators to meet" (p. 160).

There are more and more digital tools and apps available to the teachers and learners. One possible tool for the use in the classroom is interactive textbooks or tutorials. Interactive tutorials are described as:

> "a document, software, or other media on the Internet created for the purpose of instruction for any of a wide variety of tasks. Interactive tutorials usually have the following characteristics: a presentation of content, a method of review where the user follows on screen instructions (and in some cases watch short instruction movies) whereupon user does tutorial exercises and gets feedback depending on his actions, and transition to additional modules or sections" (Hansson, 2008, p. 115).

Interactive tutorials combine several features, multimodal resources, and different instructional designs, for example having the facility to integrate interactive widgets or apps amongst other things. The advantage over traditional textbooks is the "overt interactive content" that interactive tutorials allow (Baldwin, 2015, p. 2).

One example for an interactive tutorial would be so-called e-books. E-books are publications made available in digital form consisting of text, images, or both, that are readable on computers and other electronic devices (e.g. Amazon Kindle). However, many e-books lack certain features that more advanced interactive tutorials have as they do not include a number of touchpoints where the reader can interact, watch videos, listen to audio sequences, click on links, answer quizzes, and consume other interactive content.

From the perspective of teacher training at university level, there are still many advantages to working with interactive e-books. Fyfe (2014) states the following:

> "[e]-books have the potential to engage with three key strategic priorities common to most universities: to enhance the student experience and academic outcomes within an increasingly competitive environment; to drive innovation in learning, teaching and research; and to help to use space and human resources more effectively and efficiently" (p. 2).

The creativity of the teacher, and the content of the e-books created are key elements for the successful integration of e-books in the classroom (Johnson & Vanspauwen, 2015).

Interactive e-books have been shown to be popular with students because of their convenience (Walton, 2014) and the fact that they are portable (Frederick, 2015) and always available (Jeong, 2012). E-Books in particular correlate with the definition of 'mobile learning' due to their accessibility on mobile devices (Gitsaki et al., 2013). Having access to several e-books on a single device creates an uncomplicated arrangement for the learning process of students. Other benefits include the possibility of searching content through key words, the possibility of creating links to other digital content, and the ability to copy and paste sections directly from the text (Wu & Chen, 2011). E-books reinforce both distance and part-time learning modes and can meet high demand reading list access (Riha & LeMay, 2016).

From a specific language learning perspective, interactive e-books can help students with all the language skills because presentation materials are more understandable and facilitate long-term memory "by using multiple sensory channels to put forward information" (Kim, 2014, p. 311). Interactive e-books can contain diverse presentations of multimodal content that not only help students enhance their listening, speaking, reading, and writing skills, but also their understanding of how information and communications technology can support learning. Furthermore, e-books can encourage flexibility in teaching as students can work individually at their own pace.

As Rao (2019) and others (Gaskill & Hansen, 2014) have pointed out, Apple's iBook (usually in combination with an iPad) can be considered as one of the most advanced e-books currently available, as it provides many of the interactive features described above. Even more, educators can also become authors themselves and create iBooks with their own content and materials, for instance using the application iBooks Author. iBooks Author is an iBook authoring application from Apple Inc, only available for Mac OS and thus only accessible on Apple devices. By using the application, an educator "need not be a technology genius or have experience with textbook layout since templates are provided for several types of organisation" (Baldwin, 2015, p. 4).

Based on all these assumptions and longstanding experience with iBooks, the project consortium decided to use these interactive e-books as our main tool for providing background knowledge and in-depth insights into the specifics of the project.

4. The iBooks created in the project

Eight interactive tutorials in the form of iBooks were made available to students who took part in the project. Three of the iBooks were mandatory for the students, while the others were optional. It was estimated that the students would spend about five hours in total reading and working with each iBook.

The eight iBooks were designed to help students complete the study programme, and as such promoted the use of mobile technologies and digital methods in foreign language learning, the application of various research methods and instruments, as well as applications for reflective practices. More generally, the iBooks contained information, as well as hands-on activities and best-practice examples on a range of topics connected with the use of digital tools and applications in the area of language teaching education. Some of the activities promoted collaboration between the students of the partner institutions, where students needed to obtain information from and about the partner universities.

Working with the iBooks, the future teachers had the chance to reflect on their own learning process as well as the advantages and disadvantages of the use of digital tools in the classroom. The books are designed using a variety of diverse widgets, e.g. Bookry and Book widgets[5], which create a virtual learning environment where students can have fun while working with tasks. The widgets that can be embedded in an iBook are the key element of interactivity. They can support the use of audio on a page so the reader can listen to texts being read by a recorded voice. The widget can also create a quiz or a poll within the book. Images are integrated into the layout which underline important information. There are also links to informative websites or integrated videos, enabling the reader to find new information and ideas. Finally, every book has a feedback section at the end where students can leave comments and recommendations for improvement. The iBooks encouraged some kind of reflection task, such as a video or text, which was to be added to the student's e-portfolio.

All final versions are now published on Apple Books (links to the books can be found in Table 1).

---

5. https://bookry.com/account/login

Table 1. Overview of interactive tutorials

As far as the contents of the iBooks are concerned, the first iBook, which was mandatory, concerns the use of e-portfolios. The book discusses the definition of the term and key concepts of what teaching e-portfolios are based upon, as well as the digital communicative features that characterise e-portfolios. The tutorial also shows how to set up, create, and develop an e-portfolio. https://books.apple.com/se/book/propic-interactive-tutorial-1/id1525353237	
The second iBook, which was also mandatory, covers approaches to teaching and learning with technologies. The tutorial addresses the questions of what it means to teach and learn with technology and how to approach teaching and learning with technology in an informed way. https://books.apple.com/se/book/propic-interactive-tutorial-2/id1525354025	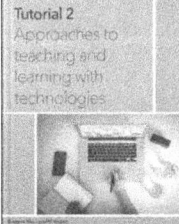
The third iBook, which was the last of mandatory iBooks, covers the subject of how to use research in language teacher education in order to develop professionally. The main focus of the tutorial is action research and the use of observation and interviews to collect data. https://books.apple.com/se/book/propic-interactive-tutorial-3/id1525354901	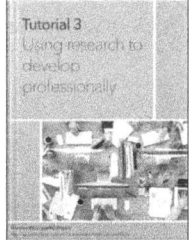
iBook Four, which was an optional choice for the students, focuses on the use of Video Enhanced Observation[6] (VEO). The tutorial explains how to use technology for peer observation and the role of feedback in the professional development of teachers. https://books.apple.com/se/book/propic-interactive-tutorial-4/id1525355755	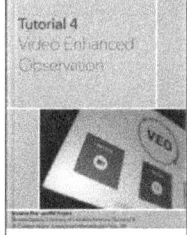

---

6. https://veo.co.uk/

Chapter 5

The fifth iBook, which was also optional, is about the use of video production in the context of language learning and teaching. The tutorial explains how to record and edit videos with the aim of helping students produce their own videos in order to integrate them into studies and future teaching. https://books.apple.com/se/book/propic-interactive-tutorial-5/id1525680492	
iBook Six was optional and covers the area of using innovative digital tools and methods. A number of digital tools are presented. The challenges of using mobile technologies are discussed, as well as ways of conceptualising the changes that technology can make to pedagogical practice. https://books.apple.com/se/book/propic-interactive-tutorial-6/id1525356644	
iBook Seven, also optional, looks at how to use iBooks and iBooks Author in language teacher education. The possibilities of using e-books in second language learning and teaching are presented and exemplified. https://books.apple.com/se/book/propic-interactive-tutorial-7/id1525360479	
Finally, the optional iBook Eight relates to the framework of CPD and discusses some further aspects of it in the context of language teacher education. https://books.apple.com/se/book/propic-interactive-tutorial-8/id1525357929	

5. Student reactions

In this section, we present some student reactions to using e-books generally, as well as the specific iBooks created as part of the proPIC study programme. Data was collected from student replies and comments to an online survey comprising ten mostly open questions. Another source is an online survey carried out by one of the participating students and as part of a Bachelor's thesis from the University of Education Karlsruhe, mainly looking at the use of the interactive tutorials (Avşar, 2018). Finally, the data includes input during short (online) interviews with some participating students, and discussion groups held at some partner universities as part of local courses.

Data collected from students express many positive arguments for the use of iBooks generally, such as an increase in pupil motivation, the benefits of using iBooks to cover the various language skills, the high levels of interactivity, the exposure to authentic language use, and the fact that e-books addressed all learner types and their different study habits. Allowing students to make their own iBooks was seen as a way of increasing student levels of motivation. As far as the learning activities that could be used in an iBook for language learning, a wide range of suggestions were made. These included podcasts, digital storytelling, videos, audio books, games, pictures, vocabulary and pronunciation practice, grammar tasks, writing, quizzes, and questionnaires, as well as other types of interaction between students.

The students regarded accessibility as one of the positive reasons to use iBooks, along with the fact that they take up less space than printed books. Respondents stated that they like the design and layout of iBooks, especially their interactivity and multimedia integration.

The majority of students felt that iBooks were effective tools in the field of language education. Reasons given were the high level of interactivity, a user-friendly design, and the multimodal features of most e-books. The multimodal features were also felt to foster student motivation. Many argued that the interactive nature of iBooks, and the fact that they can be shared online, meant that students are able to exchange ideas and work collaboratively.

Most of the respondents mentioned that they had no experience in creating an iBook. In addition, a number of other challenges in using iBooks were mentioned.

These include the time needed to create an iBook, finding or creating iBooks that fit the curriculum, getting pupils to use new media, and the availability of devices as well as technical problems and issues. Students stressed the importance of teacher support when integrating iBooks into the classroom. One respondent stressed, for example, the importance of explaining the functions of an iBook to the students but recognised too that this is time consuming.

The students also provided their thoughts on the specific iBooks created as part of the proPIC study programme. More generally, the contents of the iBooks were seen as relevant to the aims of the study programme. The students liked the choice of material in the tutorials and appreciated, too, the fact that the tutorials contained an overview of tools that are available for creating a digital portfolio, and for language teaching connected to mobile technology. The tools that were most appreciated were VEO and the tools and methods which the participating students had tried during the study week. Most respondents regarded the multimedia integration within the tutorials as very helpful.

Despite these positive remarks, many student comments concentrated on the fact that the participants who did not have an Apple device had difficulties accessing the iBooks. If students did not have an Apple device, they could only work with PDF formats of the tutorials and as a result lost the interactivity of the original iBooks. Spelling errors in the iBooks, as well as problems with links to videos not working – especially in the first version – were also mentioned by students.

6.   Discussion

The findings presented here show that because of participating in the programme, the majority of the prospective teachers had in general a positive attitude towards the use of iBooks in the classroom with a majority stating that they would appreciate using iBooks in other university courses in the future. The respondents were aware of the benefits of iBooks in the field of education and were positive about the possibilities, tools, and features that iBooks can offer, both generally and for language learning and teaching in particular.

Many of the comments on the advantages mentioned by respondents mirror those found in previous research, with aspects such as convenience, portability, accessibility, and interactivity being mentioned (Frederick, 2015; Gitsaki et al., 2013; Jeong, 2012; Walton, 2014).

The findings also show that the majority of the prospective teachers enjoyed working with the iBooks and felt that many of the tutorials in the iBooks were useful in helping the students navigate the proPIC study programme. The contents were perceived as high quality and relevant to their professional development. One student commented, for example, that "[e]verything is evaluated by teachers and trainers. There is a good mix between theory and practice". In line with Baldwin's (2015) comments on the interactive content that these tutorials allow, students appreciated the multimedia integration within the tutorials. One respondent, for example, liked "[t]he different media and methodology. It was [a] really diverse way of working, watching a video, then reading a text and afterwards filling in a mind map". Another commented that they appreciated the integration of videos and audio files, because "I am a learner who learns very well when the material is supported by audio examples".

Despite these positive comments, however, many of the participants did not feel prepared to use iBooks in their own teaching and consequently felt unsure as to whether they would use them in future or not. This finding reflects conclusions in earlier research which has shown that students continue to indicate a preference for using the printed book (Myrberg, 2017; Walton, 2014). Another issue that many students commented on concerned the fact that the participants who did not have an Apple device had difficulties accessing the iBooks. For one of the students, not having early access in the beginning of the project meant that they were "unable to do at least half of the activities included in the interactive tutorials during the course". Here, teacher educators need to be more concerned with providing students with access to a wide range of online tools and digital devices, when, at the same time, students should be given more support as well

Chapter 5

as more and better training on using mobile technology at schools. We will discuss some of these issues below and explore some other lessons we have learned from creating and using the iBooks during the proPIC project.

7. Reflections after the creation and use of iBooks during the proPIC project

After discussions amongst partners and feedback given on the iBooks from students, we have the following thoughts on the creation and use of the iBooks during the proPIC project.

- Prospective teachers have a positive attitude towards the use of iBooks in the field of education and these tools can offer many possibilities for language learning and teaching in particular.

- There is a widespread gap between student needs and current teacher levels of competence in this area. Many of the students in this study felt unsure about how to create an iBook and needed more hands-on experience in how to do so.

- The fact that iBooks published with the help of iBook Author are only compatible with Apple devices adversely affected the learning process of the students and their perception of possible advantages of iBooks. The use of other tools would overcome this problem.

- iBooks should not be like normal printed books. They should not be too long and contain too much text.

- The videos included as links in iBooks should not be more than five minutes long.

- iBooks should use icons and symbols to signpost tasks, and a wide use of widgets.

8. Conclusion

Based on our experiences and the feedback from students and project partners, we conclude that e-books, especially the more advanced devices such as Apple's iBooks, can play an important role in the professional development of prospective teachers. The students who took part in the proPIC project see the advantages of iBooks in terms of convenience, portability, accessibility, as well as interactivity. Those prospective teachers can also see the possibilities that iBooks can offer in the field of education in general and for language learning and teaching in particular. It is, however, important that students get more hands-on opportunities to create and use iBooks within teacher education in order to bridge the gap between student needs and current teacher levels of competence. The digital competences of prospective teachers are not as great as some teacher educators might think, which is why we see a need to include digital tools with different kinds of pedagogical functions in teacher education as well in the professional development of (future) teachers in general.

During the COVID-19 pandemic, the use of cloud-based applications has been a great benefit. The students have been able to stay at home and still be part of a group assignment; publishing an iBook is only one example. The possibility of collaboratively editing a video online has also been a great positive option for the students. When working with such online cloud-based applications it is important that the students have access to the paid version of the application, which is normally necessary if you want them to be able to have complete possibilities to edit and save their work.

References

Attwell, A. (2022). *e-book*. Encyclopaedia Britannica. https://www.britannica.com/technology/e-book

Avşar, B. (2018). *Promoting innovation and collaboration among future teachers of English at secondary schools*. Published Bachelor Thesis, University of Education, Karlsruhe Germany.

Baldwin, A. (2015). Developing an interactive textbook using iBooks Author. *Federation of Business Disciplines Journal, 3*(2015), 1-12.

Frederick, D. E. (2015). On e-Books in academic libraries: an article based on a presentation at the Library 2.014 Conference. *Library Hi Tech News, 32*, 12-15. https://doi.org/10.1108/LHTN-02-2015-0015

Fyfe, C. (2014). E-books in higher education: a strategic priority? In H. Wood-Ward (Ed.), *E-books in education: realising the vision* (pp. 1-7). Ubiquity Press. https://doi.org/10.5334/bal.a

Gaskill, M., & Hansen, D. T. (2014). Using iBooks to create 21st century learning materials/lessons for use on iPads. In M. Searson & M. Ochoa (Eds), *Proceedings of SITE 2014--Society for Information Technology & Teacher Education International Conference* (pp. 2807-2808). Association for the Advancement of Computing in Education (AACE). https://www.learntechlib.org/primary/p/147353/

Gitsaki, C., Robby, M. A., Priest, T., Hamdan, K., & Ben-Chabane, Y. (2013). A research agenda for the UAE iPad initiative. *Learning and Teaching in Higher Education: Gulf Perspectives, 10*(2), https://doi.org/10.18538/lthe.v10.n2.162

Hansson, T. (2008). *Handbook of research on digital technologies: innovations, methods, and ethical issues.* IGI Global/Information Science Reference. https://doi.org/10.4018/978-1-59904-970-0

Hoinkes, U., & Clausen, K. (2022). Getting curious and gaining knowledge through transnational collaboration in foreign language teacher education. In G. Schwab, M. Oesterle & A. Whelan (Eds), *Promoting professionalism, innovation and transnational collaboration: a new approach to foreign language teacher education* (pp. 83-106). Research-publishing.net. https://doi.org/10.14705/rpnet.2022.57.1384

Jeong, H. (2012). A comparison of the influence of electronic books and paper books on reading comprehension, eye fatigue, and perception. *The Electronic Library, 30*(3), 390-408. https://doi.org/10.1108/02640471211241663

Johnson, P., & Vanspauwen, N. (2015). *Teaching language classes: using iBooks author and the iPad.* https://itunes.apple.com/us/book/teaching-language-classes-using-iBooks-author-and-the-ipad/id777953566?mt=11

Kim, J. (2014). iBooks author: potential, pedagogical meanings, and implementation challenges. (Conference presentation). *The Annual Convention of the Association for Educational Communications and Technology* https://members.aect.org/pdf/Proceedings/proceedings14/2014i/14_15.pdf

Kırkgöz, Y. (2014). The use and uptake of information and communication technology: a Turkish case of an initial teacher education department. In J. E. Atiken (Ed.), *Cases on communication technology for second language acquisition and cultural learning* (pp. 141-171). IGI Global. https://doi.org/10.4018/978-1-4666-4482-3.ch011

Mann, S., & Webb, K. (2022). Continuing professional development: key themes in supporting the development of professional practice. In G. Schwab, M. Oesterle & A. Whelan (Eds), *Promoting professionalism, innovation and transnational collaboration: a new approach to foreign language teacher education* (pp. 15-44). Research-publishing.net. https://doi.org/10.14705/rpnet.2022.57.1382

Myrberg, C. (2017). Why doesn't everyone love reading e-books? *Insights, 30*(3), 115-124. https://doi.org/10.1629/uksg.386

Rao, H. (2019). *iBooks: making a valuable classroom technology with multi-touch books* [Conference session]. Online Learning Consortium (OLC) Accelerate Conference, Orlando, FL, United States.

Riha, E. C., & LeMay, D. (2016). Saving students money with ebooks: a cross-departmental collaboration between interlibrary loan and course reserve. *Technical Services Quarterly, 33*(4), 386-408. https://doi.org/10.1080/07317131.2016.1203644

Walton, E. W. (2014). Why undergraduate students choose to use e-books. *Journal of Librarianship and Information Science, 46*(4), 263-270. https://doi.org/10.1177/0961000613488124

Wu, M., & Chen, S. (2011). Graduate students' usage of and attitudes towards e-books: experiences from Taiwan. *Program, 45*(3), 294-307. https://doi.org/10.1108/00330331111151601

6. Developing an innovative and collaborative assessment framework for proPIC Europa

Alison Whelan[1] and Paul Seedhouse[2]

1.   Introduction

As discussed in Mann and Webb (2022, Chapter 1 this volume), each proPIC partner adopted an individual approach to integrate the project requirements into their academic programmes, using their own institute's frameworks of teaching and learning.

> "Partnerships in education are increasingly used to promote a joint navigation of complex dynamics and problematic situations that emerge in our multicultural and multilingual educational landscape. Indeed, the European Commission places stronger emphasis on building so-called strategic partnerships with the aim 'to support the development, transfer and/or implementation of innovative practices as well as the implementation of joint initiatives promoting cooperation, peer learning and exchanges of experience at European level' (European Commission, 2020, p. 100)" (Oesterle, Cuesta, & Whelan, 2021, n.p.).

However, in some instances, the creation of common resources, frameworks, and assessment criteria can be problematic, as each European institution in a partnership adheres to national and local guidelines and academic programmes.

---

1. Newcastle University, Newcastle-upon-Tyne, United Kingdom; alison.whelan2@newcastle.ac.uk; https://orcid.org/0000-0001-6272-6497

2. Newcastle University, Newcastle-upon-Tyne, United Kingdom; paul.seedhouse@newcastle.ac.uk

How to cite: Whelan, A., & Seedhouse, P. (2022). Developing an innovative and collaborative assessment framework for proPIC Europa. In G. Schwab, M. Oesterle & A. Whelan (Eds), *Promoting professionalism, innovation and transnational collaboration: a new approach to foreign language teacher education* (pp. 147-189). Research-publishing.net. https://doi.org/10.14705/rpnet.2022.57.1387

Chapter 6

In this chapter, we aim to examine whether commonality can be found across different institutions' approaches to assessment in language teacher education, and whether elements of individuality in these unique settings can be incorporated into a common framework, which can then be used as a model to be adapted to suit each partner's needs and requirements. The background of our research was a collaborative development of an evaluation framework using a variety of already existing frameworks, e.g. the CEFR (Council of Europe, 2001) and the iPAC framework (Kearney, Schuck, Burden, & Aubusson, 2012). Together with the University of Karlsruhe in Germany (PHKA), we explored each of the existing assessment frameworks already used to evaluate projects we were aware of, and those used on a national or Europe-wide scale to assess skills such as information communication technology competence and language proficiency. In this chapter we aim to answer the following questions.

- Q1: To what extent can a common assessment framework be developed which encompasses the individual and combined requirements of the partner institution and the project output criteria?

- Q2: How successful might a common assessment framework be in meeting the individual and combined requirements of the partner institutions and the project output criteria?

- Q3: To what extent does a European partnership retain both individuality and commonality when developing an overall framework for assessment and evaluation that can serve as a blueprint for partners to devise and use in their individual context in the field of language teacher education?

2. Literature review

2.1. Developing an effective assessment and evaluation framework

A key component in any project which aims to develop a person's skills, competences, or knowledge is the development of an effective, reliable, and robust assessment framework. In a transnational project like proPIC, the developers of such a framework can draw on their network of colleagues in order to access sources of knowledge that might otherwise be missed, frame research agendas in response to a broad range of needs and expertise, and disseminate the results of research. A drawback of some evaluation frameworks is that they often focus on single aspects of a course, rather than on the programme as a whole (Chmiel, Laurent, & Hansez, 2017). As this project incorporated many aspects of blended learning or hybrid learning (Bliuc et al., 2012; Graham, 2006), it was necessary to develop a framework which integrated digital technologies and allowed partners to incorporate a variety of resources, tools, and learning activities around a learner-centred pedagogy (Garrison & Vaughan, 2008; Stein & Graham, 2014). We therefore followed a development procedure suggested by Chmiel, Shaha, and Schneider (2017), to establish robust evaluation principles and standards, give them a structure and ensure all partners are involved in the development, and define what to measure and select the appropriate tools (p. 173).

2.2. Key criteria of effective frameworks in transnational partnerships

Definitions of an effective assessment framework vary, but at the heart is always the concept of drawing together ideas and theories into a working relationship which can adapt to suit the purpose, audience, and output. According to Bower and Vlachopoulos (2018), "[a]t their most basic level, frameworks and models assist in translating academic theory into operational practice" (p. 102), while Hsu and Ching (2015) define a framework as delineating "the conceptual relationships among components and hypotheses grounded in related theories" (p. 102).

In this line, Gross Stein, Stren, Fitzgibbon, and MacLean (2001) outline three key facets of an effective framework, stating that they should

> "produce new knowledge through transdisciplinary research as they are experienced across international boundaries in different contexts;

produce 'operational' knowledge, acquired through context-bound interactions among multiple sectors of expertise, and disseminate knowledge by blurring the boundaries between participants and researchers, thereby ensuring that 'global' knowledge is introduced locally, and that 'local' knowledge shapes and, at times, redefines global knowledge" (p. 4).

A transnational framework design must meet the individual needs of the partners as well as the overall requirements of the project. Healey, Flint, and Harrington (2014) suggest that in higher education, an assessment or evaluation framework is most effective when, amongst other criteria, "it is used to engage students in productive learning; students and lecturers become responsible partners in learning and assessment; and assessment provides inclusive and trustworthy representation of student achievement" (p. 22). The concept of assessing students' achievement was core to the proPIC framework, but the needs were varied, and assessment was not as simple as providing students with certification of participation (Broadfoot & Black, 2004). Rather, the assessment framework aimed to facilitate and direct the students in their own learning processes and allow each partner to evaluate and refine their own institutional teaching practices (Boud et al., 2010; Villarroel et al., 2018; Wiliam, 2007).

Alongside the academic requirements of each partner, there was a desire for their engagement in the project and their eventual assessed outputs to "develop students' lifelong learning abilities for sophisticated relativist thinking and autonomous complex decision-making" (McLean, 2018, p. 2, in Thomas, Ansari, & Knowland, 2019, p. 547). These skills and competences are essential for not just prospective language teachers, but also for well-informed global citizens.

2.3. Maintaining individuality in a common framework

A transnational partnership is a network of individual institutions, sharing some commonality but with many singular needs and characteristics. Gross Stein et al. (2001) define a network such as this as "a spatially diffuse structure, with no rigidly defined boundaries, consisting of several autonomous nodes sharing common values or interests, linked together in interdependent exchange relationships" (p. 4). In each 'node', the differing institutional environments will impact effective assessment design and use and can in fact enable or constrain it, as "lecturers manage tensions, agendas and requirements at institutional, departmental and personal levels" (Meyer et al., 2010, in Thomas et al., 2019, p. 547).

As part of another Erasmus+ project, Kearney et al. (2012) developed the iPAC evaluation framework through a rigorous process which included needs analysis, interviews, and surveys with potential users and feedback from workshop participants (Burden & Kearney, 2017; Kearney, Burden, & Rai, 2015).

The design of the iPAC framework was adapted and modified as a result of the information gathered, and this enabled the final output to suit all needs. However, the finished framework was a standalone output, intended to be used by all partners, irrespective of their individual needs and requirements. It was clear that like the iPAC project, constant communication and revisions made through consultation with and feedback from all partners would be essential in proPIC, but unlike iPAC, the final framework would need to be individualised to suit each partner's requirements. This will be explored in the next section.

3. How can a common assessment framework be developed which encompasses the individual and combined requirements of the partner institution and the project output criteria?

It became clear as we began to look at developing a framework that many factors needed to be taken into consideration, the two key areas being the individual requirements of each partner, and the combined requirements of the project output criteria. We will examine these requirements in the two sections which follow.

3.1. Examining the individual requirements of the five partners

Two challenges presented themselves when we began to consider how to develop an assessment framework which would effectively serve the diverse needs of five different institutions in four European countries.

3.1.1. Challenge 1: the different elements of the proPIC programme

Each partner institution used a variety of different materials and resources with their students, and collated their outputs using different media, some digital and some physical. Alongside this, students were asked to keep a reflective e-portfolio, although these differed somehow across the partners in the time committed to them and the resulting quality (for more information on this part, see Clausen & Hoinkes, 2022, Chapter 10 this volume). In each institution, these elements were already assessed in different ways, and some elements were not generally assessed at all (Table 1).

Table 1. The five elements of the proPIC course, the materials used and the desired outputs

Parts of the study programme	Materials	Outputs
Face-to-face meetings CPD framework	Student and partner feedback	Concept – final CPD version and partner materials
Blended learning units Interactive tutorials	Student and partner feedback	Template(s) – final version of tutorials
Study week	Student and partner feedback	Framework – final study week guidelines
Reflection process	e-portfolios	Criteria – proPIC evaluation framework
Create products	Student outputs	Criteria – proPIC evaluation framework

3.1.2. Challenge 2: the variety of curricula and requirements of the students

Each partner's cohort of students were from different courses, spanning different time frames (Table 2). The students at three of the partner institutions were accredited for their involvement as the programme formed part of their official studies, being embedded either into the curriculum or the course. For example, in Germany (PHKA and University of Kiel – CAU), outputs were not graded, though courses would still be accredited as part of a course module (pass/fail).

Table 2. The five partners' students were from different courses of varying durations and accreditations

Partner	Name of course	Duration of course	Extracurricular; integrated (course embedded); separated (curriculum embedded)	Voluntary participation; unaccredited module; accredited module
1	State exam (teacher training)	3-4 years	Separated (curriculum embedded)	Accredited
1	BA / MA Teacher training	2-3 years	Separated (curriculum embedded)	Accredited
2	Ma Teacher training	2-3 years	Separated (curriculum embedded)	Accredited
3	BA Teacher training	2-3 years	Separated (curriculum embedded)	Unaccredited
4	MA Adult education	2-3 years	Integrated (course embedded)	Accredited
5	PGCE (Teacher training)	1 year	Extracurricular	Voluntary
5	MA EIP / TESOL (for teaching languages outside UK)	1 year	Extracurricular	Voluntary
5	PhD Education	3 years	Extracurricular	Voluntary
5	BA MFL	4 years	Extracurricular	Voluntary

These individual requirements for each partner's cohort needed to be taken into account, as an assessment framework would need to gauge the different types and qualities of outputs and provide formal evaluation which could be mapped onto an institute's own assessment framework in order to properly accredit the students.

3.2. Meeting the combined requirements of the project output criteria

The requirements of the proPIC project were divided into two tasks: process orientation, to reflect the process of the programme on the side of the students and educators; and product orientation, namely criteria against which the outcomes produced (e-portfolios and outputs) could be measured.

The framework was intended to help higher education educators to judge success and improvements, as well as grade students for accreditation. The use of an assessment framework would allow the study programme to be integrated effectively against a set of validated criteria.

4. Development of a framework which integrated the varying needs

Existing sources were used as starting points for this framework: the CEFR and iPAC frameworks as discussed above: the SOLO Taxonomy (Biggs & Collis, 1982), DigComp 2.1 (Carretero, Vuorikari, & Punie, 2017), and the Level 5 Reference System (INTRASOFT International, 2016).

Feedback on the initial use of the framework was discussed at the transnational meeting, leading to a series of critical conversations about the framework requirements, the differing partner needs, and the terminology used. The collaborative feedback and review cycle data allowed the authors to adapt the framework to generate a model, which each partner then adapted to suit their own context while retaining commonality across the partnership to allow comparison between institutions.

In this section, we will refer to the frameworks which were used to guide and inform the development of the proPIC framework and will identify the challenges and issues which emerged throughout the process.

4.1. Meeting the product brief – assessing different components of an output

The first issue which emerged was the product brief. The student output comprised several components, including an e-portfolio, a digital product, and participation in a transnational study week. This made assessment more complex than evaluating a single product, and partners immediately commented on the difficulty of judging work which (1) had been completed without access to an assessment framework, and (2) had been completed on a multi-structural level with no opportunity to enhance the work through collaboration or higher level thinking. It was recognised by the partners that criteria needed to be given prior to the start of the cohort, and all students need to be producing similar standards of output for similar purposes.

The second issue which emerged involved the diverse outputs which students were asked to produce. Although the partner institutions encouraged their students to regularly contribute to a personal e-portfolio, using a variety of platforms including Google Sites, Wixx, and WordPress, these were not always discussed with or monitored by the module leaders or teachers, and as a result, the quality varied across the individual cohorts as well as across the partners. On examination of the e-portfolios[3] which were produced by the first two cohorts of students, one partner commented in their initial email feedback that

> "the e-portfolio is a tool to show and see that the student has carried out a reflective practice and has developed a derivative learning process. In this sense, the e-portfolio is a tool not only to show the outputs, but also to develop specific reflections about what this specific output means from a Continuing Professional Development (CPD) point of view. The output, by itself, implies learning, but adding a reflection about what, how and why learning came provokes a greater CPD".

---

3. http://www.propiceuropa.com/students.html

Another added that they "would have a problem to assess the e-portfolio without having a discussion with the student".

It was therefore felt that an evaluation framework designed to assess an e-portfolio would have different criteria than one designed to assess a digital output such as a podcast, website, or video, as there would be varying levels of reflective practice, theoretical input, and engagement with research, both academic and personal. Therefore, the question arose: should the e-portfolio component and the digital output component be assessed separately or together, and could one framework cover the criteria for both components?

4.2. The use of linear, 'academic' assessment frameworks

The final issue which emerged was the design and purpose of academic assessment criteria. Much of the student output was multimodal, and though there were elements of thinking on a multi-structural, relational, or even extended abstract level, this was difficult to assess across all students' work equally. One partner commented that "critical engagement [in one particular output] was not at a high level, especially because [the student] does not link her experience with theoretical aspects. She is too focussed on her personal experience". A linear, academic assessment framework is perhaps unable to effectively evaluate work not written in an essay format, with reference to literature sources and detailed enquiry methodologies.

The problem identified here was that many of the existing frameworks being used by the partner universities to evaluate the students on their courses (particularly those for whom proPIC formed an accredited module) were academic in nature and designed to assess linear pieces of writing, rather than the more multimodal outputs produced for the project. Therefore, the existing systems were unsuitable for our needs and it was necessary to devise our own framework derived from our research and the partner feedback. Key characteristics of a potential proPIC framework were:

- integration of differing student, course, and institution needs;

- assessment of formal outputs including digital and multimodal products, and reflective outputs including digital e-portfolios; and

- recognition of the core elements of teacher training (development of professional knowledge, professional practice, and professional attitudes) as well as development of reflection, critical dialogue, and digital competence and confidence.

5. The development process: sequential versions of the framework

In the initial version of the framework, we attempted to use a cyclical design to emphasise the connected nature of the various criteria (Figure 1).

Figure 1. October 2019 – Version 1 (cyclical format)

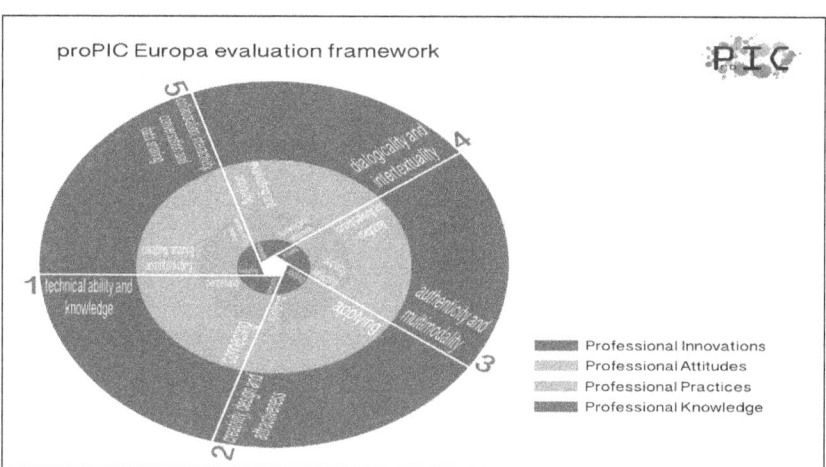

However, we decided that a tabulated framework would allow us to better incorporate the core elements and characteristics we had identified, as shown in Table 3.

Table 3. November 2019 – version 1 (linear format)

	Professional Knowledge		Professional Practices		Professional Attitudes		Professional Innovations
5	Evaluation	Full understanding, further literature application of conceptual knowledge and engagement with theory,	Developing, constructing, transferring	Engagement with the teaching and learning process, and demonstrating the impact of theorised practice leading to phronesis (practical wisdom); developing own techniques/ approaches/ strategies	Creating, sharing and interacting	Critical insight and reflection into how professional or academic thinking has been influenced examination of the learning process, showing what learning occurred, how learning occurred, and how newly acquired knowledge altered existing knowledge	Collaboration, interactivity, conversation and data sharing
4	Synthesis	Generalizability or transferability of the study to other contexts, critical engagement with a range of sources	Discovering, acting independently	Searching for the appropriate digital tools and opportunities for your purpose and audience	Evaluating and critiquing	Exploration and critique of assumptions, values, beliefs, and/or biases, and the consequences of action (present and future)	Dialogicality and intertextuality
3	Analysis	How the relevant digital tools, skills and theory relate to each other	Deciding, selecting	Finding and using tools and instruments that are suitable for purpose	Conceptualising and integrating	Attempting to understand, question, or analyse learning and events	Authenticity and multimodality
2	Application	Understand the relationships between pedagogical theory and practice and how to apply the theory to practice	Applying	Make use of tools and instruments in accordance with the needs of specific target groups	Applying	Application of learning to a broader context of personal and professional life, beginning to examine, appraise, compare, contrast, plan for new actions or response, or propose remedies to use in and outside structured learning experiences	Creativity, design and attractiveness

1	Comprehension	Remembering and understanding relevant literature, studies and theories	Perceiving	Recognise digital and mobile tools, perceive different teaching and learning strategies.	Connecting	Demonstrating acquisition of new content from significant learning experiences. evidence of gaining knowledge, making sense of new experiences, or making linkages between old and new information	Technical ability

The content of Version 1 (Table 3) was based on discussions between PHKA and Newcastle University (UNEW) as to what the proPIC programme was aiming to achieve and what the students needed to learn, demonstrate, and produce. This was divided, we felt, into four areas of competence: development of professional knowledge; demonstration of professional practices; understanding and awareness of professional attitudes; and application of professional *innovations*. This last term indicated the digital mobile technologies which the students were introduced to and encouraged to develop their skills and confidence in using.

This prototype was disseminated to the other partners, along with a sample digital output and a sample e-portfolio for them to establish whether the framework could be suitable as an assessment tool. We asked partners to consider how effective the framework would be to assess an output and e-portfolio by a student randomly selected from Cohort 2, and invited feedback on its potential success and its limitations. Partner feedback on the initial use of this framework was then discussed at the transnational meeting in November 2019, leading to a series of critical conversations about the framework requirements, the differing partner needs, and the terminology used.

5.1. Creating a common framework – changes between Versions 1 and 2

Version 1 featured Levels 1-5 which were removed in Version 2 as not all partners required a numeric levelling system. The vertical criteria used

Chapter 6

are from Bloom et al.'s (1956) original taxonomy, with nouns used in this hierarchy of learning objectives and a slightly different set of criteria titles arching across all the core elements (professional knowledge, practices, attitudes, and innovations). Version 2 replaced these with criteria from Anderson, Krathwohl, and Bloom's (2001) revised taxonomy. The verbs used emphasise a more active, dynamic approach to learning and better represent the project objectives. The criteria descriptions were adapted to better match these. The biggest change was the fourth column – professional innovations to professional solutions. This change in terminology will be discussed later in this chapter.

5.2. Creating a common framework – changes between Versions 2 and 3

Version 2 was discussed in more depth at the transnational meeting, and its potential weaknesses explored. The highest level of learning criteria, creating and sharing, was altered to creating and transferring, and the description expanded to include 'making connections across theory and practice' (see Table 4 and Table 5).

Table 4. November 2019 – Version 2 (linear format)

	Professional knowledge	Professional practices	Professional attitudes	Professional solutions
Creating and sharing	Using conceptual knowledge to generate and share new ideas and concepts	Demonstrating the impact of theorised practice by developing own tools, methods and strategies for teaching and learning	Examining the learning process, showing what learning occurred, how learning occurred, and how newly used content altered existing knowledge	Innovating and collaborating to create interactive and original content
Evaluating and synthesising	Generalizability, transferability and critical engagement of relevant tools, concepts and theories to other contexts	Reflecting on and relating the use of different tools, methods and strategies for teaching and learning to other contexts	Exploring and critiquing the experience of applying new content	Redefining and sharing content, and developing expertise through reflection and critique

Analysing	Understanding the relationship of relevant tools, concepts and theories	Understanding why, when and how to use certain tools, methods and strategies for teaching and learning in a specific context	Conceptualising and questioning new content	Modifying content and integrating strategy, diversification, developing awareness, curiosity and willingness
Applying	Knowing how to apply relevant tools, concepts and theories to practice	Making use of different tools, methods and strategies for teaching and learning in accordance with the needs of the specific context	Beginning to examine, appraise, compare, contrast, and plan new content for further actions or response,	Augmenting content through exploration of new tools and methods, with meaningful use and variation of these
Comprehending and understanding	Remembering and understanding relevant tools, concepts and theories	Recognising different tools, methods and strategies for teaching and learning	Internalising and making sense of new content from significant teaching and learning experiences.	Substituting old content for new, and developing growing awareness and curiosity of new tools and methods

Table 5. November 2019 – Version 3

	Professional Knowledge	Professional Practices	Professional Attitudes	Professional Solutions
Creating and transferring	Using conceptual knowledge to generate and share new ideas and concepts	Demonstrating the impact of theorised practice by developing own tools, methods and strategies for teaching and learning	Examining the learning process, showing what learning occurred, how learning occurred, and how newly used content altered existing knowledge	Innovating and collaborating to create interactive and original content
Evaluating and synthesising	Generalizability, transferability and critical engagement of relevant tools, concepts and theories to other contexts	Reflecting on and relating the use of different tools, methods and strategies for teaching and learning to other contexts	Exploring and critiquing the experience of applying new content	Redefining and sharing content, and developing expertise through reflection and critique

Chapter 6

Analysing	Understanding the relationship of relevant tools, concepts and theories	Understanding why, when and how to use certain tools, methods and strategies for teaching and learning in a specific context	Conceptualising and questioning new content	Modifying content and integrating strategy, diversification, developing awareness, curiosity and willingness
Applying	Knowing how to apply relevant tools, concepts and theories to practice	Making use of different tools, methods and strategies for teaching and learning in accordance with the needs of the specific context	Beginning to examine, appraise, compare, contrast, and plan new content for further actions or response,	Augmenting content through exploration of new tools and methods, with meaningful use and variation of these
Comprehending and understanding	Remembering and understanding relevant tools, concepts and theories	Recognising different tools, methods and strategies for teaching and learning	Internalising and making sense of new content from significant teaching and learning experiences.	Substituting old content for new, and developing growing awareness and curiosity of new tools and methods

The collaborative feedback and review cycle allowed the authors to adapt the framework, generating a final generic model with input from all partners, with learning objective criteria and descriptions of how this would be visible in students' work.

Creating an agreed-upon generic framework was a core feature of our approach: this basic grid covered all the requirements of the programme but could be adapted by partners according to their needs (to create their own 'bespoke framework') though still based on a common framework. This generic meta-framework would then be implemented by institutions to create specific assessment frameworks with levels where appropriate. The next stage was therefore for partners to adapt the model into bespoke 'local' frameworks which will be discussed in the next section.

6. To what extent could the creation of a common assessment framework be successful in meeting the individual and combined requirements of the partner institutions and the project output criteria? How did the partners adapt the meta-framework to their institutional requirements for assessment?

The common framework seen in Version 3 is unlike the assessment frameworks that we explored in the development stage. This section will examine to what extent a common assessment framework could be successful in meeting the individual and combined requirements of the partner institutions and the specific project output criteria, and how the partners adapted the generic meta-framework into a more effective and appropriate bespoke framework for their institutional requirements for assessment, yet retained the core purpose and concepts of the generic framework.

6.1. Data collection and analysis

Qualitative data was collected throughout, consisting of transcribed Swivl audio/video recordings of meetings, multimodal feedback data (video, audio, screencast, presentation, email, and Padlet), and a working document (accessible by all partners on Google Docs) with the outputs of the transnational meeting[4]. This was analysed using a thematic analysis approach, a technique for synthesising qualitative data through coding (Boyatzis, 2009). Firstly, transcribed qualitative data was coded using an iterative review method. Key data points were then extracted, and these were synthesised into themes, which were analysed using a grounded theory approach (Glaser, Strauss, & Strutzel, 1968). Grounded theory is concerned with generating theories regarding social phenomena and developing a "higher level understanding that is grounded in, or derived from, a systematic analysis of data" (Lingard, Albert,

---

4. This data was collected during the transnational meeting held in Barcelona from 6-8 November 2019.

& Levinson, 2008, p. 459). It is therefore effective where social interactions and experiences are being studied to explain the collaborative creation of an evaluation framework.

Data will be presented and discussed in two parts: firstly, key points from discussions which took place at the transnational meeting, during which all partners were able to put forward their opinions and ask questions; and secondly, outputs from the subsequent small group discussions during which partners worked in national teams to adapt the common framework presented into a local framework which better suited individual needs.

6.2. Discussion

After the partners had been shown the Version 3 common framework (Table 5) developed by PHKA and UNEW at the transnational meeting in Barcelona (November 2019), the floor was opened to discussion and partners were invited to give feedback and share their views on the suitability and potential effectiveness of the framework in their own context. The following themes were extracted from the transcript of the discussion and identified as key topics for examination by the partners:

- overall assessment and evaluation needs of the project;
- terminology with different meanings or connotations;
- partner-specific requirements regarding courses and students;
- framework design process;
- student reflection and action on feedback provided; and
- specific assessment and evaluation of innovation and creative outputs.

6.2.1. Theme 1: overall assessment and evaluation needs of the project

Students were required to submit two key outputs as a result of their involvement in proPIC: digital outputs and e-portfolios. These were evaluated across all three cohorts in the final project report in order to understand the impact of the project's CPD programme, interactive tutorials, and study week opportunities on the student. In some partner institutions, students' overall achievement provided accreditation on their formal teacher training programme.

> "All of this [rubric] has to be used as a basis for discussion. Even in [UNEW's] case where they volunteered taking part in the project for fun, it's so nice to have the discussion with them at the end of it, a feedback session to let them know what they scored, what they've done, why we've given them a particular level of grades and what can be done, and for those of you [partners] who are accrediting this process, it gives you a springboard for feedback, specific feedback, in specific areas. So we had to combine a lot of different aspects to create one overall framework [...] you can create a more individualised version that is suitable" (Audio recording from transnational meeting, UNEW).

However, partners had differing levels of familiarity with the different elements of the project. Partners in Barcelona already used and assessed e-portfolios in their teaching training courses, whereas other partners were new to them as an element of a course which needed to be assessed along with other, more formal elements. CAU commented that assigning an overall grade was too complex:

> "it was very hard for me to evaluate, because I was also overwhelmed with the results and I said ok, they did a really good job, I think it's very difficult to say this one gets 2.3, this one gets 1.7, it was very hard, so I just said, ok, they did it, they did it well, they got it, that's it. [When asked if they give feedback afterwards:] For the second cohort yes, for the first one, no. For the second, we met and they showed their e-portfolios to the group. Actually, the feedback was about the project and the e-portfolio, not only the e-portfolio" (Audio recording from transnational meeting, CAU).

University of Borås (HB), in contrast, already incorporated e-portfolio use into their curriculum and felt confident in their assessment methods, stating that a reflective portfolio was a compulsory part of the university course, worth 1.5 credits, and that written feedback on this reflection was given. HB and

Chapter 6

Universidad de Barcelona (UB) then discussed how they also used a range of techniques for feedback, including peer evaluation.

> "We use rubrics for peer evaluation, so it's easier, so you can do both, you can do the normal evaluation or you can do the peer evaluation" (Audio recording of transnational meeting, UB).

> "We don't have that much time to give feedback as teachers, so we give the opportunities to our students to give feedback on each other, so they also improve the way of giving feedback in the future when they become teachers to their pupils" (Audio recording of transnational meeting, HB).

Because HB and UB students were used to developing e-portfolios and giving each other feedback, as well as being assessed on their reflection, incorporating this aspect into their proPIC course was easier than perhaps for their UK and German colleagues. There was therefore a wide variety in the quality of e-portfolios being produced across all project partners. This led to a debate as to whether e-portfolios could or should be evaluated alongside more tangible outputs, and indeed whether such evaluation was even effective in providing "trustworthy representation of student achievement" given its individual nature (Boud et al., 2010, in Thomas et al., 2019, p. 547). HB summarised their perception of the role of evaluation of e-portfolios:

> "my conclusion was we shouldn't use these criteria [in the generic framework in Table 4] to evaluate the students' e-portfolios, because the product is where they are going to bring all these things together, in a way the portfolio is mainly the part of the process of getting there so it would be a reflection […]. The portfolio from our perspective should be just a place to reflect and discuss ideas, not to reach those goals that we describe here […]. What reflection means for the individual is individual, so you can't actually assess and say you haven't reflected, you can see if they are reflective, but not grading their reflections" (Audio recording from transnational meeting, HB).

6.2.2. Theme 2: terminology with different meanings or connotations

Much research has been done into formative assessment and evaluation practice in higher education, but the terms *assessment* and *evaluation* proved controversial for some of the partners. Looking at the local translations of the terms, it is noticeable that the Catalan language has only one word for both terms – 'avaluació'. This is unlike the other languages in the project: the Swedish term for assessment, 'bedömning', also translates as valuation or rating, suggesting a numerical value can be assigned, while 'utvärdering' is used for evaluation and stems from the word for appraisal or appreciation. In German, the difference between the terms is similar to the Swedish: 'Bewertung' for assessment has the equivalent meaning of valuation, whereas 'Auswertung' for evaluation carries the sense of interpretation, analysis, or appraisal, though in a German academic context, the English term 'evaluation' is also used.

This leads us to consider how a common framework can be created if the purpose of that framework is unclear to all partners and if indeed the meaning of the term used to describe the framework can be interpreted in different ways. The discussion seemed to reflect how partners were assessing/evaluating their students and if grades or credits were awarded as a result of participation, or if non-numerical feedback was given.

> "I think it's unfair to assess people's reflections, because they have got different levels. (HB)
>
> That's actually why we called it evaluation framework, not assessment criteria, because that's what we thought, you cannot. (UNEW)
>
> Can't we also call it feedback framework? (CAU)
>
> Evaluation and feedback framework? (UNEW)
>
> Yeah, feedback framework. (UB)

Chapter 6

> Feedback framework, because it helps us to see, to give these comments, but not to assess it, evaluate it. (CAU)
>
> Yes, a kind of framework with ideas to give feedback. (UB)
>
> Would it be possible to say common framework for feedback and assessment? (UB)
>
> It's nice, feedback and evaluation, trying to avoid assessment. (UNEW)
>
> Assessment, does it always include a grade? (CAU)
>
> But it always contains a level, percentage. (PHKA)
>
> Even if it's just implied, you're implying that they've done well or not so well. (UNEW)" (Audio recording from transnational meeting).

Other terms used had different connotations for the partners. One of these was the term *innovation*, which PHKA and UNEW embedded into the common framework as one of four aspects of professional learning along with knowledge, practices, and attitudes. PHKA and UNEW examined the existing frameworks and established that teacher training required the acquisition of professional knowledge; the progression of professional practices; and the development of professional attitudes. These are the core aspects of teachers who can put their knowledge into practice and have the ability to reflect and respond appropriately to their professional requirements and responsibilities, and link to the idea of the acquisition of knowledge leading to professional competence (Eraut, 1994). However, there is a fourth aspect which goes further than reflection, and involves the teacher in professional collaboration, interaction and dialogue which can result in a change or improvement in practice; allows the teacher to incorporate multimodal and authentic materials and technologies; and enables the teacher to express creativity through their use of teaching and learning methods and resources. This aspect was termed professional innovations. Though the word innovation may more generally be linked to 'newness', such as a new concept, idea, or method, in this framework we defined it as the use of approaches, methods, or technologies which demonstrated the growth and development of the trainee teacher, outside the three main strands of learning (that is, knowledge, practice, and attitude – see also Mann & Webb, 2022, Chapter 1 this volume).

> "So basically or based on this we called it professional knowledge now, professional practices and professional attitudes and we kind of had the first three strands as a basis, so we started with this and we discussed a lot the words we would use a lot and we couldn't really, we didn't have the fourth strand at the beginning, we just added this strand because something is missing here, because that was the innovative bit. So the blue one we added, basically we added the blue strand, professional innovations, so for a long time we discussed three columns and there was something missing we thought and we couldn't really find what was missing so we put it underneath, we put it on top, but then we said no it's actually part of the whole framework professional innovations, it needs to go in the whole framework as such" (Audio recording of transnational meeting, PHKA, Germany).

However, the term 'innovation' here became blurred with the term 'competence'. Were we aiming to establish in this strand of the framework exactly what the teacher could now **do**, in other words, what skills or techniques (digital or otherwise) that they were now competent in, or to establish if and how the teacher could now reflect on and use the knowledge and practice that they had developed, with this phronesis helping them to take creative risks, try new approaches, and both understand and talk about their learning from the process? Both of these meanings would be 'new' for the trainee teacher – new competences, new practical wisdom – but it was decided to alter the term to 'professional solutions' as a compromise.

> "Can I say something? I have a problem with the word innovation, sorry, I don't like it, because it goes beyond what you are trying to do here, I don't know what would be the solution, I think here what you are talking about is professional digital competence. (UB)

> I think we did say competence first, then we changed it to innovations. (UNEW)
>
> Because innovation is much more than the digital part, here if you go, you know, it's digital competence... But talking about innovation, to keep the word innovation has to do with originality as well, and you know, innovation, it depends on where you start from. As P3 [HB] was saying it would not be new for them, but it's a new thing for me maybe, maybe yes, it is a new thing for me to do" (UB) (Audio recording from transnational meeting).

It is noticeable that in the final local versions of the framework, this entire column is omitted by PHKA and UB, and reverts to 'professional innovations' in the version by CAU (see Table 7).

6.2.3. Theme 3: partner-specific requirements regarding courses and students

As discussed previously, partners had integrated the project into their course and curriculum in different ways. When developing the framework, we kept in mind the key outputs of the proPIC project and the skills students would develop and display as a result of the process, regardless of their partner-specific requirements: digital skills development, transnational collaboration, and dialogic reflection.

> "So this meant that we were trying to develop something that would evaluate the overall product, or project, with a digital product that has to show evidence of some sort of digital skills and digital competences with the dialogic reflection that needed to show some critical engagement with literature, some critical engagement with theory, some really kind of deep thought on all of this, that also appealed or applies to all partner situations, all the different cohorts and all our different types of students, it was quite tricky" (Audio recording from transnational meeting, UNEW).

Partners were focussed on how the framework could be used in their own context with their own students, particularly if formal grading was required in their courses. They tried to assimilate the framework into their own current assessment and feedback system. The comments and discussions used in this chapter illustrate how difficult it is to attain commonality across several partners with differing needs. Those students gaining credits need to have grades given which enable them to progress through their course, and often students do not want or have the time to do extra work for no credits. Equally, students undertaking a non-accredited programme voluntarily need to have something to show for their participation. This meant that some partners needed a framework which was levelled and/or graded for accreditation, and others needed to give more general constructive feedback. The aim of the framework was that it could be used by professionals in a range of institutions, but our discussion showed clearly that individual partner requirements were prioritised above common project aims, despite the development of the framework drawing on the outputs produced by each partners' students:

> "yes, we have to keep the focus, what we want is a framework that other professionals can use as an orientation, based on the outputs, so I think it is important that we remember this, we will not be able to develop something that suits everyone... And it is based on the outputs that were created in this project, I mean that's what we did, that's the data we had also developing this. We looked at the outputs that were created and the e-portfolios, that's why we asked for your contribution to send us all the outputs and e-portfolios and that's what we included here, so the data basis was the student outputs and of course the theory" (Audio recording from transnational meeting, PHKA).

Is complete commonality across a number of institutions possible, when each partner has their own individualised requirements and must adhere to their own country's academic procedures and protocols? Or, by necessity, must there be a local version of a common framework which partners feel confident meets their own particular needs?

Chapter 6

6.2.4. Theme 4: student reflection and action on feedback provided

Each partner's students received feedback during the process, and there was discussion on how this compared with the feedback they received throughout their course according to each institution's procedures.

> "I think in some cases, students integrate and improve a lot [...] the entries [of their e-portfolio], because most of the feedback are questions for reflection, some different things regarding their beliefs, because they normally start describing some of their beliefs about teaching and learning, and the Spanish teaching profession and then we start introducing questions to get reflection, so then some people introduce more explication, but some of them have not done much, I think this depends on the case [...]. Sometimes it's like I try to stimulate as much as possible and sometimes if they improve every single thing I tell them, I think it's maybe too much, so I just focus on the main things that are there. If we consider a portfolio as the starting point, there are some guidelines or some development goals, it's nice to get back to them, so I maybe focus on that and how the first feedback goes back to the starting point, so that are my main steps"

(Audio recording from transnational meeting, UK).

For a student at a partner institution where this kind of formative feedback is a regular part of the assessment and evaluation process, including this element in the proPIC assessment framework would be both useful and expected.

For partners who have no time or capacity incorporated into their course for regular feedback on reflection, or for partners where the students are from different courses and take part in the project voluntarily, this is a more complex element to manage and may be omitted from local versions of the framework (see Table 6, Table 7, Table 8, Table 9, Table 10, Figure 2, and Figure 3).

6.2.5. Theme 5: specific assessment and evaluation of innovation and creative outputs

The outputs produced by students varied depending on how much time they were able to devote to the project, which partner institution they belonged to, and which they attended as part of their study week, as well as on whether they were expecting to receive formal accreditation for their work. The common factor across the outputs, however, was an element of creativity: students were dissuaded from producing an academic paper and instead directed towards a multimodal output, using skills including video production, digital content editing, and social media.

> "Well this was the things that we also discussed, because in this project the purpose was that the students create a creative and innovative output. This was the last issue we talked about, the innovative bit. Because, of course you can have a paper, a traditional paper, but in this very project, we said that the students should create some kind of creative product at the end for which they use mobile technologies. So, this was also the last thing we discussed, the innovative character of the output or the project. How to assess this. Which we couldn't really find anywhere. (PHKA)

> But the thing about innovation is tricky, because we've got students who think that they have created something very innovative and during the process they discover that somebody has already done it. (HB)

> And innovation in itself has to be, it has to be combined with all of these other criteria, because an Instagram account is not innovative anymore. Everybody has an Instagram account, we all stick photos on an Instagram account, a blog, a podcast, all these things are quite old hat now. (UNEW)

> At the same time, if we look at it from a language learning perspective, maybe some of the things they are doing are innovative compared to what other teachers in the field are doing, it's all relative. (HB)

Chapter 6

> It is relative, but we have to focus on this project now, we have to focus on the courses we have, then we can open it up, then we can say okay how will we use it in our own institution or course in particular. First, we have to compare the courses we have in this project, compare the students of this project and their outputs" (PHKA) (Audio recording from transnational meeting).

Again, the discussion above demonstrates that it would be complex to use the same framework to evaluate students from different institutions who may have received different initial instruction on the project, had different criteria to meet for their course, and worked with different partners both in their home institution and their study week institution. Our own differing perspectives on what classes as innovative will mirror those of the students.

6.3. Outputs from national partner teams, adapting common framework to local requirements

The generic Version 3 framework (Table 5) was taken by each partner team and examined to see how it could meet their specific requirements. Each partner team then adapted the common framework into a bespoke framework, adding a grading system where necessary, altering or omitting certain criteria, and changing the terms used to suit their individual needs. These bespoke partner frameworks are shown in the section below.

6.3.1. PHKA, Germany

PHKA's intended and actual outputs were in general multimodal and demonstrated a variety of mobile technologies. These included web pages and blogs, video tutorials, Instagram accounts, videos, interactive Google Docs, e-books, podcasts, and screen-recorded WhatsApp interviews. Their local framework (Table 6) reflected this need to assess digital tool use and innovative content.

Table 6. Local framework of PHKA

	Content and language	**Use of digital tools**	**Content presentation**
Creating and sharing 80-100 %	Using conceptual knowledge and a proficient level of professional language to generate and share new ideas and concepts	Demonstrating the impact of theorised practice by developing own tools using format-specific criteria	Innovating and collaborating to create interactive and original content
Evaluating and synthesising 60-80 %	Generalizability, transferability and critical engagement of relevant concepts and professional language	Relating the use of different formats to specific contexts	Redefining and sharing content, and developing expertise through reflection and critique
Analysing 40-60 %	Understanding the relationship of concepts and professional language	Understanding why, when and how to use certain formats	Modifying content and integrating strategy, diversification, developing awareness, curiosity and willingness
Applying 20-40 %	Knowing how to apply relevant tools, concepts and theories to practice	Knowing how and making use of relevant tools with the needs of the specific format	Augmenting content through exploration of new tools and methods, with meaningful use and variation of these
Comprehending and understanding 0-20 %	Remembering and understanding relevant concepts, theories and basic linguistic phrases containing some professional language	Understanding and recognising relevant tools and format-specific criteria	Substituting old content for new, and developing growing awareness and curiosity of new tools and methods

6.3.2. CAU, Germany

CAU focussed their local framework (Table 7) on their use of video production, which featured heavily in both their teacher training course and in their implementation of the proPIC programme. Their final column, for which they reverted to the initially presented 'professional innovations' title, was designed to assess film production under two categories of creativity: the challenges of foreign language use and a change of perspective and overcoming technical limitations.

Table 7. Local framework of CAU

		Professional Knowledge Linkage to PCK (professional content knowledge) Definition of a content-relevant problem Basic skills in filmmaking (media competence)		Professional Practices Film concept, topic and structure Storyboarding as well as intellectual concept Educational and pedagogical value		Professional Attitudes Sense giving in the media framework Documentary input Personal message, engagement	Professional Innovations Successful elaboration of the chosen film category Creativity I (challenges: foreign language use and change of perspective) Creativity II (overcoming technical limitations)
5	Evaluation	Full understanding, further literature Application of conceptual knowledge and engagement with theory	Developing, constructing, transferring	Engagement with the teaching and learning process, and demonstrating the impact of theorised practice leading to phronesis (practical wisdom); Developing own techniques/ approaches/ strategies	Creating, sharing and interacting	Critical insight and reflection into how professional or academic thinking has been influenced Examination of the learning process, showing what learning occurred, how learning occurred, and how newly acquired knowledge altered existing knowledge	Collaboration, interactivity, conversation and data sharing

4	**Synthesis**	Generalizability or transferability of the study to other contexts, critical engagement with a range of sources	**Discovering, acting independently**	Searching for the appropriate digital tools and opportunities for your purpose and audience	**Evaluating and critiquing**	Exploration and critique of assumptions, values, beliefs, and/or biases, and the consequences of action (present and future)	Dialogicality and intertextuality
3	**Analysis**	How the relevant digital tools, skills and theory relate to each other	**Deciding, selecting**	Finding and using tools and instruments that are suitable for purpose	**Conceptualising and integrating**	Attempting to understand, question, or analyse learning and events	Authenticity and multimodality
2	**Application**	Understand the relationships between pedagogical theory and practice and how to apply the theory to practice	**Applying**	Make use of tools and instruments in accordance with the needs of specific target groups	**Applying**	Application of learning to a broader context of personal and professional life, beginning to examine, appraise, compare, contrast, plan for new actions or response, or propose remedies to use in and outside structured learning experiences	Creativity, design and attractiveness
1	**Comprehension**	Remembering and understanding relevant literature, studies and theories	**Perceiving**	Recognise digital and mobile tools, perceive different teaching and learning strategies.	**Connecting**	Demonstrating acquisition of new content from significant learning experiences. evidence of gaining knowledge, making sense of new experiences, or making linkages between old and new information	Technical ability

Chapter 6

6.3.3. HB, Sweden

HB noted that they planned to use the criteria to help us give feedback on the outputs created by their Cohort 2 students, presenting the criteria to Cohort 3 as well as using it in order to make possible amendments to their current course plan. The criteria would be used generally to give feedback on portfolios. They did not add a grading system to the framework, deciding to use it as a feedback tool rather than an assessment tool. Their local framework (Table 8) was the most similar to the common framework presented to the group.

Table 8. Local framework of HB

	Professional Knowledge	**Professional Practices**	**Professional Attitudes**	**Professional Solutions**
Creating and sharing	Using conceptual knowledge to generate and share new ideas and concepts	Demonstrating the impact of theorised practice by developing own tools, methods and strategies for teaching and learning	Examining the learning process, showing what learning occurred, how learning occurred, and how newly used content altered existing knowledge	Innovating and collaborating to create interactive and original content
Evaluating and synthesising	Generalizability, transferability and critical engagement of relevant tools, concepts and theories to other contexts	Reflecting on and relating the use of different tools, methods and strategies for teaching and learning to other contexts	Exploring and critiquing the experience of applying new content	Redefining and sharing content, and developing expertise through reflection and critique
Analysing	Understanding the relationship of relevant tools, concepts and theories	Understanding why, when and how to use certain tools, methods and strategies for teaching and learning in a specific context	Conceptualising and questioning new content	Modifying content and integrating strategy, diversification, developing awareness, curiosity and willingness

Applying	Knowing how to apply relevant tools, concepts and theories to practice	Making use of different tools, methods and strategies for teaching and learning in accordance with the needs of the specific context	Beginning to examine, appraise, compare, contrast, and plan new content for further actions or response	Augmenting content through exploration of new tools and methods, with meaningful use and variation of these
Comprehending and understanding	Remembering and understanding relevant tools, concepts and theories	Recognising different tools, methods and strategies for teaching and learning	Internalising and making sense of new content from significant teaching and learning experiences	Substituting old content for new, and developing growing awareness and curiosity of new tools and methods

6.3.4. UB, Spain

UB's framework (Table 9) omitted the final column completely, focussing on the three core strands of professional knowledge, practices, and attitudes. They then began to develop a separate evaluation system for their e-portfolio assessment (see Figure 2). As e-portfolio use and design played a key part in their teacher training programme, they prioritised this element and aimed to find a way that the e-portfolio could help students to consider and reflect upon their development of the three core strands.

Table 9. Local framework of UB

		Professional knowledge		Professional Practices		Professional Attitudes
5	Evaluation	Full understanding, further literature Application of conceptual knowledge and engagement with theory,	Developing, constructing, transferring	Engagement with the teaching and learning process, and demonstrating the impact of theorised practice leading to phronesis (practical wisdom); developing own techniques/ approaches/strategies	Creating, sharing and interacting	Critical insight and reflection into how professional or academic thinking has been influenced Examination of the learning process, showing what learning occurred, how learning occurred, and how newly acquired knowledge altered existing knowledge

Chapter 6

4	Synthesis	Generalizability or transferability of the study to other contexts, critical engagement with a range of sources	Discovering, acting independently	Searching for the appropriate digital tools and opportunities for your purpose and audience	Evaluating and critiquing	Exploration and critique of assumptions, values, beliefs, and/or biases, and the consequences of action (present and future)
3	Analysis	How the relevant digital tools, skills and theory relate to each other	Deciding, selecting	Finding and using tools and instruments that are suitable for purpose	Conceptualising and integrating	Attempting to understand, question, or analyse learning and events
2	Application	Understand the relationships between pedagogical theory and practice and how to apply the theory to practice	Applying	Make use of tools and instruments in accordance with the needs of specific target groups	Applying	Application of learning to a broader context of personal and professional life, beginning to examine, appraise, compare, contrast, plan for new actions or response, or propose remedies to use in and outside structured learning experiences
1	Comprehension	Remembering and understanding relevant literature, studies and theories	Perceiving	Recognise digital and mobile tools, perceive different teaching and learning strategies.	Connecting	Demonstrating acquisition of new content from significant learning experiences. evidence of gaining knowledge, making sense of new experiences, or making linkages between old and new information

Figure 2. E-portfolio evaluation system of UB

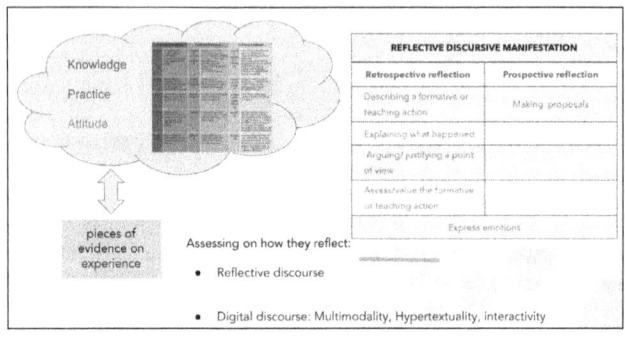

180

6.3.5. UNEW, UK

UNEW retained the common framework but added a scale to demonstrate the increasing competency of the participants as they moved up from the lowest row of descriptors (dependent/descriptive/uncritical/less complex) to the top row of descriptors (independent/analytical/critical/complex – Table 10). As the project was voluntary and was an extracurricular activity, the teachers would circle the appropriate descriptor in each category, giving the participant the ability to see what they could do to achieve the next level. In addition, written feedback would give extra information and could potentially be combined with video/audio feedback (see Figure 4). No grading system was needed, as the framework was merely a feedback tool and not used for accreditation. Finally, the student would receive a certificate of participation (Figure 3). These documents could be used as part of their teacher training or personal portfolio to demonstrate that they had developed knowledge, practices and skills in an extra-curricular programme which broadened their experiences outside the Master of Arts, post doctorate, or postgraduate certificate in education course they were following.

Figure 3. Certificate of Participation (UNEW)

Certificate of Participation

This is to certify that

NAME OF STUDENT

has completed the Erasmus+ proPIC Europa programme at Newcastle University between November 2019 and June 2020, and has achieved the knowledge, practices and skills as detailed on the accompanying feedback document.

Professor Paul Seedhouse: Programme Director

Date: 30 June 2020

Table 10. Local framework of UNEW

		Professional knowledge	Professional practices	Professional attitudes	Professional solutions
Independent/Analytical/Critical/Complex ↑ ⋮ ↓ Dependent/Descriptive/Uncritical/Less complex	Creating and sharing	Using conceptual knowledge to generate and share new ideas and concepts	Demonstrating the impact of theorised practice by developing own tools, methods and strategies for teaching and learning	Examining the learning process, showing what learning occurred, how learning occurred, and how newly used content altered existing knowledge	Innovating and collaborating to create interactive and original content
	Evaluating and synthesising	Generalizability, transferability and critical engagement of relevant tools, concepts and theories to other contexts generalizability, transferability and critical engagement of relevant tools, concepts and theories to other contexts	Reflecting on and relating the use of different tools, methods and strategies for teaching and learning to other contexts	Exploring and critiquing the experience of applying new content	Redefining and sharing content, and developing expertise through reflection and critique
	Analysing	Understanding the relationship of relevant tools, concepts and theories	Understanding why, when and how to use certain tools, methods and strategies for teaching and learning in a specific context	Conceptualising and questioning new content	Modifying content and integrating strategy, diversification, developing awareness, curiosity and willingness
	Applying	Knowing how to apply relevant tools, concepts and theories to practice	Making use of different tools, methods and strategies for teaching and learning in accordance with the needs of the specific context	Beginning to examine, appraise, compare, contrast, and plan new content for further actions or response	Augmenting content through exploration of new tools and methods, with meaningful use and variation of these

Comprehending and understanding	Remembering and understanding relevant tools, concepts and theories	Recognising different tools, methods and strategies for teaching and learning	Internalising and making sense of new content from significant teaching and learning experiences	Substituting old content for new, and developing growing awareness and curiosity of new tools and methods

Figure 4. Feedback Sheet of UNEW

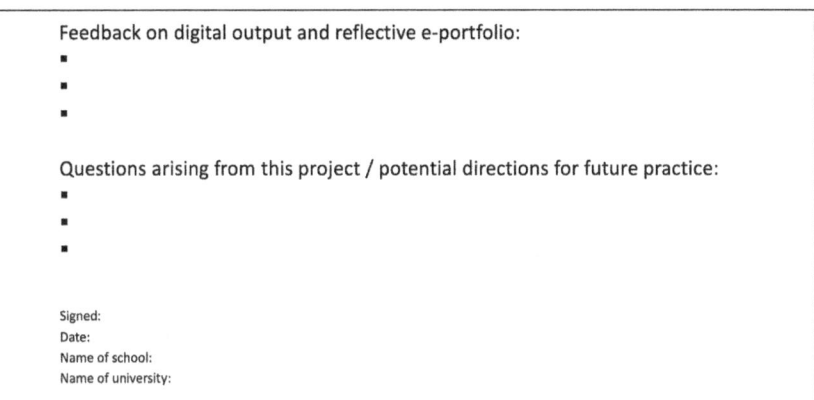

7. To what extent does a European partnership retain both individuality and commonality when developing an overall framework for assessment and evaluation that can serve as a basis for partners to devise and use in their individual context in the field of language teacher education?

As discussed throughout the chapter, there is a necessity in a European partnership for partners to embrace and encourage commonality, yet also have the ability to modify materials or models created for common use to ensure that they meet individual needs and requirements. There is a process of convergence and divergence undertaken by the partners. Pelkonen and

Terävainen-Litardo (2013) discuss the perceived increasing Europeanisation in higher education, driven in their view by the 2000 Lisbon Strategy[5] and the 1999 Bologna Declaration[6], as one reason for this transnational convergence, encouraging universities across Europe to collaborate and coordinate policies and practice. Certainly, one of the goals of the proPIC project was transnational collaboration, and it was important to consider and incorporate all of the varying partner needs as the framework was developed. As Khalifa and Sandholz (2012) note, the "breaking of barriers amongst countries around the world and building ties" (p. 344) is essential when universities collaborate on research and curriculum initiatives. Partners in the proPIC programme commented on the positive working relationships that were developed and the joint vision that we all shared in regard to the objectives and aims of the project.

However, when partners viewed the framework from their individual perspectives, the resulting discussion led to a situation where 'otherness' was experienced, but instead of leading to misunderstanding and conflict, this divergence served as a facilitator

> "for critical thinking and professional development. In line with Smith (2016), as well as Groundwater-Smith (2017), [discussion of this nature] is guided by the belief that fruitful partnerships [do not emerge] by chance but need to be initiated and scaffolded" (Oesterle et al., 2021, n.p.).

Partners were connected by the common ground of needing to provide assessment and feedback to students, and the challenges of the project such as the "lack of time to develop, trial and collaboratively research innovative learning and teaching scenarios (Mann & Walsh, 2017)" (Oesterle et al., 2021, n.p.). The positive relationships developed allowed the discussion to be critical without causing conflict. The decision to allow all partners to diverge from

---

5. http://www.europarl.europa.eu/activities/committees/studies.do?language=EN

6. http://www.ehea.info/page-ministerial-conference-bologna-1999; p. 53

the common framework and amend it to suit their individual needs meant that the results retained both the commonality across all institutions and the individuality required to make the framework usable and effective.

8. Conclusion

The development of a common assessment framework was an essential aspect of this project, as it enabled partners to reflect on their students' requirements and expectations, and how, as educators, they were supporting and scaffolding students in their reflection as well as their knowledge and practice development. Throughout the development of the framework, partners experienced a series of lexical and conceptual misunderstandings, conflicts of opinion, and differing views on the needs and abilities of their students.

By drawing on existing frameworks, we were able to identify the core factors of effective assessment and evaluation for trainee teachers and by examining the different university models and methods, and combining these with aspects of the existing frameworks, we felt that the common framework developed had the potential to be used by all partners to some extent. Though the framework was developed in a convergent manner, bringing together this variety of existing frameworks and the different course structures, curriculum models and student backgrounds of each partner institution, it was obviously necessary to allow partners to diverge from this common framework to assert their individuality. This brought us to the conclusion that an entirely common framework may not be possible in the context of a transnational partnership, as institutional requirements and needs are simply too diverse. However, it also showed that a common framework developed without a numerical grading system could then be adapted to suit both credit bearing and non-credit bearing courses, and this gave flexibility in how it was used.

Unfortunately, with the cancellation of Study Week 3 due to the global COVID-19 pandemic preventing all travel taking place, partners were not able to test the framework against submitted outputs and student e-portfolios, though it is hoped that all partners learnt from the development process and have taken away aspects of the framework to use in their teaching and assessment practices.

In our view, a common framework will always require adaptation into bespoke frameworks to fit individual needs, as one size does not fit all, but a coherent and dynamic partnership can work together to consolidate individual requirements and harmonise them into a common solution which works for all partners if they have a strong working relationship, built on regular collaboration and constructive critical discourse.

References

Anderson, L. W., Krathwohl, D. R., & Bloom, B. S. (2001). *A taxonomy for learning, teaching, and assessing: a revision of Bloom's taxonomy of educational objectives*. Longman.

Biggs, J., & Collis, K. (1982). *Evaluating the quality of learning: the SOLO taxonomy*. Academic Press.

Bliuc, A. M., Casey, G., Bachfischer, A., Goodyear, P., & Ellis, R. (2012). Blended learning in vocational education: teachers' conceptions of blended learning and their approaches to teaching and design. *The Australian Educational Researcher, 39*(2), 237-257. https://doi.org/10.1007/s13384-012-0053-0

Bloom, B. S., Engelhart, M. D., Furst, E. J., Hill, W. H., & Krathwohl, D. R. (1956). *Taxonomy of educational objectives: the classification of educational goals*. David McKay Company.

Boud, D., Sadler, R., Joughin, G., James, R., Freeman, M., Kift, S., & Dochy, F. (2010). *Assessment 2020: seven propositions for assessment reform in higher education*. Australian Learning and Teaching Council. https://www.uts.edu.au/sites/default/files/Assessment-2020_propositions_final.pdf

Bower, M., & Vlachopoulos, P. (2018). A critical analysis of technology-enhanced learning design frameworks. *British Journal of Educational Technology, 49*(6), 981-997. https://doi.org/10.1111/bjet.12668

Boyatzis, R. E. (2009). Competencies as a behavioral approach to emotional intelligence. *Journal of Management Development, 28*(9), 749-770. https://doi.org/10.1108/02621710910987647

Broadfoot, P., & Black, P. (2004). Redefining assessment? The first ten years of assessment in education. *Assessment in Education: Principles, Policy & Practice, 11*(1), 7-26. https://doi.org/10.1080/0969594042000208976

Burden, K., & Kearney, M. (2017). Investigating and critiquing teacher educators' mobile learning practices. *Interactive Technology and Smart Education, 14*(2), 110-125. https://doi.org/10.1108/ITSE-05-2017-0027

Carretero, S., Vuorikari, R., & Punie, Y. (2017). *DigComp 2.1: the digital competence framework for citizens with eight proficiency levels and examples of use.* European Commission. https://publications.jrc.ec.europa.eu/repository/bitstream/JRC106281/web-digcomp2.1pdf_%28online%29.pdf

Chmiel, N., Laurent, J., & Hansez, I. (2017). Employee perspectives on safety citizenship behaviors and safety violations. *Safety science, 93*(2017), 96-107. https://doi.org/10.1016/j.ssci.2016.11.014

Chmiel, A. S., Shaha, M., & Schneider, D. K. (2017). Introduction of blended learning in a master program: developing an integrative mixed method evaluation framework. *Nurse education today, 48*, 172-179. https://doi.org/10.1016/j.nedt.2016.10.008

Clausen, K., & Hoinkes, U. (2022). Filmmaking by students or rethinking thinking. In G. Schwab, M. Oesterle & A. Whelan (Eds), *Promoting professionalism, innovation and transnational collaboration: a new approach to foreign language teacher education* (pp. 233-242). Research-publishing.net. https://doi.org/10.14705/rpnet.2022.57.1391

Council of Europe. (2001). *Common European framework of reference for languages: learning, teaching, assessment.* Cambridge University Press. https://rm.coe.int/1680459f97

Eraut, M. (1994). *Developing professional knowledge and competence.* Psychology Press.

European Commission. (2020). *Erasmus+ programme guide.* https://erasmus-plus.ec.europa.eu/sites/default/files/2021-09/erasmus_programme_guide_2020_v3_en.pdf

Garrison, D. R., & Vaughan, N. D. (2008). *Blended learning in higher education: framework, principles, and guidelines.* Jossey-Bass/Wiley. https://doi.org/10.1002/9781118269558

Glaser, B., Strauss, A., & Strutzel, E. (1968). The discovery of grounded theory; strategies for qualitative research. *Nursing Research, 17*(4), 364. https://doi.org/10.1097/00006199-196807000-00014

Graham, C. R. (2006). Blended learning systems: definition, current trends, and future directions. In C. J. Bonk & C. R. Graham (Eds), *Handbook of blended learning: global perspectives, local designs* (pp. 3-21). Pfeiffer Publishing.

Gross Stein, J., Stren, R., Fitzgibbon, J., & MacLean, M. (2001). *Networks of knowledge: collaborative innovation in international learning*. University of Toronto Press.

Groundwater-Smith, S. (2017). Partnerships, networks and learning in educational research: contested practices. In R. McNae & B. Cowie (Eds), *Realising innovative partnerships in educational research theories and methodologies for collaboration* (pp. xvii-xix). Sense Publishers.

Healey, M., Flint, A., & Harrington, K. (2014, July). *Engagement through partnership: students as partners in learning and teaching in higher education*. Higher Education Academy. https://documents.advance-he.ac.uk/download/file/63

Hsu, Y.-C., & Ching, Y.-H. (2015). A review of models and frameworks for designing mobile learning experiences and environments. *Canadian Journal of Learning and Technology, 41*(3), 1-22. https://doi.org/10.21432/T2V616

INTRASOFT International S.A. (2016). REVEAL – social media verification [Erasmus+ Project]. https://revealproject.eu/

Kearney, M., Burden, K., & Rai, T. (2015). Investigating teachers' adoption of signature pedagogies. *Computers & Education, 80*, 48-57. https://doi.org/10.1016/j.compedu.2014.08.009

Kearney, M., Schuck, S., Burden K., & Aubusson, P. (2012). Viewing mobile learning from a pedagogical perspective. *Research in Learning Technology, 20*(1), 1-17. https://doi.org/10.3402/rlt.v20i0.14406

Khalifa, M., & Sandholz, S. (2012). Breaking barriers and building bridges through networks: an innovative educational approach for sustainability. *International Journal of Environmental and Science Education, 7*(2), 343-360.

Lingard, L., Albert, M., & Levinson, W. (2008). Grounded theory, mixed methods, and action research. *BMJ Clinical Research, 337*, 459-461. https://doi.org/10.1136/bmj.39602.690162.47

Mann, S., & Walsh, S. (2017). *Reflective practice in English language teaching. research-based Principles and practices*. Routledge.

Mann, S., & Webb, K. (2022). Continuing professional development: key themes in supporting the development of professional practice. In G. Schwab, M. Oesterle & A. Whelan (Eds), *Promoting professionalism, innovation and transnational collaboration: a new approach to foreign language teacher education* (pp. 15-44). Research-publishing.net. https://doi.org/10.14705/rpnet.2022.57.1382

McLean, H. (2018). This is the way to teach: insights from academics and students about assessment that supports learning. *Assessment & Evaluation in Higher Education, 43*(8), 1228-1240. https://doi.org/10.1080/02602938.2018.1446508

Meyer, L. H., Davidson, S., McKenzie, L., Rees, M., Anderson, H., Fletcher, R., & Johnston, P. M. (2010). An investigation of tertiary assessment policy and practice: alignment and contradictions. *Higher Education Quarterly, 64*(3), 331-350. https://doi.org/10.1111/j.1468-2273.2010.00459.x

Oesterle, M., Cuesta, A., & Whelan, A. (2021). *The value of transnational partnerships in teacher education - promoting professionalism and innovation*. ECER 2021. https://eera-ecer.de/ecer-programmes/conference/26/contribution/51472/?

Pelkonen, A., & Teräväinen-Litardo, T. (2013). Convergence and divergence in research, higher education and innovation policies: an analysis of nine European countries. In T. Erkkilä (Ed.), *Global university rankings*. Palgrave Macmillan. https://doi.org/10.1057/9781137296870_4

Smith, K. (2016). Partnerships in teacher education - going beyond the rhetoric with reference to the Norwegian context. *CEPS Journal, 6*(3), 17-36. https://doi.org/10.25656/01:12510

Stein, J., & Graham, C. (2014). *Essentials for blended learning: a standards based guide*. Routledge. https://doi.org/10.4324/9780203075258

Thomas, M. S. C., Ansari, D., & Knowland, V. C. P. (2019). Educational neuroscience: progress and prospects. *Journal of Child Psychology and Psychiatry, 60*(4), 477-492. https://doi.org/10.1111/jcpp.12973

Villarroel, V., Bloxham, S., Bruna, D., Bruna, C., & Herrera, C. (2018). Authentic assessment: creating a blueprint for course design. *Assessment & Evaluation in Higher Education, 43*(5), 840-854. https://doi.org/10.1080/02602938.2017.1412396

Wiliam, D. (2007). Keeping learning on track: formative assessment and the regulation of learning. In F. K. Lester (Ed.), *Second handbook of mathematics teaching and learning* (pp.1053-1098). Information Age.

7 Approaches to the development of pre-service language teachers' e-portfolios

Azahara Cuesta[1], Jaume Batlle[2], Vicenta González[3], and Joan-Tomàs Pujolà[4]

1. Introduction

Pre-service training of language teachers requires tools that foster the development of teaching competences, and the construction of their teacher identities. One crucial tool in that respect is the e-portfolio. Thus, in the framework of the proPIC Europa project[5], the e-portfolio is a dynamic artefact in which students collate learning evidence that helps to construct their teacher identity. In this chapter, we present the concept of the e-portfolio as it has been applied in the proPIC project, together with the associated learning objectives and constituent elements. In the sections that follow, we look at the e-portfolio from the perspective of the common formative actions carried out across the participating Higher Education Institutions (HEIs) and the specific actions implemented in each context, which were based in the context of the overall study programme[6] (see Hoinke & Clausen, 2022, Chapter 3 this volume). We will also present some of the outcomes, showcasing a number of e-portfolios that were constructed by the pre-service teachers participating in the project.

---

1. Universitat de Barcelona, Barcelona, Spain; azaharacuestagarcia@ub.edu; https://orcid.org/0000-0002-3530-1255

2. Universitat de Barcelona, Barcelona, Spain; jaumebatlle@ub.edu; https://orcid.org/0000-0002-7429-9768

3. Universitat de Barcelona, Barcelona, Spain; vicentagonzalez@ub.edu; https://orcid.org/0000-0002-5262-9500

4. Universitat de Barcelona, Barcelona, Spain; jtpujola@ub.edu; https://orcid.org/0000-0002-8664-432X

5. http://www.propiceuropa.com

6. http://www.propiceuropa.com/io3-study-programme.html

How to cite: Cuesta, A., Batlle, J., González, V., & Pujolà, J.-T. (2022). Approaches to the development of pre-service language teachers' e-portfolios. In G. Schwab, M. Oesterle & A. Whelan (Eds), *Promoting professionalism, innovation and transnational collaboration: a new approach to foreign language teacher education* (pp. 191-212). Research-publishing.net. https://doi.org/10.14705/rpnet.2022.57.1388

Chapter 7

1.1. H2 The e-portfolio: a dynamic tool

For the purpose of this study, we adopt the definition of e-portfolios given by Kunnari and Laurikainen (2017), who state that:

> "e-Portfolios are **student-owned digital** working and learning **spaces** for **collecting, creating, sharing, collaborating, reflecting** learning and **competences**, as well as **storing assessment** and **evaluation**. They are **platforms** for students to follow and be engaged in their personal and **career development**, and **actively** interact with **learning communities** and different **stakeholders** of the learning process" (p. 7; emphasis added by the authors).

This concept of digital portfolio or e-portfolio stresses its **process-oriented, dynamic**, and **reflective** nature. Thus, the e-portfolio is understood in terms of the processes that take place during its creation and should not be considered a static tool, i.e. just for assessment. It is not merely a finished product or a series of outcomes; rather, it serves as a basis for ongoing feedback throughout the various phases of one's training. In this regard, an e-portfolio can be considered a learning strategy in itself, a tool for reflective practice or a resource to help developing pre-service teachers' professional identity. It is thus seen as an effective tool for professional development, not simply a folder in which to compile pieces of evidence of the learning process. Learning and self-assessment processes that facilitate reflection on learning activities and teaching practices are particularly relevant in the development of an e-portfolio (Bozu, 2012). As a digital tool, the e-portfolio enables students to enrich their individual learning process by sharing them with others, building their own knowledge while also contributing to the construction of a common knowledge base. The e-portfolio also provides tutors with a straightforward means of monitoring and guiding the creative process (Pujolà & González, 2021).

The pre-service teachers' e-portfolio compiles evidence of the different **training cycles** that make up the overall learning process (Pujolà, 2019). The first cycle requires each pre-service teacher to describe their unique starting point: the situation in which they find themselves at the beginning of a study programme, setting out their prior training and knowledge, the objectives they are pursuing, and how they intend to achieve them. The exercise provides a snapshot of what each student has achieved up to that point and the challenges they have set themselves for the duration of the programme (Pujolà & González, 2008). This snapshot is a point of reference to which students can return to assess their progress. As they complete the study programme, the pre-service teachers begin a new cycle in which they review the degree to which their initial objectives have been achieved, collecting examples of completed learning activities and reflecting on the outcomes, as well as defining new challenges. The study programme proceeds through successive cycles until its completion, at which point the pre-service teachers conduct an overall review of each cycle to establish a global self-assessment of their learning process. The pieces of evidence incorporated into the e-portfolio must be illustrative of their learning process and should be accompanied by each pre-service teacher's reflections on why each example was selected and what impact it has had on their training (see Figure 1).

As explained by Sayòs and Torras (2019, p. 29), drawing on Cole, Ryan, Kick, and Mathies (2000) and on Pérez Gómez (2016), reflection in e-portfolios must clearly establish the relationship between the evidence presented and the scope and quality of the learning activity. Students should also highlight the individual metacognitive processes and the group socio-affective processes employed, assess their attainment of the desired competences, and set future targets for personal and professional development.

Continuous reflection on the learning process through the structured presentation of individual texts obliges pre-service teachers to record aspects of their training that are not necessarily reflected in the course activities. In other words, in addition to the theoretical content of the training syllabus, they must also record and reflect on the competences they have been required to develop. The self-reflective nature of the e-portfolio enables students to critically examine the programme content, the learning process and their own skills and competences (González & Montmany, 2019, p. 18f.).

Chapter 7

Figure 1. Dynamic representation of an e-portfolio (Pujolà, 2019, p. 71)

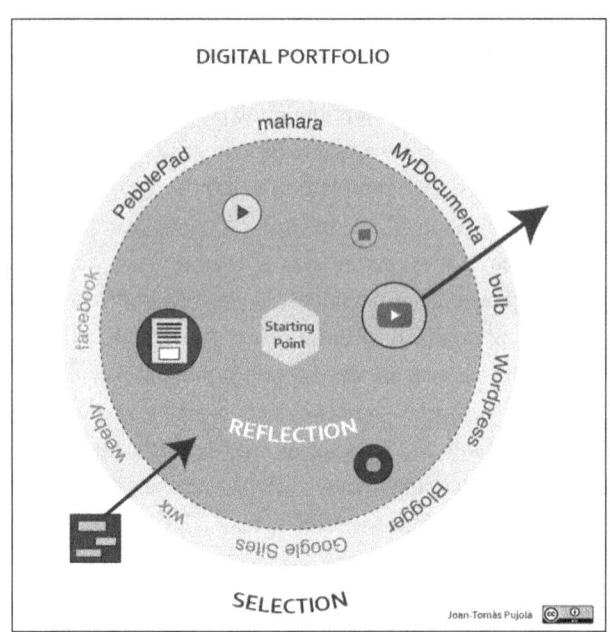

1.2. Key aspects of the e-portfolio

The four key aspects of the e-portfolio are attributed to its digital format. That is to say, the e-portfolio is **interactive, multimodal,** and **hypertextual,** and **offers the potential to create communities of practice or learning communities** (see Figure 2).

The interactive nature of the e-portfolio translates into the interplay built between pre-service teachers and the chosen interface. This choice can also contribute to the development of digital teaching competence and digital communication skills by channelling conversations across other learners' e-portfolios. The interactivity is also provided by internal and external hyperlinks which the users can interact with if they feel they need them. Moreover, hypertextuality allows the information compiled in the e-portfolio to be presented sequentially or with

194

a meaningful structure, so readers can create their own itinerary when examining its content. Hypertext also enables the author to guide the reader along suggested itineraries, within the e-portfolio itself and in other sources if external links are included (Gilster, 1997, in Pujolà & Montmany, 2010).

Figure 2. The key aspects of an e-portfolio: features of interactivity, multimodality, and hypertextuality

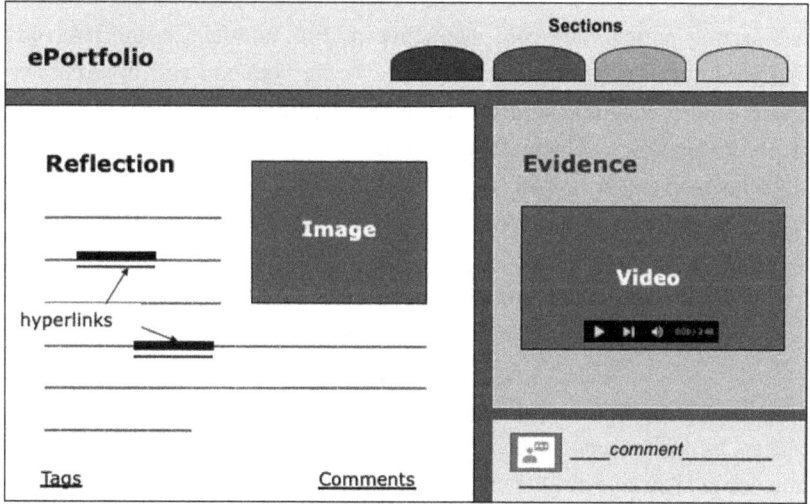

As a multimodal tool, the e-portfolio facilitates the construction of discourses beyond the exclusive use of linguistic messages (Kress, 2010). The confluence of different modes (spoken, written, static and moving images, etc.) can bridge the gulf between orality and writing by encouraging users to employ a range of digital modes that intertwine to create far richer texts.

Finally, the e-portfolio offers pre-service teachers the potential to create learning communities (Coll, Bustos, & Engel, 2008) using digital platforms, which are designed to facilitate comments (see Figure 2) or content sharing with other learners and the programme's teaching staff. It works like social media: Authors can make their content visible or provide access to it via a link. Most platforms allow each learner to browse other learners' portfolios, leave comments, and

Chapter 7

make suggestions. They also provide space for group reflection and the joint creation of content. By building their own learner communities, pre-service teachers can even establish a structure for peer evaluation.

2. Pedagogical implementation of e-portfolios within the proPIC study programme

This section presents the core interactive proPIC tutorial, i.e. the Interactive Tutorial 1, on e-portfolio development and the common and differentiating aspects of the pedagogic implementation of e-portfolios across the participating HEIs: Pädagogishe Hochschule Karlsruhe (GER KA/PHKA), Christian Albrechts Universität zu Kiel (GER KI/CAU), Hoegskolan i Borås (SWE, HB), Universitat de Barcelona (SPA/UB), and Newcastle University (UK/UNEW).

2.1. Developing a common framework for creating teacher e-portfolios

Interactive Tutorial 1 (see Figure 3) introduces the participating pre-service teachers to the concept and functions of a teaching e-portfolio. Furthermore, it provides guidance for the first steps of creating their own portfolios.

Figure 3. Interactive Tutorial 'e-portfolio'[7]

7. https://books.apple.com/us/book/propic-interactive-tutorial-1/id1525353237

The theoretical framework of the tutorial encompasses the conceptualisation of the e-portfolio and its links to reflective practice and Continuing Professional Development (CPD), stressing its process-oriented, dynamic, reflective, evidence-based, and digital nature. The tutorial also defines the principal types of e-portfolios – working, showcase, assessment – and their respective characteristics, and presents their general structure (a starting point, a collection of evidence, and a conclusion). In line with the objectives of the project, particular focus was placed on the digital dimension of the e-portfolio, looking at the specific text building strategies available (hypertextuality, multimodality, interactivity), as well as the discursive processes put into practice in the students' self-reflection (including description, explanation, argumentation, and retrospective and prospective evaluation).

Figure 4. Excerpts from the e-portfolio interactive tutorial

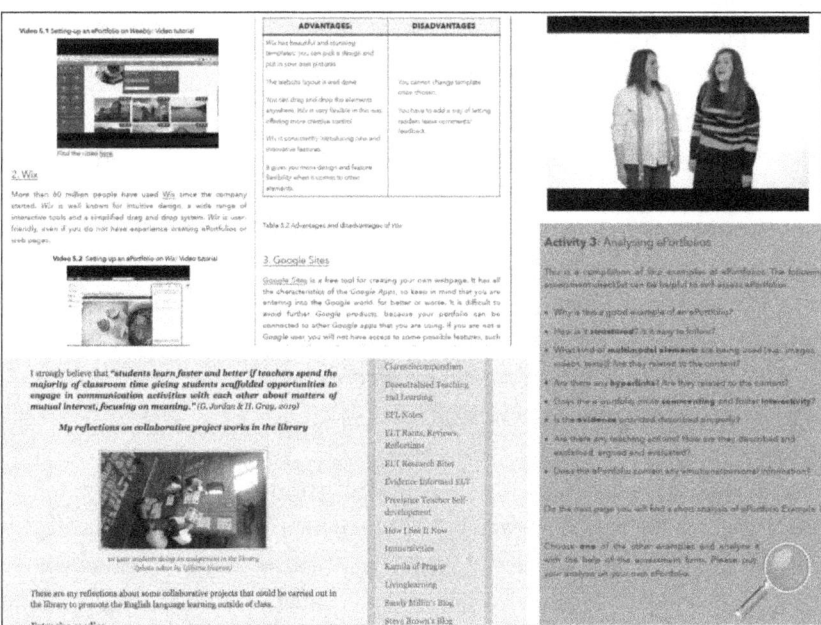

The tutorial provides a series of resources and activities designed to help the student teachers make informed decisions when creating and developing

Chapter 7

their e-portfolios. It offers detailed descriptions of suitable digital platforms, summarising their respective advantages and disadvantages. This information is complemented by a series of multimedia resources, including video tutorials on how to use each of the platforms presented. It further comprises video capsules with practical recommendations from teachers who use e-portfolios professionally, and self-assessment checklists. The tutorial also includes a series of guided activities to help students define the starting point for their e-portfolios. These activities encourage the students to reflect on their prior teaching-learning experiences and on observation and critical analysis using specific e-portfolio models and examples (see Figure 4 above).

2.2. E-portfolio implementation in proPIC: commonalities and differences

The different approaches (integrated or separated versions) used to implement the proPIC study programme at the participating HEIs influenced how the e-portfolio concept was interpreted at each institution and how the pedagogical implementation of this tool was designed. The different pedagogical activities employed to support pre-service teachers in the creation of their e-portfolios considered the different profiles, needs, and training goals of pre-service teachers in their respective learning contexts. As a result, e-portfolios were used in shared pedagogical activities among institutions, such as classroom observation, as well as across a variety of distinct activities, specific to each institution.

2.2.1. Commonalities of e-portfolio implementation within the proPIC study programme

The creation of an e-portfolio was one of the common requirements for all participants in the project. It was linked to the final student output: the design of a classroom research project or a teaching proposal based on the innovative use of digital tools. This is consistent with the understanding of the e-portfolio as a key tool within a broader training process rather than a standalone assessment tool for a single experience or event (see the *introduction* section of this chapter).

One of the fundamental approaches of the project was to consider both the e-portfolio and the final student output as means for achieving the core proPIC objectives: acquiring experience with digital tools through a variety of language teaching practices and reflecting on the didactic strategies that entail the use of these tools. On the one hand, creating the e-portfolio provides pre-service teachers the chance to reflect on their own research projects or teaching proposals. Consequently, it opens a discussion of the benefits and added value of the collaborative and innovative use of digital tools through their own teaching practice. On the other hand, building an e-portfolio is a means of experiencing the significance of communication 2.0 (González & Montmany, 2019), as well as a way of exploring the potential that digital tools offer in this digital communication process. A particular focus was therefore placed on the multimodality of e-portfolios and the student teachers' outputs.

An open and flexible approach was taken to setting guidelines and requirements for the use of e-portfolios across the proPIC project. This is consistent with the conceptualisation of the e-portfolio as a dynamic product (see Figure 1). Trainee teachers were commonly free to choose both the digital platform on which to create it and the pieces of evidence they wish to include or discard throughout the learning process. In line with the learning philosophy of proPIC, pre-service teachers had the final say on almost all key decisions in the creation of their e-portfolios: the digital platform used (web or blog), the content, the structure, and the number and type of examples of evidence. Pre-service teachers were also free to decide how to approach the reflective component of the project, choosing between self or joint reflection and working with written, spoken, or dialogic forms of reflection. Although pre-service teachers were not specifically given directions in the selection of evidence to include in their e-portfolios, they were expected to use multimodal content. Furthermore, all the participating HEIs stressed the importance of establishing a clear link between this collection of evidence, language learning, and each student teacher's professional experience. Thus, pre-service teachers were expected to demonstrate the significance of each example in their learning process and to focus particularly on the learning experiences from the study week part of the programme.

Chapter 7

The participating HEIs used varying teaching methods throughout the different stages of the project in order to help the students to prepare the e-portfolios: by local face-to-face sessions at the start and at the end of the project and by periods of independent online work through interactive tutorials and during the study week. The diverse teaching input developed in the HEIs presented some shared aspects. It consisted of activities and resources intended to foster reflection or reflective practice and the creation of the e-portfolio, which required pre-service teachers to establish a digital discourse, define a suitable structure, and select the appropriate learning evidence. The specific characteristics of activities and resources can be broadly classified as follows.

- Guided joint or self-reflection, achieved by prompting questions: This was carried out in face-to-face sessions and via Slack, with classmates from the same institution or students from the same cohort at other participating universities. The student teachers were invited to reflect on a wide range of topics, examining previous teaching and learning experiences, experiences related to technology and specific methodological approaches, reflective practice, beliefs and values concerning education, and so on. Reflection was centred on discussion of static images (see Pujolà & González, 2022, Chapter 9 this volume) or videos created by individual students or groups or on joint experiences carried out by students at different institutions over the course of study week, such as team microteaching (SWE/HB), the design of group mobile-based tasks (SPA/UB), or Video Enhanced Observation (VEO) of classroom practice (UK/UNEW).

- Use of web-based e-portfolios[8]: Students were able to work with examples of e-portfolios produced by participants in proPIC. These resources served as the basis for activities to examine the characteristics and structure of a teaching e-portfolio, 'communication 2.0' (González & Montmany, 2019), and the reflective strategies deployed in the creation of these tools.

---

8. http://www.propiceuropa.com/students.html

- Audio-visual input: Students had access to video tutorials on how to create an e-portfolio on different platforms. They could also access video case studies presenting the work and teaching e-portfolios of practising teachers who employ reflective teaching, dialogic reflection and observation-based reflection in the classroom.

- Conceptual input: To introduce the methodology of reflective practice, students were provided with a review of various tools (diaries, ad hoc observation, critical incidents, etc.) and different models and procedures for employing them in reflective practice (reflective teaching phases, written versus spoken and dialogic reflection, sentence starters to initiate reflection according to the specific approach adopted, etc.).

One of the project's outputs was the creation of a system of proPIC assessment criteria[9] (see Whelan & Seedhouse, 2022, Chapter 6 this volume), which was adopted at each institution for the combined assessment of e-portfolios and student outputs. This system was implemented in different ways at each institution in order to focalise supervision of the e-portfolios on the basis of their role in assessment design. It was used at all participating institutions as a resource for providing feedback. In some cases, it was additionally employed as a grading tool. In this vein, supervision, feedback, and coaching for the creation of e-portfolios in proPIC can be summarised as follows.

- Supervision in the different phases of the process: Monitoring progress with the creation of e-portfolios was carried out at different points in the study programme at each participating institution. All universities devoted specific attention to the e-portfolios and the final output during each study week.

- Online (synchronous and asynchronous) and face-to-face feedback: Different forms (written, spoken, audio-visual, see Figure 5) and different tools (e.g. self-assessment checklists) were considered for

---

9. http://www.propiceuropa.com/io5-assessment-criteria.html

Chapter 7

giving students feedback on the construction of their e-portfolios. The feedback itself focused mainly on the digital and reflective competencies developed in relation to the various outputs and on the illustrative collection of evidence selected by students, although the emphasis on each type of evidence varied across institutions.

- Collaborative feedback by different agents: In addition to self-assessment, students received feedback from local and international proPIC teaching staff, from teachers of different subjects, and, in the case of Universitat de Barcelona (SPA, UB), also from a specific e-portfolio tutor. Activities were also organised to promote collaborative feedback on the e-portfolios produced both between peers and through joint reflection between students and teachers (see Figure 6). These sessions were held during the study week and as face-to-face local activities.

Figure 5. Examples of written and audio-visual feedback (P4-SPA, P1-GER KA)

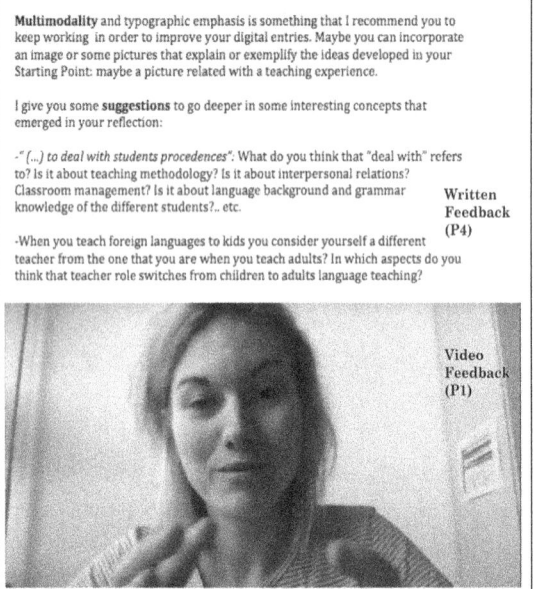

Figure 6. 'Show and tell your e-portfolio': collaborative feedback during study week in Spain (P4, SPA)

2.2.2. Differences of e-portfolio implementation in the different proPIC study programme versions

Figure 7 shows the differences in the implementation of e-portfolios between the versions of the proPIC study programme at the participating HEIs. The specific differences in the project learning objectives for each context had a bearing on the learning requirements considered in implementing the e-portfolio in class.

The adaptation of the e-portfolio to the particular needs of each learning context highlighted differences in the way the tool was considered for the purpose of assessment design and in its relationship to the other learning outcomes. As seen in Figure 7, the e-portfolio was integrated into the assessment process in different manners. At GER KI/CAU for example, the grade assigned to the e-portfolio accounted for 60% of the overall grade, with the research project or teaching proposal accounting for the remaining 40%. At SWE/HB, the e-portfolio carried a study load equivalent to 1.5 of the overall 7.5 credits awarded for the subject.

Figure 7. E-portfolio implementation in the different versions of the proPIC study programme

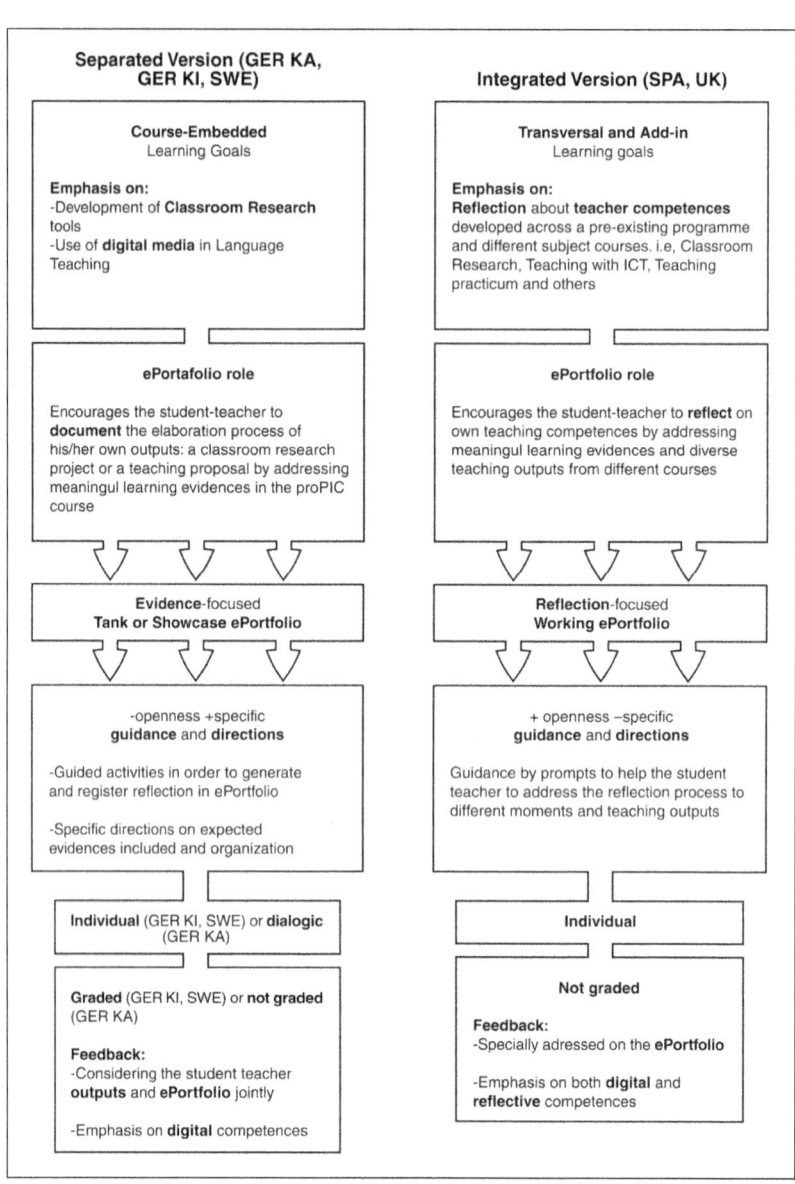

Another key difference can be found in the extent to which the pre-service teachers were guided through the creation of their e-portfolios. Guidelines were set at all institutions but varied in specificity and restrictiveness according to the academic profiles of the participants. One interesting difference was the possibility offered at GER KA/PHKA of creating the e-portfolio both as an individual task and as a dialogic group undertaking. In the latter format, design of the site and the selection of learning evidence and reflections were carried out in a group. However, each student could also incorporate an individual space into it.

3. Development of e-portfolios during the proPIC project: examples and evidence of the learning process

Over the duration of the project, 43 e-portfolios were produced by the participants in the first two cohorts[10] (16 in the first cohort, 27 in the second) using various platforms (see Table 1). All participants, except for students of a single cohort from GER KA/PHKA taking a specific training course at one institution, were free to make their own choice of platform for the creation of their e-portfolios. It should be noted, however, that the most commonly chosen platforms were those described and recommended in the e-book written specifically for the project (see Section 7.2), so students were guided by the teaching staff and the interactive tutorial to some degree.

The e-portfolio interactive tutorial also provided specific explanations of the objectives pursued by the construction of a reflective e-portfolio and the sections the final product should contain. As a result, all of the participants' e-portfolios have the same general structure: the description of a starting point, the presentation of a series of learning activity examples, reflections on the content of the examples, and an action plan that sets out the intended

---

10. Unfortunately, only a small number of examples are available for the third cohort, as completion of the course was interrupted by the outbreak of the COVID-19 pandemic. These examples will not be considered in describing the characteristics of the e-portfolios constructed during the project.

professional development path after completion of the proPIC project. Within this structure, a certain level of variation was present due to the different ways in which the e-portfolio had been integrated in the study programmes at each institution.

Table 1. Digital platforms used to construct e-portfolios and number of students per university

Platform	Universities					Total number of students
	GER KA P1	GER KI P2	SWE P3	SPA P4	UK P5	
Google Sites	8	6		1	4	19
Weebly	5	3			4	12
Blogger			5	5	1	11
Wix		3		6		9
Wordpress		2		1		3
Github				1		1
Blogg			1			1
Google docs	1					1

In setting out their starting points, all students essentially gave a general presentation of their individual profiles as pre-service foreign language teachers. For instance, SWE/HB offered a reflection on the teaching-learning process and on what it means to be a foreign language teacher. Other participants chose to describe the learning objectives of the different courses in the proPIC framework. GER KI/CAU, for example, gave a description of the proPIC project itself and the learning objectives for his particular course. Where the proPIC course was not specifically related to the content of a participant's degree programme, the learning objectives expressed were more closely aligned with the transnationality and internationalisation of the proPIC project and with the chance to learn about the educational realities of other countries. Considerable variation can be observed in the texts of the starting points, which range from brief personal descriptions and summaries of prior teacher training to longer, more substantial reflections on the personal significance of creating an e-portfolio and the participant's expectations of the course.

One of the elements that exhibits the greatest variation in the composition of the different e-portfolios is the choice of learning examples and pieces of evidence of professional development. Each student teacher chose the pieces of evidence that related directly to her/his training and was therefore guided to some degree by the nature of the course through which their home institution participated in the proPIC project. For example, some pieces of evidence reflected learning activities carried out during courses leading up to study week that were related to general proPIC concerns such as professional development through information and communication technology and the significance of reflective practice. However, most learning activity samples presented in the e-portfolios were taken from the study week itself (see also Schwab & Oesterle, 2022, Chapter 4 in this edited volume). This evidence, developed during the week-long stay at a partner university, can be classified into two blocks: on the one hand, learning examples related to professional development as language teachers, and on the other hand, learning examples that focused on social aspects or cultural experiences.

The activities classified in the first block varied according to the host university, reflecting general differences between their study programmes. For example, while students who travelled to Barcelona, like Ziyun (UK/UNEW), incorporated evidence of activities carried out over the week, such as an activity using the Genially app or the use of VEO for class observation, students who visited Kiel incorporated videos they had created over the course of the week or videos of group interviews with teaching staff from the host institution. In most cases, however, students chose to structure the learning evidence in their e-portfolios in the form of daily entries, recording examples of their learning activities and the associated reflection in tabs corresponding to the days of the week.

Interestingly, students also used their e-portfolios to record images and occasional reflections on the social and intercultural side of their experience. Some e-portfolios featured images of social activities carried out during the different programmes, such as group meals or sightseeing, and, more commonly, group photographs and images of the authors with their new classmates. Leona (GER KI/CAU), for example, who completed the study week in Borås, presents photographs of her class group at the university, the image of a cup of tea and

Chapter 7

cake – illustrating the famed Swedish *fika* – and a photograph of the majestic hall in Gothenburg Central Station. The reflective portfolio, then, could also be configured as a logbook or travel journal to illustrate the significance of study week in a more personal and experiential way.

Looking at the different activities carried out during the study week, many portfolios focused particularly on the final activity carried out during the short stay (the study programmes at each of the participation institutions were designed to culminate in the completion of a final activity). For example, in Kiel and Borås, students worked in groups to develop final products such as an educational video, while in Barcelona the final product was the e-portfolio itself, which was developed as a digital tool for professional development and reflective practices. These final activities were carried out over the course of the week and were recorded in the e-portfolios, which chart the development of each activity and students' reflections on their progress. Elisa (SPA/UB), for example, uploaded a video along with her e-portfolio to explain how she created and edited an instructional video on the design of audio-visual materials for foreign language teaching. In other examples, students were asked to carry out a research project within the proPIC course, which was also documented in the e-portfolios. Morten, Stephanie and Natalie (GER KA/PHKA) explain their research project, focusing on the theme of classroom management in an international context.

A certain degree of variation was also observed in the reflections related with the learning examples. In some cases, students were expected to base their reflections specifically on the evidence presented in their e-portfolios, whereas in others these reflections were more general, focusing on the sum of activities carried out over a whole day. In reflecting on their work, the students essentially sought to conceptualise the significance of the activities carried out during the study week for their professional development as foreign language teachers. Ken (UK/UNEW), for example, reflects on the fourth day of his short stay in Kiel, focusing on a seminar organised with local students. In his e-portfolio, he highlights having had the opportunity to discuss professional development with students of the host institution and explains that the resulting reflections on the meaning of feedback in teaching were highly significant to his professional development.

Most of the pre-service teachers completed their e-portfolios at the end of the teacher training. In these cases, the final reflection generally contains a closing message and a global evaluation of the study week, as demonstrated in the video created by Özge (GER KI/CAU). In other portfolios, a plan of action was established, setting out how each student teacher intends to continue their professional development after proPIC. Phillipp (GER KI/CAU), for example, in his closing remarks, raises the theme of lifelong learning and the need to keep working in order to consolidate the intercultural education derived from his stay in Barcelona. It should be noted, however, that the majority of the e-portfolios did not contain a message of this type as many students ended proPIC with a presentation of their research project, which marked the culmination of the study programme. One such example is Laura (GER KI/CAU), who discusses the final research project of her bachelor's degree studies, which focuses on approaches to pronunciation in foreign language classrooms across different countries.

As described in this section, the e-portfolios constructed in the framework of the proPIC project generally contained the characteristic elements of a reflective e-portfolio for professional development in teaching (Cuesta, Batlle, González, & Pujolà, 2020). While not all the e-portfolios contained every typical element, there was evidence of reflective practice and clear testimony of professional development by the authors across all cases and contributions. Each of the pre-service teachers was clearly committed to building a highly multimodal document and most of them used a wide range of multimodal elements to present their learning evidence and reflections. The e-portfolios frequently contain images – predominantly of activities or experiences – and videos – either of audio-visual products prepared for the project or of a relevant experience. Similarly, each e-portfolio has a particular design that reflects the platform on which it was constructed, showing that the trainee teachers had the chance to experiment with different digital platforms for the task, which was another of the project's initial learning objectives.

4. Conclusions

One of the main challenges in this project was to bring together the flexibility of a learning tool such as the e-portfolio and the international diversity of the project consortium, as well as the diverse learning requirements that exist at each partner institution. The experience has underlined the importance of conceptualising the e-portfolio as a tool for initiating meaningful processes of reflective practice(s) and feedback for pre-service teachers, drawing on actions with sufficient scope to involve language teachers with highly diverse profiles and backgrounds. From the teacher educator perspective, the experience has shown that discussing and finding common ground in regard to what each of the partners understands when talking of an e-portfolio is a challenge. It can thus be noted that the e-portfolio is not merely a standalone assessable outcome but rather a starting point for CPD, the development of a teaching identity and the building of a wider community of practice.

This transnational experience of e-portfolio creation opens several areas for future work, including the in-depth examination of assessment and feedback strategies and their role in the development of e-portfolios in educational contexts like the proPIC project. It will be particularly interesting to study how feedback can be harnessed to enrich the reflective processes of pre-service teachers, integrating different perspectives on teaching practice in a specific teaching community. Another area of interest that emerged is the potential of the dialogic e-portfolio and the benefits of collaborative reflection. In this regard, a focus of future research could be analysing the affordances as well as the constraints (e.g. time management, workload, or difficulties finding shared interests or needs) emerging while developing a dialogic student teacher or teacher educator e-portfolio.

References

Bozu, Z. (2012). *Com elaborar un portafolis per millorar la docència universitària. Una experiència de formació del professorat novel*. Octaedro. https://octaedro.com/wp-content/uploads/2019/07/quadern23.pdf

Cole, D. J., Ryan, C. W., Kick, F., & Mathies, B. K. (2000). *Portfolios across the curriculum and beyond*. Corwin Press.

Coll, C., Bustos, A., & Engel, A. (2008). Las comunidades virtuales de aprendizaje. In C. Coll & C. Monereo (Eds), *Psicología de la educación virtual* (pp. 299-320). Morata.

Cuesta, A., Batlle, J., González, V., & Pujolà, J. T. (2020). *ePortfolio* [iBook]. iTunes. https://books.apple.com/us/book/propic-interactive-tutorial-1/id1525353237

Gilster, P. (1997). *Digital literacy*. John Wiley & Sons Inc.

González, V., & Montmany, B. (2019). Iniciarse en el ámbito de los portafolios digitales. In J. T. Pujolà (Ed.), *El portafolio digital en la docencia universitaria* (pp.11-23). ICE-Octaedro. https://octaedro.com/libro/el-portafolio-digital-en-la-docencia-universitaria/

Hoinke, U., & Clausen, K. (2022). Getting curious and gaining knowledge through transnational collaboration in foreign language teacher education. In G. Schwab, M. Oesterle & A. Whelan (Eds), *Promoting professionalism, innovation and transnational collaboration: a new approach to foreign language teacher education* (pp. 83-106). Research-publishing.net. https://doi.org/10.14705/rpnet.2022.57.1384

Kress, G. R. (2010). *Multimodality: a social semiotic approach to contemporary communication*. Routledge.

Kunnari, I., & Laurikainen, M. (2017). *Collection of engaging practices one-Portfolio process*. Häme University. https://drive.google.com/file/d/0BxEnFq7yUumMUGV2V2VxVmNaNFU/view?resourcekey=0-6g5Qm50JBkNON7-MgdPTEQ

Pérez Gómez, A. I. (2016). (Ed.). *El portafolios educativo en educación superior*. Akal.

Pujolà, J. T. (2019). *El portafolio digital en la docencia universitaria*. ICE-Octaedro. https://octaedro.com/libro/el-portafolio-digital-en-la-docencia-universitaria/

Pujolà, J. T., & González, V. (2008). El uso del portafolio para la autoevaluación en la formación continua. *MONOGRÁFICOS MarcoELE, 7,* 92-110. https://marcoele.com/el-uso-del-portafolio-para-la-autoevaluacion-en-la-formacion-continua-del-profesor/

Pujolà, J. T., & González, V. (2021). El portafolio digital docente en la formación en línea de profesores de ELE: una experiencia de acompañamiento. In M. Alcocer & Z. Bozu (Eds), *El portafolio del profesorado en educación superior.* . Universidad de Rosario.

Pujolà, J. T., & González, V. (2022). Images to foster student teachers' reflective practice and professional development. In G. Schwab, M. Oesterle & A. Whelan (Eds), *Promoting professionalism, innovation and transnational collaboration: a new approach to foreign language teacher education* (pp. 223-232). Research-publishing.net. https://doi.org/10.14705/rpnet.2022.57.1390

Pujolà, J. T., & Montmany, B. (2010). Más allá de lo escrito: la hipertextualidad y la multimodalidad en los blogs como estrategias discursivas de la comunicación digital. In J. M. Pérez Tornero, J. Cabero Almenara & L. Vilches (Eds), *Congreso Euro-Iberoamericano "Alfabetización Mediática y Culturas Digitales"* (pp. 1642-1657). Universidad de Sevilla, Gabinete Comunicación y Educación (UAB). https://idus.us.es/handle/11441/57564;jsessionid=E1548CE0198A01455083F58DE6B93A03?

Sayòs, R., & Torras, F. (2019). Promover el aprendizaje reflexivo y la autonomía de aprendizaje a través del portafolio digital. In J. T. Pujolà (Ed.), *El portafolio digital en la docencia universitaria* (pp. 27-43). ICE-Octaedro. https://octaedro.com/libro/el-portafolio-digital-en-la-docencia-universitaria/

Schwab, G., & Oesterle, M. (2022). The proPIC study weeks: experiencing transnational exchange. In G. Schwab, M. Oesterle & A. Whelan (Eds), *Promoting professionalism, innovation and transnational collaboration: a new approach to foreign language teacher education* (pp. 107-130). Research-publishing.net. https://doi.org/10.14705/rpnet.2022.57.1385

Whelan, A., & Seedhouse, P. (2022). Developing an innovative and collaborative assessment framework for proPIC Europa. In G. Schwab, M. Oesterle & A. Whelan (Eds), *Promoting professionalism, innovation and transnational collaboration: a new approach to foreign language teacher education* (pp. 147-189). Research-publishing.net. https://doi.org/10.14705/rpnet.2022.57.1387

Part 3.

# Personal pronouns as linguistic features in the construction of pre-service language teacher identity

Azahara Cuesta[1] and Jaume Batlle[2]

1. Introduction

One of the affordances of the proPIC project is the opportunity to create a transnational community of teaching practice (Guo & Lei, 2019) and to foster collaborative professional development between pre-service language teachers at different European universities. The project also provided a suitable framework in which pre-service teachers could engage meaningfully in 'identity work' (Yazan & Lindahl, 2020). The study of teacher identity is a key area of research into teaching-learning processes in foreign language learning and is intrinsically necessarily linked to professional development. Analysing this facet of teaching practice helps to understand how pre-service teachers, from the earliest stage of their training onwards, learn to become teachers and develop as professionals.

Reflective practice can help student teachers to comprehend the educational setting into which they are transitioning and to understand their own identities as teachers. Traditionally, the activities used to facilitate reflective practice have been largely based on written reflections, for example, in the form of class diaries or teaching portfolios. However, several authors have stressed the value of interactive reflective practice deriving from collaborative and dialogic reflection (Farr, Farrell, & Riordan, 2019; Mann & Walsh, 2017). Particularly

---

1. Universitat de Barcelona, Barcelona, Spain; azaharacuestagarcia@ub.edu; https://orcid.org/0000-0002-3530-1255

2. Universitat de Barcelona, Barcelona, Spain; jaumebatlle@ub.edu; https://orcid.org/0000-0002-7429-9768

How to cite: Cuesta, A., & Batlle, J. (2022). Personal pronouns as linguistic features in the construction of pre-service language teacher identity. In G. Schwab, M. Oesterle & A. Whelan (Eds), *Promoting professionalism, innovation and transnational collaboration: a new approach to foreign language teacher education* (pp. 215-221). Research-publishing.net. https://doi.org/10.14705/rpnet.2022.57.1389

important in this type of 'identity work' is the stimulation of reflective practice through multimodality (Yazan & Lindahl, 2020), especially when this includes the use of images (Bessette & Paris, 2020). This approach to reflective practices enables trainee teachers to develop personal practical knowledge based on their own teaching and learning experience and, in particular, the awareness of their individual teaching identities that has been attained through this experience (Clandinin, 2013). Reflection stimulated by the description and interpretation of images generally takes the form of metaphorical and argument construction, establishing a connection between what is observed in the image and the pre-service teacher's personal experience (Birello & Pujolà, 2020).

In order to discern how reflective practice functions in an interactive context (Mann & Walsh, 2017), this chapter offers an initial approach to understanding how pre-service teachers construct and represent their teacher identities, using a series of interactions designed to stimulate joint reflection in the framework of the proPIC project. The analysis focuses on the use of personal pronouns as a means of understanding the arguments on which the participating students construct their individual teacher identities (Farr et al., 2019). We first identify the personal pronouns that the students use to transmit their teacher identities and then provide examples of how these identities are developed by using the pronouns in the course of the reflective interaction. Due to restrictions in space, findings will only be shown along one sample description.

2. Method

Data were collected during the study week of the second cohort of the project at the University of Barcelona, in May 2019. Participants were 12 foreign language student teachers (aged 20-44) from five other institutions in the proPIC consortium. The corpus contains a total of nine video-recorded interactions with a total length of one hour and 47 minutes and 14,594 words. All of the interactions were developed as semi-structured discussions carried out to encourage the student teachers to reflect on diverse self-selected images that represented different ways to understand what it is to be a foreign language teacher and its implications for foreign language teaching (see Pujolà & González, 2022, Chapter 9 this volume).

The analysis draws primarily on Corpus Linguistics-Conversation Analysis (CL-CA) as an approach to understanding teacher professional identity (Walsh, Morton, & O'Keeffe, 2011). This approach allows us firstly to consider the range of personal pronouns used by the student teachers in interaction and the associated components that constitute the emergence of their teacher identities. This first phase of the analysis was carried out from a CL perspective, using the AntConc programme. In the second phase, interactions were analysed following a CA approach to examine in depth the relationship between the emergence of teachers' identities and the interaction in which it unfolds: the reasons why the student teachers use the pronouns in a certain way and at a certain moment.

3. Results

Analysis of the data reveals a significant use of personal pronouns: as illustrated in Table 1, they account for five of the 30 most recurring words in the corpus. The most frequent is 'you' (n=370), followed by 'I' (n=262), 'we' (n=105), and 'they' (n=84). The figures provide the basis for preliminary observations about the use of the pronouns, although they will not be covered in detail in this chapter. More systematic corroboration of these findings will be given in further studies, using a CL approach combining occurrence analysis with the study of lexical combinations.

First, we see that 'you' recurs more frequently than 'I'. This suggests that the student teachers tend to engage more readily in group interaction than expressing their views in direct statements. Instead, they put forward arguments that establish a position. They speak less about their experiences and more about their reflections on a given learning context, seeking to involve the interlocutor using the first-person plural 'we'. Attempts to involve the interlocutor in group discussion are articulated more commonly with the pronoun 'you' than with 'we', suggesting that the pre-service teachers do not consider themselves a group *per se* but they wish to encourage their interlocutors to discuss a specific reality: the experience of being a teacher.

Table 1. Top 30 recurring words in the corpus

1	541	the	11	236	is	21	105	what
2	399	yea	12	212	so	22	95	but
3	370	you	13	200	em	23	94	ok
4	336	it	14	175	mm	24	91	language
5	309	that	15	147	of	25	90	can
6	268	a	16	146	this	26	87	or
7	262	I	17	143	in	27	87	think
8	257	and	18	116	are	28	86	one
9	257	to	19	111	have	29	84	they
10	240	like	20	105	we	30	83	do

Figure 1 invites us to imagine a fight between two sumo fighters of different ages, which the participants extrapolate to the relationship between a teacher and their students. As we can see in the extract from the interaction (Figure 2), the participants disagree as to whether a contest is established between teachers and students. This idea, formulated by S (details not shown), is questioned by M, who asks S to confirm whether she agrees or not with the underlying notion of competition (lines 01-02). This request prompts a clarification by S (line 05), in which she confirms that she does not agree with the idea that teachers and students are in competition. Despite the change-of-state token used by M (line 06), S goes on to provide an explanation in which she clarifies the reasons for her misalignment with the image. In formulating her arguments, S displays a particular teacher identity that can be classed as a 'language-related identity' (Pennington & Richards, 2016, in Farr et al., 2019), since it is rooted in her linguistic difficulties as a non-native speaker of the language that she teaches.

Figure 1. Image used as the basis for reflective interaction

Source: 呂布の痔: https://bokete.jp/odai/3234998

Figure 2. Extract from reflective interaction activity

```
Extract (1) ID1_SZMO_1'17''-4'08''
01.  M: >but but< (.) did you mean exactly when you said you would
02.     not agree with the with the message?
03.  S. (I see) (.) em:
04.  Z: [(   )
05.  S: [to the- to the fact that they are competitives.
06.  M: ah (.) ok=
07.  S: =so (.) it's- (.) because it's like: (.) em: for- for me it's
08.     not (1.0) language learning is not really like:
09.  Z: like a: [yea
10.  S:         [yea- (.) >you´re< challenging yourself (.) that's
11.     true but (0.3) language is challenging you
12.  M: ok=
13.  S: =you know what I mean?
14.  M: yea
15.  S: so (0.5) you are challenging yourself to: (.) em: (.) get on
16.     (.) >get on (hard)< (.) get- get updated and em: learn: the
17.     vocab but- (1.0) basically (.) the language (.) itself
18.     shouldn't be (0.8) em:: (0.5) em (.) shouldn't be a challenge
19.     itself (.) as language em: (0.5) is (so) too pragmatic to
20.     ↑be a challenge
21.  M: mhm
22.  S: or too- too pragmatic (.) to em:: to say (.) that I hav- I-
23.     (0.4) I can't take this challenge
24.  M: mhm
```

As observed in the extract, three personal pronouns are involved in the construction of teacher identity. First, in setting out her argument, S begins by stressing that what she is saying reflects her own view (for me, line 07). However, in presenting a situation to exemplify her point and explaining the reasoning behind it, S uses the second person personal pronoun (>you´re< challenging yourself, line 10). The argument, then, is developed using a pronoun with which all the participants in the conversation can identify: S is exemplifying a specific

219

reality but constructs it as a shared reality rather than a personal one (in the latter case they would instead use the first-person personal pronoun). This form of argumentation with the personal pronoun 'you' involves the interlocutors in the scenario, encouraging them to see themselves reflected in the specific reality it depicts. However, once S has set out the argument that exemplifies her epistemic status, she returns to the use of the first-person singular pronoun (**I** can't take this challenge, line 23).

In the extract, teacher identity emerges in interaction through the way in which the speaker explains her understanding of the reality presented in the image. S sets out a specific position using the first-person pronoun but goes on to give the reasons for her argument in the second person. This reasoning, in the form of exemplification, is a strategy for sharing personal practical knowledge with the interlocutor with the aim of establishing a shared epistemic position. With 'language is too pragmatic to be a challenge' S seems to share her own understanding of foreign language learning as a 'practical' endeavour, further than an 'abstract' or theoretical challenge unaffordable by the language learner. The teacher's language-related identity (Pennington & Richards, 2016 in Farr et al., 2019) is co-constructed through this process of argumentation and search for shared epistemic positions with the interlocutor.

4. Conclusions

The notion of transnational continuing professional development promoted by proPIC Europa has made it possible to examine how the participating pre-service teachers construct their language teacher identities through reflective practice and interaction. This preliminary approach to the data has allowed us to observe how the identity of a language teacher is established through the construction of epistemic arguments and standpoints in which pronouns play a decisive role: Speakers use them to denote a position and to situate others in the arguments they construct. Further extracts and research are required, however, to learn more about the use of personal pronouns in interactive reflective practice from both CL and CA approaches.

References

Bessette, H. J., & Paris, N. A. (2020). Using visual and textual metaphors to explore teachers' professional roles and identities. *International Journal of Research & Method in Education*, *43*(2), 173-188. https://doi.org/10.1080/1743727X.2019.1611759

Birello, M., & Pujolà, J. T. (2020). The affordances of images in digital reflective writing: an analysis of preservice teachers' blog posts. *Reflective Practice*, *21*(4), 534-551. https://doi.org/10.1080/14623943.2020.1781609

Clandinin, D. J. (2013). Personal practical knowledge: a study of teachers' classroom images. In Ch. J. Craig, P. C. Meijer & J. Broeckmans (Eds), *From teacher thinking to teachers and teaching: the evolution of a research community* (pp. 67-95). Emerald. https://doi.org/10.1108/S1479-3687(2013)0000019007

Farr, F., Farrell, A., & Riordan, E. (2019). *Social interaction in language teacher education*. Edinburgh University Press.

Guo, S., & Lei, L. (2019). Toward transnational communities of practice: an inquiry into the experiences of transnational academic mobility. *Adult Education Quarterly*, *70*(1), 1-18. https://doi.org/10.1177/0741713619867636

Mann, S., & Walsh, S. (2017). *Reflective practice in English language teaching: research-based principles and practices*. Routledge. https://doi.org/10.4324/9781315733395

Pennington, M. C., & Richards, J. C. (2016). Teacher identity in language teaching: integrating personal, contextual and professional factors. *RELC Journal*, *47*(1), 5-23. https://doi.org/10.1177/0033688216631219

Pujolà, J.-T., & González, V. (2022). Images to foster student teachers' reflective practice and professional development. In G. Schwab, M. Oesterle & A. Whelan (Eds), *Promoting professionalism, innovation and transnational collaboration: a new approach to foreign language teacher education* (pp. 223-232). Research-publishing.net. https://doi.org/10.14705/rpnet.2022.57.1390

Walsh, S., Morton, T., & O'Keeffe, A. (2011). Analyzing university spoken interaction: a CL/CA approach. *International Journal of Corpus Linguistics*, *16*(3), 325-345. https://doi.org/10.1075/ijcl.16.3.03wal

Yazan, B., & Lindahl, K. (2020). (Eds.). *Language teacher identity in TESOL. Teacher education and practice as identity work*. Routledge. https://doi.org/10.4324/9780429342875

9 Images to foster student teachers' reflective practice and professional development

Joan-Tomàs Pujolà[1] and Vicenta González[2]

1. Introduction

This chapter deals with a small-scale study that focuses on the analysis of the student teachers' evidence gathered from the first task of the Barcelona study week of the proPIC project. The task, called 'One picture and One thousand words', consists of selecting an image that represents the student teachers' conception of Additional Language (AL) teaching and an explanatory text that accompanies it to clarify interpretation. The main objective of this task is to prompt student teachers to use the image-text relationship to express their beliefs about the complex process of AL teaching, and to make the metacognitive effort to verbalise this relationship.

There is already a number of studies that analyse the use of images in narrative inquiry research in teacher education to reveal student teachers' roles as professionals in the field of AL, their teaching methods, and professional identities (Birello & Pujolà, 2020; Chik, 2018; Kalaja & Melo-Pfeifer, 2019; Melo-Pfeifer & Chik, 2020). Analysis of the images that student teachers select to show their perception of AL teaching can help them to understand how they develop their role as teachers in the first stages of their professional development (Bessette & Paris, 2019). In addition, having to describe these images can foster student teachers' reflective practice and metacognitive processes, which

---

1. Universitat de Barcelona, Barcelona, Spain; jtpujola@ub.edu; https://orcid.org/0000-0002-8664-432X

2. Universitat de Barcelona, Barcelona, Spain; vicentagonzalez@ub.edu; https://orcid.org/0000-0002-5262-9850

How to cite: Pujolà, J.-T., & González, V. (2022). Images to foster student teachers' reflective practice and professional development. In G. Schwab, M. Oesterle & A. Whelan (Eds), *Promoting professionalism, innovation and transnational collaboration: a new approach to foreign language teacher education* (pp. 223-232). Research-publishing.net. https://doi.org/10.14705/rpnet.2022.57.1390

stimulate teachers' awareness and allow their beliefs about teaching and learning to emerge (Costa Ribas & Manzan Perine, 2017).

The elicitation of metaphors of pre-service teachers to articulate their conceptions of teaching and learning is also a powerful reflective task in teacher education (Leavy, McSorley, & Boté, 2007; Saban, Kocbeker, & Saban, 2007). In addition, metaphors can be expressed in diverse representational systems or modes, such as the visual mode (Forceville, 2008), and thus, visual metaphors can also be exploited for reflective practice in teacher education. An image used as a visual metaphor can foster reflection but also expand different complex and opaque meanings which would certainly need clarification. When working with visual metaphors in teacher education, many authors combine visual and textual data which help to clarify the visual interpretation of metaphorical images (Bessette & Paris, 2019; Costa Ribas & Manzan Perine, 2017; Hamilton, 2016). Thus, using both images and written texts to describe participants' conceptions of AL teaching provided the contextual frame for the current study.

2. Methodology

The objective of this exploratory study is to analyse the images as visual metaphors for reflective purposes that participants used in the first task during the study week of the first and second cohorts of student teachers attending the University of Barcelona in 2018 and 2019. Out of a total of 20 participants, 17 images were selected because they included a reflective written text, which is needed to disambiguate misinterpretations in the analysis.

The qualitative analysis was carried out in two phases, as below.

- **First phase**. A descriptive analysis of the image was carried out according to the following criteria: type of image, focus of agent (teacher or learner), content, and metaphoric conception. The criteria of analysis were established following an inductive approach to try to achieve the research objective. This initial phase led us to establish categories that would facilitate the analysis of the images and group them accordingly. In this phase, both authors of the study labelled categories separately and then agreed on a consensus to achieve internal validity. Five categories were identified taking into account their metaphorical conception: openness, collaboration, process, construction, and challenge, and the images were classified accordingly.

- **Second phase**. A thematic analysis approach (see Braun & Clarke, 2006) was followed to identify relevant themes and keywords from the student teachers' written reflections. The information of the written text allows researchers to contrast it with the information portrayed by the image. In this way, researchers could validate or refute the interpretation of the visual metaphors.

3. Results and discussion

The data include 17 images, ten photos, and seven drawings which were all taken from the web. They portray both learners and teachers, with an emphasis on the learner since the teacher is portrayed only in four images. The use of the images as visual metaphors is the main strategy student teachers used to help them represent the abstract and complex conception of AL teaching. The images were classified considering the relation between the content of the image and the conception that they represent. Following an inductive approach of analysis, the images can be grouped into the following five categories: openness, collaboration, process, construction, and challenge.

3.1. Openness

Openness is shown by six images that contain maps and world globes (for example, Figure 1) to imply that teaching AL broadens the learners' vision, opens the learners' minds, and develops their intercultural competence.

Chapter 9

Figure 1. Image[3] similar to the one used by student teacher D

This conception of AL teaching coincides with what student D describes:

> "I think as foreign language teachers we should encourage our students to follow their goals, to broaden their horizon, to be open-minded to other cultures and people who speak a different language than we do".

3.2. Collaboration

Collaboration is the second relevant notion that includes three images which show the need to design collaborative tasks that enhance interaction as a key to improve students' communicative skills including negotiation and mediation.

---

3. Source: Photo by Alyssia Wilson, https://unsplash.com/photos/8O0_aFy72KY

The three images in this category represent children from different ethnicities in a circle holding hands (see example in Figure 2).

Figure 2. Image[4] similar to the one used by student teacher G

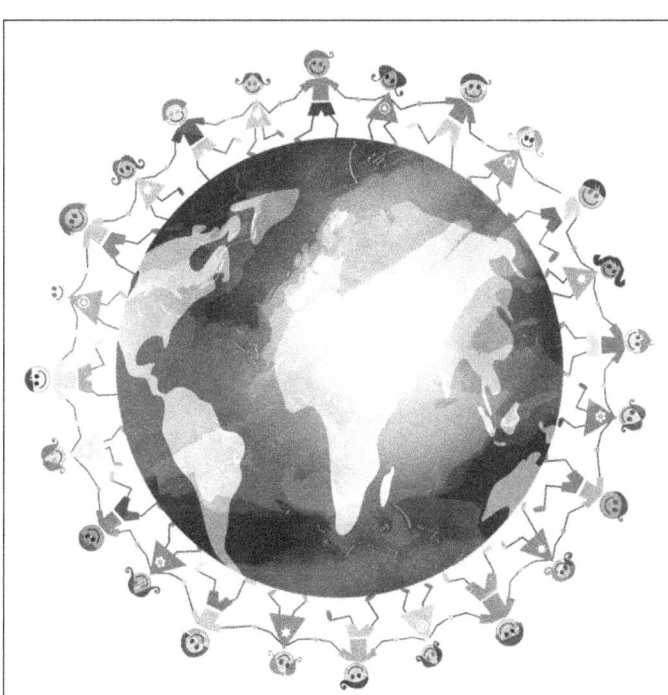

In her text, student teacher G describes the literal representation of the image and emphasises the idea of teaching AL as a key factor to achieve a better world:

> "I believe that teaching foreign languages and cultures can be a good starting point towards a more peaceful way of togetherness in the world. This is well visualised in the picture I chose because only by acting hand in hand can we change something about the way of living together in the world".

---

4. Source: Prawny from https://pixabay.com/es/illustrations/niños-juventud-niños-pequeños-5133287/

3.3. Process

The third category, **process**, also includes three images that portray paths or roads, either straight (see Figure 3) or circular.

Figure 3. Image[5] similar to the one used by student teacher K

These images show the perception of AL teaching as a **process**. This process is detailed in their written texts that describe two diverse aspects:

> "I think a way in beautiful setting represents the situation in the classroom, where the class stands in front of the street and has to **walk together the path in the right direction**" (emphasis added, Teacher K).

> "This picture should symbolise the will and encourage of teachers to **break out of their comfort zone** trying **something new** in their lessons and going a new path they didn't go before" (emphasis added, Teacher T).

---
5. Source: https://pixabay.com/es/photos/la-carretera-%c3%a1rbol-paisaje-viaje-2593616/

As we can see, the same type of image can reflect two different conceptions: In Text 1, the path leads to following a more prescriptive approach to teaching while in Text 2 it is a way to discover new avenues of teaching.

3.4. Construction

AL teaching seen as a **construction** is portrayed by four images that show the idea of rising, growth, or building, as shown in Figure 4.

Figure 4. Sketch of the image selected by student teacher M

In this category, student teachers focus their attention on the teaching process related to Bruner's scaffolding of learning (Wood, Bruner, & Ross, 1976), as student teacher M comments:

> "[s]econd language teaching is just like the teachers help students to build the bridge brick by brick. It also helps students to build connection between their mother tongue and the new language".

The idea of teaching as construction in her text is reinforced in two main ideas: on the one hand, the succession of phases through the relationship with the use of construction materials and on the other hand, in the literal and metaphorical meaning of scaffolding.

Chapter 9

3.5. Challenge

Despite having only one instance (see Figure 5, a sumo wrestler facing a little sumo boy ready to fight) the last category is worth mentioning as the image reflects the teachers' **challenge** to empower the language learner with the necessary knowledge and skills to face new challenges in their learning process.

Figure 5. Image selected by student teacher F

Source: 呂布の痔: https://bokete.jp/odai/3234998

Student teacher F comments:

> "For me, teaching is about equipping students for the world, not just the job or the university – and the challenge is to give them the courage to face every problem armed with their knowledge and curiosity, no matter how insurmountable it may seem. I root for the underdog, because I want every student to have the confidence to try, even fail, but then try again until they win. It's easy to teach someone who wins every time, but it's a vocation to turn those with the potential to win into those with the ability to win".

4. Conclusion

This exploratory study carried out of a task using images underlies the importance of visual metaphors as a teacher training tool for reflective practice. Images, if used as visual metaphors, serve to trigger student teachers' reflections to elicit their teacher identity construction at the pre-service stages of their professional development. The images selected by student teachers show that they are deeply ingrained in shared beliefs about AL teaching and learning. They illustrated AL teaching with key concepts such as openness, collaboration, process, construction, and challenge, which denote that the student teachers in this study have already comprehended and integrated them into their belief system. In addition, the coincidence in the type of images selected reveals that the visual metaphors they used reflect similar conceptions despite coming from different countries and training programmes. Although this study does not allow generalisations to be drawn due to the small number of participants, it does allow us to affirm that this type of reflective task using visual metaphors can be relevant and meaningful in teacher education to examine student teachers' beliefs about AL teaching and learning in the development of their teaching competence as reflective practitioners.

References

Bessette, H. J., & Paris, N. A. (2019). Using visual and textual metaphors to explore teachers' professional roles and identities. *International Journal of Research & Method in Education, 43*(2), 173-188. https://doi.org/10.1080/1743727X.2019.1611759

Birello, M., & Pujolà, J. T. (2020). The affordances of images in digital reflective writing: an analysis of preservice teachers' blog posts. *Reflective Practice, 21*(4), 534-551. https://doi.org/10.1080/14623943.2020.1781609

Braun, V., & Clarke, V. (2006). Using thematic analysis in psychology. *Qualitative Research in Psychology, 3*(2), 77-101. https://doi.org/10.1191/1478088706qp063oa

Chik, A. (2018). Beliefs and practices of foreign language learning: a visual analysis. *Applied Linguistics Review, 9*(2-3), 307-331. https://doi.org/10.1515/applirev-2016-1068

Costa Ribas, F., & Manzan Perine, C. (2017). What does it mean to be an English teacher in Brazil? Student teachers' beliefs through narratives in a distance education programme. *Applied Linguistics Reviews 2018, 9*(2-3), 273-305. https://doi.org/10.1515/applirev-2017-0002

Forceville, C. (2008). Metaphors in pictures and multimodal representations. In R. W. Gibbs, Jr. (Ed.), *The Cambridge handbook of metaphor and thought* (pp. 462-482). Cambridge University Press. https://doi.org/10.1017/CBO9780511816802.028

Hamilton, E. (2016). Picture this: multimodal representations of prospective teachers' metaphors about teachers and teaching. *Teaching and Teacher Education, 55,* 33-44. https://doi.org/10.1016/j.tate.2015.12.007

Kalaja, P., & Melo-Pfeifer, S. (2019). *Visualising multilingual lives: more than words.* Multilingual Matters. https://doi.org/10.21832/9781788922616

Leavy, A. M., McSorley, F. A., & Boté, L. A. (2007). An examination of what metaphor construction reveals about the evolution of preservice teachers' beliefs about teaching and learning. *Teaching and Teacher Education, 23*, 1217-1233. https://doi.org/10.1016/j.tate.2006.07.016

Melo-Pfeifer, S., & Chik, A. (2020). Multimodal linguistic biographies of prospective foreign language teachers in Germany: reconstructing beliefs about languages and multilingual language learning in initial teacher education. *International Journal of Multilingualism.* https://doi.org/10.1080/14790718.2020.1753748

Saban, A., Kocbeker, B. N., & Saban, A. (2007). Prospective teachers' conceptions of teaching and learning revealed through metaphor analysis. *Learning and Instruction, 17*(2), 123-139. https://doi.org/10.1016/j.learninstruc.2007.01.003

Wood, D. J., Bruner, J. S., & Ross, G. (1976). The role of tutoring in problem solving. *Journal of Child Psychiatry and Psychology, 17*(2), 89-100. https://doi.org/10.1111/j.1469-7610.1976.tb00381.x

10. Filmmaking by students or rethinking thinking

Kyra Clausen[1] and Ulrich Hoinkes[2]

1. Introduction

As proPIC partners in Kiel, the area of expertise we brought into the project was filmmaking in teacher training as an innovative learning approach. In 2013, the so-called Viducation project[3] was launched at the Institute of Romance Studies at the University of Kiel[4] (CAU) as a reaction to the new Bachelor of Arts and Masters of Arts degree programmes in order to improve students' learning skills and core competences by creating subject-related videos. Filmmaking by students is already widely used in primary and secondary schools (Reid, Burn, & Parker, 2002), while teacher education is still hardly prepared for it (as shown for German teacher education training, Müller, 2012). The aim of this article is to present a learning approach that enables students to expand their subject knowledge in a sustainable, value-based, and personality-building way on the basis of constructivist learning theories by means of filmmaking. The framework of proPIC offered an opportunity to use this learning approach with incoming students during the study week in a workshop and to encourage all participants to produce a film themselves as a creative output. In this context, data could be collected through designing the iBook and the workshop as well as surveys and student artefacts. In the following sections, we explain the theoretical background of the learning approach 'Filmmaking by Students' and sum up

---

1. Christian-Albrechts-Universität zu Kiel, Kiel, Germany; kyraclausen@gmx.de; https://orcid.org/0000-0002-3617-9503

2. Christian-Albrechts-Universität zu Kiel, Kiel, Germany; hoinkes@romanistik.uni-kiel.de; https://orcid.org/0000-0001-5781-7722

3. https://viducation.net/

4. https://www.romanistik.uni-kiel.de/de?set_language=de

How to cite: Clausen, K., & Hoinkes, U. (2022). Filmmaking by students or rethinking thinking. In G. Schwab, M. Oesterle & A. Whelan (Eds), *Promoting professionalism, innovation and transnational collaboration: a new approach to foreign language teacher education* (pp. 233-242). Research-publishing.net. https://doi.org/10.14705/rpnet.2022.57.1391

empirical evidence of filmmaking in learning. Subsequently, we present the methodical procedure and its results in relation to this approach in the proPIC project.

2. Theoretical background

Filmmaking by students, a learning approach based on constructivist learning theories, means a context-based creation of videos for learning purposes. Kritt (2018) points out that constructivist education was developed on the basis of Dewey's pragmatic philosophy, Piaget's theory of cognitive development, and Vygotsky's cultural history approach (Kritt, 2018). Considering that learners actively construct their knowledge through individual transformation and changes in understanding (Mathieson, 2015), filmmaking is the "most appropriate technology and medium for learning and embedding new subject knowledge and understanding, and for reflecting on and reinforcing and extending that knowledge" (Reid et al., 2002, p. 18). Through the process of filmmaking – pre-production, production, and post-production – students present academic content and transform acquired concepts and principles of a particular discipline in the form of a film using storytelling and the 'language' of film (Monaco, 2009). In addition to acquiring knowledge, students train various competences, more precisely media, professional, and social and self-competence. The learning process of filmmaking is in sum the approach to address 21st century skills (Ken, 2010), as students critically question specific problems of a particular discipline and produce a creative film to communicate their understanding of the world.

3. Empirical evidence of filmmaking in learning

There is empirical evidence that filmmaking enables students to improve their learning skills and core competencies and to acquire lasting knowledge. Research focuses heavily on the use of filmmaking by students in primary and secondary schools. In 2002, the evaluation report on the BECTA Digital Video

Pilot Project (Reid et al., 2002), which involved 50 schools from across the UK, provided detailed insight into the process of learning through filmmaking and its learning outcomes. Key findings relate to increased student motivation and the development of skills such as problem solving, negotiation, reasoning, argumentation, and risk taking. Greene and Crespi (2012) investigated the use of student-created videos in higher education and found that "students appreciated the opportunity to be autonomous and to exercise personal creativity and having educational activities that are experiential, active, and entertaining" (Greene & Crespi, 2012, p. 281). Ludewig (2001) concludes that by introducing filmmaking into language teaching in higher education in terms of an intercultural perspective, students "gradually build a knowledge and understanding of other's values, attitudes and beliefs, in a very concrete and dynamic way" (p. 4).

The Viducation project at CAU strives for comprehensive competence-oriented knowledge transfer by integrating digital forms of teaching and learning and, in particular, by aligning the cultural studies components of specialised education with the subjective experiences of the learners (Hoinkes, 2020). In the form of project-based learning, students of Romance languages produce problem-oriented short films on subject-relevant topics in small groups (Hoinkes, 2020). These empirical results demonstrate that filmmaking as a learning approach contributes to continuous professional development (see Oesterle & Schwab, 2022, Chapter 2 this volume).

4. Method

4.1. Procedure

Within the framework of proPIC, we offered participating students the opportunity to study film production for learning purposes. We implemented two approaches. All participants had the opportunity to voluntarily work on the iBook on video production (Clausen & Murillo-Wilstermann, 2019) and on this basis to create a film as a creative output of their research project. In addition, the incoming students took part in a workshop on video production during the study week at CAU and produced short films during this time. We are guided by the question of how students judge the learning approach of filmmaking for their own and future teaching practice.

4.2. Participants

In theory, every proPIC participant has been invited to make a video. In this article, we consider home students who made a film on the basis of the iBook and incoming students of the study week who attended the workshop on video production. In total, three home students out of 20 produced a film as creative output, two from the second cohort and one from the third cohort. Regarding incoming students, in the first cohort, four students attended the workshop and produced one joint film; in the second cohort, 11 students produced three films in small groups of three or four.

4.3. Data collection

This article is based on qualitative data. Participants' statements on filmmaking are taken from surveys conducted during the first study week by the project coordinators via SurveyMonkey, by us as project partners via Padlet, as well as from the e-portfolios of students who made a film.

5. Results and discussion

In the following, we present how the involved students of proPIC view the learning approach of filmmaking. For the sake of clarity, we will proceed chronologically and separated by groups (incoming and home students).

In the first cohort, which started in the summer semester 2018, we offered the four incoming students a two-day workshop on video production during the study week in Kiel. The students were first introduced to the production process and different aspects of the techniques and 'language' of film (e.g.

camera angles, camera shots, camera movements). We discussed the use of filmmaking in the language classroom, with students reflecting on their own experiences during their school life. After a first input, the students were asked to generate an idea and a storyboard for a film in which they reflect on their experiences and learning outcomes of their participation in proPIC. The students wanted to produce a film together and decided to make a documentary film[5] in which they gave an insight into their activities (e.g. school visit, social event) and analysed their learning outcomes through interviews. On the second workshop day, the last day of the study week, the students were asked to edit and present their film to the proPIC partners at CAU. The students did not complete the film in the given time. The finished film was therefore linked to the proPIC website at a later date.

Although the whole production was very time-consuming, the students said that they enjoyed working in the transnational group. In particular, the creation of a common storyboard had a positive effect on the cooperation in the group: "[t]o start with I had a good time creating the story board with everyone. It was fun coming up with ideas together, we worked perfectly well as a team and I had the feeling everyone was participating and bringing in their ideas" (participant from the first cohort via Padlet). This supports the assumption that filmmaking promotes social competences.

In general, some find the filmmaking learning approach useful for teachers and future teaching:

> "[t]eachers must know about technology and use it properly to find out what it can offer them in the classroom in order to improve the learning/teaching style. So that this workshop inspired me about the resources I could get from it in my future classes and have some ideas for my research project" (participant from the first cohort via Padlet).

However, another student stated:

---

5. https://youtu.be/A5LmB4LGI0Q

> "[f]or my own professional development I wouldn't use video production in the way we used it because it is very time-consuming" (participant of first cohort via SurveyMonkey).

In the second cohort, we focused on smaller productions in a fixed time frame as a reaction to the feedback from students in the first cohort regarding time exposure. After a more interactive workshop[6] using digital tools such as Socrative[7], which served to summarise the content of the interactive tutorial on video production (Clausen & Murillo-Wilstermann, 2019), incoming students were asked to produce a maximum three-minute film[8] on the use of video in language teaching.

The students were pressed for time but later reported that they had benefited from working in transnational groups:

> "[w]e had no [sic] much time, but we had a lot of fun. […] It's been really interesting to make this video, we were four girls from different countries. We all have the same opinion about that selfproduced [sic] videos is [sic] a didactic potential, but we needed our time to agree on how to put it on a image [sic]" (participant from the second cohort via e-portfolio).

The focus on the didactic use of filmmaking inspired the students, they said, to develop skills and think about their future teaching:

> "I would like to offer as many options [formats and occasions] as possible to my students so they will never feel that they are not good enough, because they always have a choice that suits them. […] I wanna use that information when I am planning my teaching for different students, some of them may need my face in the video

---

6. https://drive.google.com/file/d/1IZVXM8IvvD3J7jYBZSsLLIpSIf3HatxB/view?usp=sharing

7. https://www.socrative.com/

8. https://youtu.be/bNBrb6Q6ZaI

(talking head) to see how I move my mouth while I pronounce the words, while others need to understand words, and using animations, like Cutout animations, is more benefitting" (participant from the second cohort via e-portfolio).

The home students were asked to work through the interactive tutorial on filmmaking (Clausen & Murillo-Wilstermann, 2019) in order to be well prepared for the production of a video as the creative output of the research project. But only in the second cohort did two students take the opportunity to present their research projects in the form of a video. The first student produced a stop-motion video[9] with PLAYMOBIL figures to explain the results of her survey on information and communications technology tools in language learning. As the participant was modelling a Spanish classroom, the participant decided to speak Spanish but present the research project in English. During the final conference in June 2020, the student presented the video, for which the participant received very positive feedback from the audience. The participant mentioned how time-consuming video productions are:

"I realised after finishing it how much we should appreciate a good movie that we see because it was a lot of work" (participant from the second cohort via e-portfolio).

Another participant produced an animated explainer video[10] on digital methods in language teaching. The participant did not make any specific comments on the film production in the e-portfolio but commented generally on the research project which is why we do not analyse these comments in this paper.

Also, in the third cohort, one student decided to present the research project in the form of a video[11]. The participant used the format of a talk show so that the actors could portray both the researcher and the test subjects. Given the

---

9. https://youtu.be/F43MUj9GEtw

10. https://youtu.be/I-kDfeNTC2Y9

11. https://propicalessa.wixsite.com/website/research-project?wix-vod-video-id=c551f0059bd64ba799b12bdd45239bba&wix-vod-comp-id=comp-k9gkmti6

limitations imposed by the spread of the coronavirus, the participant stuck to the idea but replaced the real actors with fruits and vegetables, which had been humanised by painting faces on them. The student eventually commented that she had enjoyed producing the film precisely because it was a creative way to present the research results:

> "[c]oncerning my creative product, I can conclude that it was lot of fun for me to illustrate the results of my project in a creative way and I think, one can see that in the product. To improve my video, I should have paid more attention to the language" (participant from the third cohort via e-portfolio).

6. Conclusion

The self-production of films enables students to visualise their personal approach to learning content, to arrange acquired knowledge in a video through storytelling, and to collaborate with different people in the learning process. Specifically, the positive experiences during the study weeks prove the effect of collaborative filmmaking in terms of social and intercultural competence. The participating students had to discuss their ideas in transnational groups and put themselves in the shoes of others, especially while preparing a storyboard. In addition, the students were able to further their professional development as they developed media competence in relation to the didactic use of videos in language teaching and reflected on their future role as teachers. By using a foreign language in the videos, the foreign language education students promoted their own language skills and their self-competence. Presenting a research-relevant problem or one's own research project by creating a video is an innovative approach that helps to further develop essential core areas of university teaching such as digitalisation, project work, and collaborative learning. The participants predominantly evaluate the learning approach of filmmaking as positive for teaching. But the time required has been criticised several times. The Viducation project in Kiel, which has been successful for many years (as evidenced by the continuous project duration since 2013), and the positive experiences of proPIC based on the students' feedback, provide great encouragement for the use of filmmaking by students in foreign language teacher education at universities worldwide.

References

Clausen, K., & Murillo-Wilstermann, I. (2019). *proPIC interactive tutorial 5. Video production* [iBook]. iTunes. http://www.propiceuropa.com/io4-interactive-tutorials.html

Greene, H., & Crespi, C. (2012). The value of student created videos in the college classroom. *International Journal of Arts and Science, 5*(1), 273-283.

Hoinkes, U. (2020). Kompetenzförderung und Wissensvermittlung in studentischen Filmproduktionen als Bestandteil der universitären Lehre in den neueren Philologien. In T. Heinz, B. Brouër, M. Janzen & J. Kilian (Eds), *Formen der (Re-)Präsentation fachlichen Wissens. Ansätze und Methoden für die Lehrerinnen- und Lehrerbildung in den Fachdidaktiken und den Bildungswissenschaften* (pp. 241-258). Waxmann. https://doi.org/10.31244/9783830990208

Ken, K. (2010). 21st century skills: why they matter, what they are and how we get there. In J. Bellanca & R. Brandt (Eds), *21st century skills. Rethinking how students learn*. Solution Tree Press.

Kritt, D. (2018). Teaching as if children matter. In D. Kritt (Ed.), *Constructivist education in an age of accountability*. Palgrave Macmillan US. https://doi.org/10.1007/978-3-319-66050-9_1

Ludewig, A. (2001). iMovie. A student project with many side-effects. In N. Smythe (Ed.), *Proceedings of the Apple University Consortium Conference, September 23-26, 2001 at James Cook University, Townsville, Queensland, Australia* (pp. 12.1-12.11.). https://www.researchgate.net/profile/Mark_Mcmahon3/publication/49283272_Choreograph3d_collaborative_inNovation_through_dance_and_multimedia/links/562c707808ae04c2aeb35c5a.pdf#page=115

Mathieson, S. (2015). Student learning. In H. Fry, S. Ketteridge & S. Marshall (Eds), *A handbook for teaching and learning in higher education*. Routledge.

Monaco, J. (2009). *How to read a film. movies, media, and beyond*. Oxford University Press.

Müller, I. (2012). *Filmbildung in der Schule. Ein filmdidaktisches Konzept für den Unterricht und die Lehrerbildung*. Kopaed.

Oesterle, M., & Schwab, G. (2022). Developing a framework of CPD for the context of foreign language teaching. In G. Schwab, M. Oesterle & A. Whelan (Eds), *Promoting professionalism, innovation and transnational collaboration: a new approach to foreign language teacher education* (pp. 45-79). Research-publishing.net. https://doi.org/10.14705/rpnet.2022.57.1383

Reid, M., Burn, A., & Parker, D. (2002). *Evaluation report of the Becta Digital Video Pilot project.* https://www.researchgate.net/publication/237598160

11. Impact beyond the project: exploring engagement in proPIC Europa and potential lasting impact on teaching studies and professional development

Alison Whelan[1] and Richard Baldwin[2]

1. Introduction

As seen in previous chapters, student involvement in the proPIC Europa project differed at each partner university. For some, engagement rewarded students with formal credits towards a Master's programme. For others, the project offered an opportunity to experience another education system and broaden their knowledge of mobile technologies in the language learning classroom. In this chapter, we will examine a sample of students from Newcastle University (UNEW), UK, and the University of Borås (HB), Sweden, to see if they observed an impact on their studies, their teaching careers, and/or their mindset towards language learning and teaching, after the completion of the project.

2. Background

2.1. UNEW

At UNEW, student involvement in the proPIC project was voluntary and not a mandatory component of any degree programme, which meant that students did

---

1. Newcastle University, Newcastle-upon-Tyne, United Kingdom; alison.whelan2@newcastle.ac.uk; https://orcid.org/0000-0001-6272-6497

2. Högskolan i Borås, Borås, Sweden; richard.baldwin@hb.se; https://orcid.org/0000-0001-8663-6293

How to cite: Whelan, A., & Baldwin, R. (2022). Impact beyond the project: exploring engagement in proPIC Europa and potential lasting impact on teaching studies and professional development. In G. Schwab, M. Oesterle & A. Whelan (Eds), *Promoting professionalism, innovation and transnational collaboration: a new approach to foreign language teacher education* (pp. 243-252). Research-publishing.net. https://doi.org/10.14705/rpnet.2022.57.1392

not accrue credits towards their studies. Most, therefore, participated in order to gain an insight into European education systems and for the opportunity to spend a week at a host university. Participants were required to spend their own time on the tasks and activities involved and request time away from their study programmes to attend the face-to-face sessions and the study week (see Schwab & Oesterle, 2022, Chapter 4 this volume).

Although students reported that they enjoyed their experience on the project, it appeared to be difficult for them to take time from their study programmes to attend the face-to-face sessions, and they struggled to understand the rationale behind the use of e-portfolios, as it is not common practice either in their study programmes or in their home countries.

2.2. HB

At HB, student involvement in the proPIC project was voluntary and not a mandatory component of any degree programme, as in Newcastle. The project was instead organised as an extra optional course worth 7.5 credits or as 7.5 credits equivalent to some existing credits in the existing English courses or Swedish as a second language courses for trainee teachers. Experience shows that all students participating chose to take the course as an optional course.

In terms of student participation in the proPIC project, the fact that the programme was run parallel to the students' existing studies was problematic, both in terms of attracting students to join the project as well as retaining them. This is reflected in the number of students completing the project. In Cohort 1, only five students took part in the course and of them only one completed all parts. In Cohort 2, seven students took part with all seven completing all parts of the course. For the third cohort, 11 students joined the project, but due to problems caused by the COVID-19 pandemic, the majority decided to leave the project prior to the decision being made to cancel the planned study week. Several group meetings had taken place and participants had begun the process of formulating their project ideas.

3. Data collection and analysis

One data set was collected from UNEW Cohort 2 students during a face-to-face group debriefing around one month after their participation in the project. Another data set was then collected from HB, in the form of a delayed online questionnaire sent via email to the Swedish second cohort around 14 months after they had attended the transnational study week.

3.1. Diamond 9 Ranking, Cohort 2, UNEW

Feedback was collected from UNEW Cohort 2 after the study week using a Diamond 9 approach, a recognised thinking skills tool usually carried out with nine written statements (Rockett & Percival, 2002). Eight students were given nine statements and asked to rank them in order of agreement, with the one they most agreed with at the top of the diamond, working down to the one they least agreed with. The statements in each diamond were then given a value of one (highest significance) to five (lowest significance) depending on the line of the diamond where the student allocated it.

Figure 1. Diamond 9 ranking feedback after final face-to-face session from UNEW Cohort 2 (n=8)

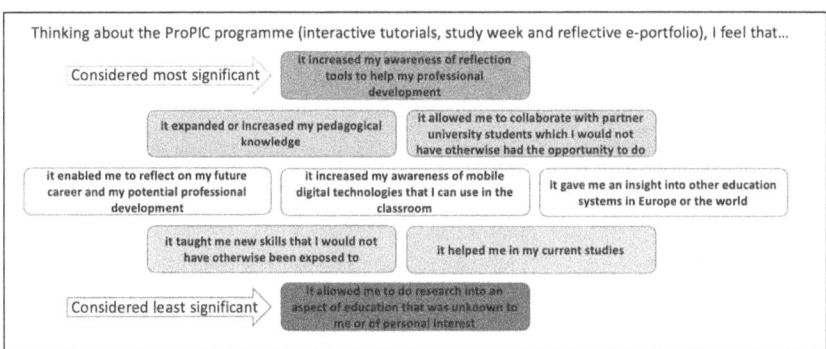

The results of the exercise were collated and presented based on the overall rank allocated to each statement. Clark (2012) explains that Diamond 9 ranking

Chapter 11

requires participants to "make explicit the over-arching relationships by which they organise knowledge, thus making their understandings available for scrutiny and comparison" (p. 223). The results of this ranking exercise are shown in the Diamond 9 above (Figure 1).

3.2. Online survey – Likert scale statements, Cohort 2, HB

An online survey was emailed to the second cohort students from HB, consisting of two sections. Firstly, students used a five-point Likert scale to respond to the nine statements used with the UNEW Cohort 2 students. This was intended to align to the Diamond 9 method, though the process of arranging the statements was missing. Unfortunately, only three responses were received due to some students having completed their course and moved on. The Likert scale responses were analysed in the same manner as in a Diamond 9 approach, arranging the statements which had been accorded the highest significance in the top rung, and those with the least significance at the bottom. As there were fewer responses (n=3), some statements had equal values and were placed on the same rung. Results are shown below (Figure 2). The two sets of responses were then assigned values and arranged into a final combined Diamond 9. Again, there were several statements which had equal value, and these were assigned to the same rung (Figure 3).

Figure 2. Diamond 9 ranking feedback from online Likert survey from HB Cohort 2 (n=3)

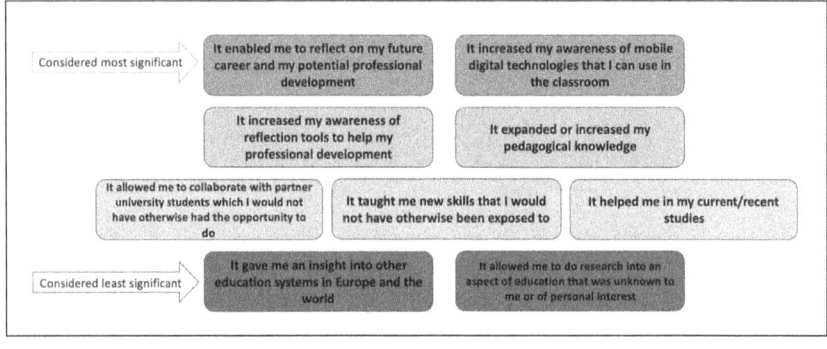

Figure 3. Diamond 9 ranking combined responses from UNEW and HB Cohort 2 (n=11)

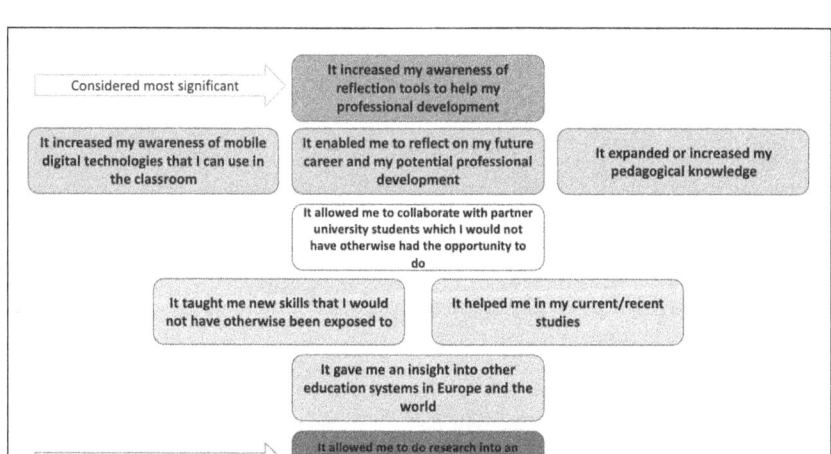

The most positive benefits recorded were increased awareness of reflection tools to help professional development; increased awareness of mobile digital technologies; an ability to reflect on future career and potential professional development; and increased pedagogical knowledge. These findings mirror those from the student evaluations (see Hoinke & Clausen, 2022, Chapter 3 this volume).

3.3. Online survey – qualitative responses, Cohort 2, HB

Qualitative data was also collected through questions about the students' experiences of their participation in the project and their perceptions of the lasting impact, which complemented the data collection and analysis discussed in Schwab and Oesterle (2022, Chapter 4 this volume). These responses were analysed using a thematic analysis approach (Braun & Clarke, 2006), extracting the key statements and arranging them into the themes that arose from the Diamond 9 responses: (1) increased awareness of digital mobile technologies;

(2) reflection on future career and professional development; and (3) expanded or increased pedagogical knowledge. The fourth potential theme, increased awareness of reflection tools to help professional practice, was not apparent in the responses.

3.3.1. Increased awareness of digital mobile technologies

"I am far more confident in using mobile technology in my classroom" (HB Respondent No. 2).

"I am a bit more aware of what different digital tools are available" (HB Respondent No. 3).

"Becoming more acquainted with various digital tools has both increased [my] confidence and knowledge on additional teaching methods" (HB Respondent No. 1).

3.3.2. Reflection on future career and professional development

"The project opened doors to so many opportunities such as travelling to another country, collaboration with students and professors from around the world and exposure to different education forms" (HB Respondent No. 1).

"It made me more confident in my approach" (HB Respondent No. 2).

"I believe the collaboration opportunities that were made during the project will be of great use in my teaching career" (HB Respondent No. 1).

"The best and lasting impact that I will take with me from the proPIC project is all of the new friends and connections I have made during the process" (HB Respondent No. 1).

3.3.3. Expanded or increased pedagogical knowledge

"My hopes in participating in proPIC were to establish connections with other students and professors from around the world, as well as increase my awareness and confidence in teaching through digital platforms. I can successfully say that I achieved both of these goals" (HB Respondent No. 1).

"I benefited a lot from the course since it broadened [my] perspectives to see and learn how other teachers/schools/systems work" (HB Respondent No. 2).

"The proPIC project has opened my eyes to collaboration opportunities within the teaching profession, both in Sweden and other countries. Working together and exchanging have been successful tools during my studies" (HB Respondent No. 1).

4. Discussion

The Diamond 9 ranking from the two data sets shows four key impacts on the students' teacher training and professional development.

4.1. Increased awareness of reflection tools to help professional practice

This was not expanded further in the qualitative comments but scored very highly from both cohorts. The proPIC project had a strong focus on developing reflection skills, with students using e-portfolios as a means to externalise their thoughts and share them with others and discussing their learning with fellow trainee teachers both using online platforms and in person during the study week. This awareness of reflection tools includes reflecting on teaching practice, future professional development, digital tools available, and how they can be incorporated in the classroom.

4.2. Increased awareness of digital mobile technologies

Most of the students surveyed scored this highly, and the qualitative comments reflected the perceived importance. Students mentioned increased confidence, awareness, and knowledge of the digital mobile technologies available, and were able to use new technologies during the study week. Combining this with their increased awareness of reflection tools means that they were able to externalise their views and experiences of these digital tools with their fellow trainees and think about how they could implement them in their differing educational environments, particularly if they observed their use in transnational contexts.

4.3. Reflection on their future career and potential professional development

The students talked about the opportunities they had encountered through involvement in the project for transnational collaboration, connection with other trainees, and exposure to other education systems and contexts. All of these experiences enable the students to consider their future career and how they can use their knowledge and skills in their own classroom contexts. This early exposure to a wider variety of experiences than they may have perhaps otherwise had will undoubtedly have an impact on their future professional development, as they mentioned how the project had broadened their perspectives and increased their awareness of the need to improve their skills in terms of the constantly evolving world of teaching and learning.

4.4. Expanded or increased pedagogical knowledge

One key aspect of the proPIC project was that many of the students took part as a voluntary or additional element to their university course. This meant that they appeared to demonstrate increased motivation from the outset, and a willingness to learn from each other, the educators involved, and from the overall experience. They were therefore open to learning new pedagogical knowledge and developing their skills and were exposed to a wider range of pedagogies than those available purely on their own course. As a result of engaging in the proPIC programme, the interaction students were able to have with educators and peers from other transnational institutions expanded their knowledge and allowed them to demonstrate new skills, learning from the theory they engaged with, but also from the implementation and reflection processes.

5. Conclusion

Overall, the students' responses clearly show the impact that the project had on their studies and their professional development. The students developed skills and acquired knowledge from engaging with the theory, observing and interacting with educational contexts during the study weeks, and using e-portfolios to document and externalise their reflection. This latter point, having the opportunity to develop their reflection skills and increase their awareness of reflection tools available to them, was the most significant impact and is a key aspect of being a teacher. One respondent stated that:

> "[participating in proPIC] is an experience and knowledge that I will have with me and mostly that we, as teachers, always have to 'step up our game'. We cannot teach in the same way we did 20 years ago. We have to be able to reach our students, meet them on their level. This is not levels of highs and lows rather than levels of evolution and development, personally and generally" (HB Respondent No. 2).

Reflecting on their practice, both through reflection-in-action and reflection-on-action (Schön, 1983), is crucial for teachers, and developing a reflective mindset with positive beliefs, motivation, and self-regulatory abilities (Blömeke & Delaney, 2012) can help a teacher to grow and adapt to educational changes, challenges, and conflicts.

Chapter 11

References

Blömeke, S., & Delaney, S. (2012). Assessment of teacher knowledge across countries: a review of the state of research. *ZDM, 44*, 223-247. https://doi.org/10.1007/s11858-012-0429-7

Braun, V., & Clarke, V. (2006). Using thematic analysis in psychology. *Qualitative Research in Psychology, 3*(2), 77-101. https://doi.org/10.1191/1478088706qp063oa

Clark, J. (2012). Using diamond ranking as visual cues to engage young people in the research process. *Qualitative Research Journal, 12*(2), 222-237. https://doi.org/10.1108/14439881211248365

Hoinke, U., & Clausen, K. (2022). Getting curious and gaining knowledge through transnational collaboration in foreign language teacher education. In G. Schwab, M. Oesterle & A. Whelan (Eds), *Promoting professionalism, innovation and transnational collaboration: a new approach to foreign language teacher education* (pp. 83-106). Research-publishing.net. https://doi.org/10.14705/rpnet.2022.57.1384

Rockett, M., & Percival, S. (2002). *Thinking for learning*. Network Educational Press.

Schön, D. (1983). *The reflective practitioner*. Basic Books.

Schwab, G., & Oesterle, M. (2022). The proPIC study weeks: experiencing transnational exchange. In G. Schwab, M. Oesterle & A. Whelan (Eds), *Promoting professionalism, innovation and transnational collaboration: a new approach to foreign language teacher education* (pp. 107-130). Research-publishing.net. https://doi.org/10.14705/rpnet.2022.57.1385

12. How can teacher educators benefit from participating in a transient transnational community?

Mareike Oesterle[1]

1. Introduction

In the professional landscape of today's teacher education, the on-going expansion of activities into a global and digital context has provoked a significant change of the traditionally stable and well-established communities in higher education (Czerniawski, 2018; Sachs, 2001). Teacher education today needs to prepare students for changing tasks and roles in increasingly digital and dynamic societies. Teacher educators need to be able to teach future teachers how to prepare their students to actively participate in such societies. The engagement in transnational networks and third-party funded projects, such as the proPIC project, is becoming steadily more important. In recent years, teacher educators have relied more and more on international partnerships. However, as Swennen and White (2021) describe, there is still a gap of systematic research focusing on communities within and outside their own institutions, as well as detailed knowledge of how they work and collaborate. Looking at the complex challenges that teacher educators face, this gap is considerable. Based on an in-depth literature review, four main challenges can be identified.

First, society is changing vastly, primarily due to an overall and intense social, technical, and cultural change. Second, teacher educators face increasing critical working conditions in many contexts across Europe and beyond, with a rising number of administrative obligations and with temporary employments, which is as Van den Besselaar and Sandström (2017) point out, predominantly restraining

---

1. University of Education Ludwigsburg, Ludwigsburg, Germany; mareike.oesterle@gmx.de; https://orcid.org/0000-0002-9458-7927

How to cite: Oesterle, M. (2022). How can teacher educators benefit from participating in a transient transnational community? In G. Schwab, M. Oesterle & A. Whelan (Eds), *Promoting professionalism, innovation and transnational collaboration: a new approach to foreign language teacher education* (pp. 253-260). Research-publishing.net. https://doi.org/10.14705/rpnet.2022.57.1393

for women. Third is the traditional image of professionals who train teachers has shifted towards a more diverse and dynamic identity. As Lunenberg, Murray, Smith, and Vanderlinde (2017) describe, being a teacher educator does not merely mean teaching teachers but implies a highly multifaceted professional identity with many areas of responsibility. Fourth, and highlighted by many in recent years (see InFo-TED, 2019), is the general lack of systematic opportunities for teacher educators.

As part of a cumulative doctoral thesis, the consortium of the proPIC project was chosen as a single case study, investigating the development, potentials, as well as challenges of interacting in a transient transnational community of teacher educators. On the basis of Mortensen's (2017) theory on transient multilingual communities, I define transient transnational communities as "social configurations where professionals from diverse sociocultural [and national] backgrounds come together (physically/[virtually]) to engage in a temporary bounded activity which results in prior agreed-upon outcomes" (Oesterle, Schwab, Hoffmann, & Baldwin, 2021, n.p.).

As this essay presents findings from some aspects of my thesis, the guiding research question was the following: *what are the perceived benefits of participating in a transient professional community?*

Having been part of the project consortium myself, I decided to use an auto-ethnographic approach to collect my data, which gave me the opportunity to understand the project community from within. The qualitative data corpus of this first part comprises 11 semi-structured interviews; multimodal partner evaluations, for example, online surveys, and Flipgrids (a kind of video pinboard), as well as relevant project documents. Data was prepared by transcribing the interviews. Afterwards, MAXQDA was used to code and analyse it. Focusing on idiographic, as well as interactional phenomena in my data analysis, I intend to contribute to two themes in particular that, according to White and Swennen (2021, p. 2), have emerged over the past ten years: knowledge of the work of teacher educators; and the professional development of teacher educators. The complexity that teacher educators face in their professional environments needs to be closely observed and analysed in order to develop new formats of research-informed practices that support them in their work and development. In line with Powell (2021, p. 63), I consider teacher educator collaboration as significant to offer potential learning opportunities. Further, it is crucial to integrate professional learning more thoroughly in the professional environment and workplace interactions of teacher educators. In this essay, interim findings will be presented.

2. Interim findings

The data analysis shows that one benefit of participating in a transient professional community is the feeling of belonging that partners described and that they reported had a positive impact on their own well-being in contrast to their regular work situations in which they often feel isolated. Six participants also referred to the low hierarchies that they witnessed in contrast to rather steep hierarchies at their home institutions. One partner stated:

> "I think a lot of people get into these projects, because they want to get away from the normal hierarchies, and pressures of work situations, so it is a kind of tolerance and feeling of belonging which I think a lot of academics miss. Actually that's probably why we get involved in such projects, because we're kind of equals, no matter what position we have, we're in the academy, in the project, we're all equals, which I think is positive for everybody involved" (partner interview, 2019, Partner #8).

In line with Mann and Walsh (2017) who emphasise the importance of intellectual conversation and collaborative dialogue, the data show that professional learning is fundamentally a social process, based on and promoted through social relationships:

> "[a]s reflective practices are a very intimate activity, professional relationships are required. Social activities promote to tie up these relationships" (final partner evaluation, partner10, July 2020, Partner #10).

Highly relevant for promoting reflective practice among the teacher educators in this sample seemed to have been the fact that through describing and in a way 'justifying' their own professional practices over and over again during project meetings, the participants became more aware of them. One partner, for example, describes this very well:

> "'[a]t our university', sentences like that gave me the opportunity to reflect on our local circumstances and reflect on my own development in terms of what kind of teacher I want to be" (final partner evaluation, anonymous, July 2020, Partner #n.a.).

In extracts like these, in a way spoken self-reflections, the partners referred to their own teaching, mentoring, supervision, as well as their own learning. In most of the extracts, the partners also gave specific examples. In some cases this also included presenting some kind of evidence to go along with it (e.g. course materials, student outputs), as well as referring to literature and research studies and sharing these with the others. Based on those findings, one important value that was pointed out by the partners is that they learned a lot about themselves through participating in this transient professional community.

The following extract illustrates a potential challenge of working in such a community on the one hand, which on the other hand was one of the most significant potentials as well:

> "I still have the feeling that everybody has a different understanding of what a portfolio is, even though we did the last meeting, we talked about it, but conceptually I think they understand something completely different" (partner interview, 2019, Partner #12).

Here, the partner describes that even after two years, the differences that existed right from the start, in regard to the terminology and concepts, had become even more visible for him. So, on the one hand, the terminology and different concepts were a challenging issue, as language – not only if it is not one's first language – is complex and culturally, as well as in our case, institutionally rooted. In particular, terms like assessment, evaluation, and feedback were highly dependent on the institutional context and conditions of our participants. Here, in such situations, the constant alternation between 'otherness' and 'sharedness' could be observed.

The next extract (Figure 1) is from the last face-to-face meeting in November 2019 and gives an example of reflective questioning. Partners were asking each other critical or prompting questions to better understand each other's beliefs and conceptions, to possibly make connections and engage in collaborative meaning-making. This example shows a data-led and theory-based discussion. It is data-led, meaning it is based on group work that took place before the discussion, in which the participants had a look at different data collected from the participating students in the project (e.g. extracts from e-portfolios, digital learning outputs). It is further theory-based, as for example as Partner #12 (blue) refers to Bloom, meaning Bloom's taxonomy that was further being documented as part of the project partners' e-portfolio. It thus portrays a suitable example of dialogic reflection.

Figure 1. Extract, Interim Findings[2]

```
#partner10: I have a problem with this part [section of the developed assessment framework], I don't see that this one is better than the other
#partner2: What do you mean?
#partner10: That seems to be better than the other, you get 80 to 100 and 60 to 80 here, but I think one can get 100 on the evaluating and synthesising, it depends on the type of task that you ask them to do, do you know what I mean?
#partner2: No
#partner12: I mean this is just based on Bloom's [Taxonomy], Bloom's the same
#partner10: I know
#partner2: So in the original Bloom's, it can be quite inter-changable
#partner10: Yeah
#partner2: If you're evaluating and synthesising you're more taking all of the available concepts, kind of making sense of them, the creating and sharing is, you're going a step further
#partner10: No no I know, I understand perfectly well and I understand Bloom, what I mean is we have to tell them to share and create to reach that, otherwise they're not going to reach that
#partner2: But they know that, they know that their products will be shared, that they have to create it and that they will be shared, or what do you mean?
#partner10: Then you mean if they are sharing, then they get 100?
#partner2: No, but the sharing does not mean, just post something on Instagram, the sharing does imply to also interact or think about organising, structuring your content in a way that it interacts with the consumer, you know?
#partner10: Really? Do you agree with that? You don't have any problems with that? I would have lot of problems
#partner2: No, but think about a webpage that is for example very interactive, you know
#partner10: But I can't grade it, you know because the fact of doing a blog or a webpage is that it's interactive, you know, you're not adding anything, it's interactive, so how can I grade that?
#partner3: I don't think, if you only post a lot of text on a webpage it's not interactive
#partner10: No, of course not
#partner3: You have to do something more, you have to do it, you interact by using a lot of links and other multimodal
#partner10: I know TR, but you've done that and then you're grading it? You see, what I am trying to say is that for me it is difficult to grade it [based on the developed framework]
#partner3: I think it's a very important point about defining or understanding the 'terms' we use
(201911_proPIC_TPM4_recording 2b, Pos. 186-187)
```

---

2. Some of the findings and interview answers used for this chapter are published in Oesterle, Schwab, Hoffmann, and Baldwin (2020); these findings were also presented in Oesterle et al. (2021).

However, this example also reveals that partners did not always understand each other perfectly – either due to language difficulties or terminological contradictions or both. Nevertheless, it must be noted that these discussions never created a negative atmosphere, but that they demonstrated trust and positive working relationships that had been established. This was often mentioned in informal conversations but most obviously in the final project evaluation, in which all participants highlighted the supporting and open partnership that had been established. Discussions like these did not appear during the first two partner meetings, so it can be assumed that the community needed time to grow and become strong enough for critical conversations.

3. Conclusions

Coming back to the question asked at the beginning, how can teacher educators benefit from their participation in a transient professional community; based on the data, I have identified four factors.

First, it can be highlighted that especially institutions acknowledge and support the participation in such communities, even though they are not research-oriented. This means allocating time, space, and possibly finances to maximise their potential usefulness.

Second, didactical content or guidelines should be developed to better scaffold reflective practices and activities that focus more on the content rather than on the management of such communities. This includes the exploration of effective tools for evaluation (e.g. a collaborative e-portfolio). In line with Groundwater-Smith (2017, p. xviii), I argue that fruitful communities are not emerging by chance, but need to be initiated and scaffolded.

Third, it seems to be crucial to explore and develop innovative and creative hybrid formats of working together. The COVID-19 pandemic in particular has provided new opportunities to collaborate and interact with each other. Accordingly, and based on the collected data, it can be stated that it is necessary to foster not only active participation but further encourage and support professionals to actively shape and reinvent their future, most likely a hybrid, professional environment. This includes the creation of virtual spaces in which professional communities can be strengthened. Partners believed it to be relevant to simplify and unify the space of communication and work.

Last but not least, I consider that promoting more research in the field of transient professional communities in education is relevant in order to find out how teacher educators and the like work and how their professional practices can be improved.

References

Czerniawski, G. (2018). *Teacher educators in the twenty-first century.* In I. Menter (Ed.), *Critical guides for teacher educators*. Critical Publishing.

Groundwater-Smith, S. (2017). Partnerships, networks and learning in educational research: contested practices. In R. McNae & B. Cowie (Eds), *Realising innovative partnerships in educational research. Theories and methodologies for collaboration*). Sense Publishers.

InFo-TED. (2019). *White paper. The importance of teacher educators: professional development imperatives*. International Forum for Teacher Educator Developmenthttps://info-ted.eu/wp-content/uploads/2019/10/InFo-TED-White-Paper.pdf

Lunenberg, M., Murray, J., Smith, K., & Vanderlinde, R. (2017). Collaborative teacher educator professional development in Europe: difference voices, one goal. *Professional Development in Education, 43*(4), 556-572. https://doi.org/10.1080/19415257.2016.1206032

Mann, S., & Walsh, S. (2017). *Reflective practice in English language teaching. Research-based principles and practices.* Routledge. https://doi.org/10.4324/9781315733395

Mortensen, J. (2017). Transient multilingual communities as a field of investigation: challenges and opportunities. *Journal of Linguistic Anthropology, 27*(3), 271-288. https://doi.org/10.1111/jola.12170

Oesterle, M., Schwab, G., Hoffmann, S., & Baldwin, R. (2020). The potentials of a transient transnational community for teacher educators' professional learning and development. *European Journal of Education Studies, 7*(8), 117-147. https://oapub.org/edu/index.php/ejes/article/view/3192/5828

Oesterle, M., Schwab, G., Hoffmann, S., & Baldwin, R. (2021). Promoting transnationalism in teacher education: how can teacher educators benefit from their participation in a transient professional community? *Conference presentation ECER 2021*. EERA. https://eera-ecer.de/ecer-programmes/conference/26/contribution/51484/

Powell, D. (2021). Teacher educator collaboration and a pedagogy of teacher education: practice architectures, professional learning, praxis, and production. In A. Swennen & E. White (Eds), *Being a teacher educator. research-informed methods for improving practice* (pp. 56-71). Routledge. https://doi.org/10.4324/9781003055457-5

Sachs, J. (2001). Teacher professional identity: competing discourses, competing outcomes. *Journal of Education Policy, 16*(2), 149-161. https://doi.org/10.1080/02680930116819

Swennen, A., & White, E. (2021). (Eds). *Being a teacher educator. research-informed methods for improving practice*. Routledge. https://doi.org/10.4324/9781003055457

Van den Besselaar, P., & Sandström, U. (2017). Vicious circles of gender bias, lower positions, and lower performance: gender differences in scholarly productivity and impact. *PLoS, 12*(8), 1-16. https://doi.org/10.1371/journal.pone.0183301

White, E., & Swennen, A. (2021). Introduction to being a teacher educator. In A. Swennen & E. White (Eds), *Being a teacher educator. research-informed methods for improving practice* (pp. 1-9). Routledge. https://doi.org/10.4324/9781003055457-1

Part 4.

13 proPIC student vignettes

Alison Whelan[1], Götz Schwab[2], and Mareike Oesterle[3]

1. Introduction

Up to this point, chapters in this volume have reflected on the proPIC Europa project primarily through the experiences and views of the educators involved. However, a major element of the project was the active and constant involvement of pre-service teachers in the study programme (see Hoinke & Clausen, 2022, Chapter 3 this volume). Throughout the project, 142 students took part and helped develop various outputs and resources. Moreover, the students contributed to our research agenda by giving their feedback, allowing us to record various sessions and meetings, and by producing a great number of diverse essays and papers. Then, towards the end of the project, students from all cohorts and all partner institutions were invited to contribute a short essay detailing an aspect of the project which had impacted their studies, their practice, and their professional development. Primarily, the students either reported on their own individual experiences in becoming a part of this transnational endeavour or presented and discussed the findings and results of their own research projects, which they worked on during the proPIC project. On examination of the submitted essays and other contributions by the participating students (e.g. Bachelor of Arts or Master of Arts theses),

---

1. Newcastle University, Newcastle-upon-Tyne, United Kingdom; alison.whelan2@newcastle.ac.uk; https://orcid.org/0000-0001-6272-6497

2. University of Education Ludwigsburg, Ludwigsburg, Germany; goetz.schwab@ph-ludwigsburg.de; https://orcid.org/0000-0003-0939-3325

3. University of Education Ludwigsburg, LudwigsburgGermany; mareike.oesterle@gmx.de; https://orcid.org/0000-0002-9458-7917

How to cite: Whelan, A., Schwab, G., & Oesterle, M. (2022). proPIC student vignettes. In G. Schwab, M. Oesterle & A. Whelan (Eds), *Promoting professionalism, innovation and transnational collaboration: a new approach to foreign language teacher education* (pp. 263-286). Research-publishing.net. https://doi.org/10.14705/rpnet.2022.57.1394

thematic strands emerged of developing knowledge and skills in the fields of language learning and teaching, digital mobile technologies, and Continuing Professional Development (CPD) and reflection. These underlying themes demonstrated that the transnational project had been effective in meeting its objective of inspiring prospective teachers "to actively engage in lifelong learning processes and to cooperatively establish a culture of self-reflection, innovation and interculturality in foreign and second language learning and teaching"[4].

Having been inspired by Mann and Walsh (2017), this chapter combines extracts of student essays and includes a choice of vignettes that help examine the project from the perspective of the students themselves, exploring their reflections on their participation and the impact this had on their studies and future careers as language teachers. Additionally, we have provided links to the complete essays as handed-in by the students on the project website[5].

2. Theme 1: developing knowledge and skills in the processes and theories of language learning and teaching – how can the transnational experiences explored in the proPIC project impact foreign language teaching and learning?

The majority of our students are going to become second or foreign language teachers. As a key rationale for our project, we tried to bring together students from different national and regional backgrounds in order to discuss their perspectives on language learning and teaching. Although teacher training across Europe is different in many respects, there is nonetheless common ground regarding what teaching is about, as Cristina described in a clear and thoughtful manner:

---

4. https://propic-portfoleo.weebly.com/study-week-i.html

5. http://www.propiceuropa.com/final-publication.html

Cristina's vignette

proPIC's values in education: How do they help to enhance students' motivation and interest?[6]

Teaching has never been easy. As teachers we are not only in charge of conveying academic knowledge, but of being capable to manage a long list of skills, such as class [organisation] and control, pedagogical and psychological coaching abilities, empathy, creativity, being innovative, self-development and, of course, in nowadays society, digital, and technological skills. Being a teacher means to constantly learn and develop professionally, but also personally. Thus, we must prepare ourselves for the various situations that we face in our daily work.

Cristina considers in this vignette her future field of work from a rather general point of view, detailing the numerous skills and competences that a prospective teacher must develop and demonstrate, both professionally and personally.

Marie-Louise went a step further and tried to look at her experience with proPIC from the perspective of a (prospective) *language* teacher. In her Master's thesis, she shed light on the role of an international study programme on the professional habits and developments of future language teachers.

Marie-Louise's vignette

Becoming Professional – the impact of international collaboration on the professional development of future language teachers[7]

The findings [of the author's MA thesis] show that a study [programme] that is aimed at fostering international collaboration among future language teachers can include workshops, dealing with projects,

---

6. http://www.propiceuropa.com/uploads/1/0/8/0/108097905/propic_book_part_iv_cristina.pdf

7. http://www.propiceuropa.com/uploads/1/0/8/0/108097905/ma_haubensak.pdf

actively engaging with contents, interviews, and discussions with experts, school visits, social events, and communication devices and digital tools. A [programme] can foster international collaboration in that it provides opportunities and time for any form of exchange among its participants, brings people together, [organises] activities in which students collaboratively work on a task and everyone contributes to a shared outcome.

In addition to that, collaborative reflections and group discussions with experts in the field of teaching can be ways in which such collaboration can be fostered. The participants' active role is especially important. Findings on how international collaboration could affect the participants' CPD have shown that a collaborative culture can evolve in which professional knowledge can be expanded, new cultural knowledge can be developed, and participants are found to be active producers of knowledge. Such collaboration can further enable professional sharing with peers, can lead to receiving feedback from peers and foster reflection processes.

The affordances which students have in order to foster collaborations and exchanges among themselves as well as with each expert and others with experience in the field (teachers, lecturers, administrators, etc.) seem to be highly important in an international study programme such as proPIC. Marie-Louise here points out the wide range of activities being offered to the participating students. Being actively engaged in these enterprises may help to become more reflective and thus more professional.

However, as professionals in the realm of foreign language teaching, and in particular English language teaching, we also need to look at the object of our teaching, i.e. the target language and how it needs to be taught. In her Master's thesis, based on a project during the study week in Spain, Felicitas dealt with the role of English as a lingua franca or international language (Waldman, Harel, & Schwab, 2019) and presented her findings in a separate paper, thereby taking a critical stance on how English has been taught in the past.

Felicitas's vignette

The intercultural speaker model: language proficiency and the 'Native Speaker' redefined[8]

English in the international context has long been a reason for discourse in [second language acquisition theory]. Little empirical work has been done however, and language policies continue to rely on the native speaker model (Seidlhofer, 2003). During the project I observed how non-native English speakers facilitate the English language to communicate interculturally on an academic level. My considerations lead me to the following questions:

What are the common linguistic standards of Intercultural Speakers of English? Once established, how do these standards apply to language education? (Siwik, 2019)

I realised quickly that it is nearly impossible to define one common version of international English that could facilitate the innate diversity that comes with Intercultural Speakers (Siwik, 2019). Nonetheless, I was able to get an insight into what intercultural communication in an academic setting looks like.

I used the guidelines for assessment of spoken performance by the *Common European Framework of Reference* (Council of Europe, 2001) in order to identify common themes among participants. I then compared these to native speaker performance in a recorded interview. What was observed was that out of the five qualitative aspects, *Range, Accuracy, Fluency, Interaction,* and *Coherence,* all remained relevant (Council of Europe). However, the way in which they were achieved differed notably. […]

---

8. http://www.propiceuropa.com/uploads/1/0/8/0/108097905/propic_book_part_iv_felicitas.pdf

Chapter 13

Overall, Intercultural Speakers were able to facilitate diverse non-native accents, different grammatical styles, and proficiency levels. If there were problems during the interaction, they could get around these difficulties using strategies such as paraphrasing, code switching, and mutual correction. They avoided ambiguity through repetition and the sensible use of idiomatic expressions. […]

Teaching the English language brings an additional responsibility to its teachers and learners. Although it may be of noble intention to use English as a tool for international communication, cultural exchange, and/or even peace efforts, it is (still?) accompanied by the bitter reality of (neo-)colonialism. Capital-based globalisation is the continuation of a system that centres the global West and its cultures as a benchmark for what is considered 'international'. Traditional approaches to literature in English promote predominantly British or American white (and often male) authors at the expense of all others. Efforts have to be made to include more postcolonial literature and authors with diverse backgrounds.

There is a need for real change in European language education. The fact that non-native English speakers outnumber native speakers to such a high degree and, due to their ability to connect with members of diverse cultures in this shared L2, they now hold the balance of power when it comes to evolving the English language and its cultural diversity. Future teachings of English to Intercultural Speakers demand that teaching techniques and methodology evolve to meet their needs.

Since the beginning of the 21st century, communicative language teaching has been enhanced with the notion of interculturality and the concept of intercultural communicative competence (Byram, 2008; Byram, Holmes, & Savvides, 2013). Languages are closely connected to the cultural background of the speaker, which plays an important role not only for one's L1 but also for each and every additional language. While this is true for every language, it needs to be considered even more when dealing with English as an L2 due to its role in history and in international communication today. In her study, Felicitas clearly highlights this and includes another dimension which is the socio-political understanding of English as a foreign language and how we deal (or do not deal) with it in European schools.

Digitalisation is certainly not limited to language teaching and its different methodological considerations. Nevertheless, it has become a prevailing topic in foreign language teacher training programmes across Europe and also became an overarching topic within the project, a theme that was tackled in multifaceted ways.

3. Theme 2: developing knowledge and skills in digital mobile technologies

In her essay, Lisha looks at using technology in language teaching and how to implement it in her own teaching while being part of the student project group.

Lisha's vignette

Digital natives: how digital technologies can influence speaking proficiency[9]

The development of technology encourages me to hold an insightful observation into the impact that technologies can make on language learning in an effective and innovative way. This is the reason why I got so excited when I received the invitation to participate in the proPIC programme, from which I can obtain the latest news about digital education and most excitingly, I can study abroad for one week at the University of Barcelona in Spain. Before the study week, some e-portfolio training was given in the study session at Newcastle University

---

9. http://www.propiceuropa.com/uploads/1/0/8/0/108097905/propic_book_part_iv_lisha.pdf

Chapter 13

> and I learned about some approaches to teaching and learning with technologies, [CPD], and more. Unfortunately, due to the outbreak of COVID-19, the trip to Spain was cancelled. However, as a postgraduate student from a TESOL [programme] at Newcastle University, there are so many other ways for me to continue my interest. Hence, I created an English website for improving students' oral proficiency based on the framework of task-based language teaching. It is at the very initial stage of my website and I will create more related content in the future. I will also share my beliefs into what makes an effective teacher.

As was the case all over the globe, the pandemic had a massive impact on students and their opportunities to take part in student programmes such as proPIC. Although our programme included much more than a five-day study week abroad, this can certainly be considered a highlight of our project (see also Schwab & Oesterle, 2022, Chapter 4 in this volume). Therefore, it is no surprise that Lisha was quite disappointed not to be able to go to our partner university in Barcelona. Nonetheless, she seemed to profit greatly from taking part in the programme at her home institution, and she put particular effort into creating a website in order to foster her digital and methodological competences.

Digital competence can be taught in many ways. In our project, we decided to provide basic knowledge and competences via the use of iBooks, compiled by all the partners in proPIC (see also Baldwin & Ruhtenberg, 2022, Chapter 5 in this volume). The effect and impact of the iBooks were researched in a Bachelor's thesis by Birnur.

> **Birnur's vignette**
>
> *Promoting innovation and collaboration among future teachers of English at secondary schools*[10]

---

10. http://www.propiceuropa.com/uploads/1/0/8/0/108097905/avsar_2018.pdf

Living in the new age where technology is an integral part of everyday life and new media an important tool, teaching is getting more and more towards the use of innovation in educational settings. The emerging changes in the global economy, due to development of new technologies, retails the evolution of new skills in our education system in order to prepare students for their future life. Therefore, the integration of the use of such technologies in teacher training is vitally important, in order to prepare prospective teachers for the use in their own classrooms. The proPIC course integrated as an example the interactive books in the syllabus, giving future teachers the opportunity to work with emerging technologies. Prospective teachers could figure out which features, tools, and apps can be integrated in iBooks while learning the subject matter of the books. Getting to know iBooks as a tool for language learning and teaching, prospective teachers could experience the advantages and disadvantages of their use in the classroom which gave them first-hand experience.

The results of the survey [conducted in the context of the author's BA] showed that the integration of this tool in the proPIC course caused in general a positive attitude towards the use of iBooks in the classroom. Future teachers who participated in this project are aware of the benefits iBooks entail in the field of education and think that the use of iBooks can improve students' understanding and engagement, caused by their own experience. This shows that in order to foster the professionalism of prospective teachers the integration of emerging technologies in university courses is inevitable. Even if difficulties occur while using new tools, the effect of gaining new experience and developing critical thinking pose an enrichment for the future teachers, which is the presupposition for the effective application of such technologies in language learning and teaching. Not only the integration of technologies in the classroom is essential, but also the motivation and competencies of teachers to use iBooks in a meaningful way. The elation of future teachers to use iBooks for their own teaching paired with the know-how they need can lead to a positive effect on students' learning process.

Chapter 13

Looking at how participating students in all four European countries managed with the iBooks was the main focus of Birnur's survey. For most of the students, it was the first time that they came across this tool, especially as we started our project before the onset of the global pandemic when digital tools were less commonly used in most European countries. All in all, students appreciated the fact that they were presented with state-of-the-art technology. They managed to get along without significant problems, gained insights into their advantages and disadvantages, and learned about the opportunities of using iBooks (or similar applications) in their own classrooms.

As iBooks represented only one tool that we promoted in our project, students had to deal with other applications as well. Mercedez, a student originally from the US, reported on how she developed her digital competences over time, i.e. before and during the time as a participant in the project.

Mercedez's vignette

Using mobile technologies in the classsroom to aid learning: creating a digital escape room[11]

proPIC played a significant role in my professional development as it helped me understand how to use digital tools in the classroom to aid student's learning. [...]

In 2017, I was accepted onto a teaching [Master's programme] at the University of Barcelona. There, I had the amazing opportunity to take classes that encouraged students to learn using digital tools. Professors J. and O. taught me just how effective digital tools could be in helping students understand, whether in the classroom or through distance learning. We did a project in collaboration with students from the University of the Háskóli Islands, and used *Google Docs, Google Slides, Canva, WhatsApp,* and other similar platforms to deliver our

---

11. http://www.propiceuropa.com/uploads/1/0/8/0/108097905/propic_book_part_iv_mercedez.pdf

lessons, while students used the same digital resources to complete their assignments. […]

Going to Karlsruhe was the perfect supplement to my studies in Barcelona. The contribution of knowledge from my proPIC peers, our group discussions, presentations, and school visits truly resonated with me, having a lasting impact on how I teach. This is especially true now that we, as educators, have been forced to adopt these new forms of teaching due to the pandemic. Times change, and we need to adapt. […]. I am proof that acquiring knowledge does not only come from classroom experience. I had plenty of experience in the classroom prior to the pandemic. However, without the knowledge gained through my studies at the Universitat de Barcelona and my study week in Karlsruhe, I would not have been able to teach effectively via distance learning during the pandemic. This is because instead of focusing on the design, development, and delivery of subject matter, I would have been preoccupied with simply learning how to use the digital tools that would enable me to teach effectively.

In conclusion, it is crucial that educators spend time learning about digital tools that will improve the quality of their lessons. They must consider researching the numerous applications, websites, and software that can and should be used by students to promote autonomous learning. Looking back on my first teaching experiences, I realise that although I was very comfortable using technology, I could have helped students develop greater skills if I were able to better implement the use of digital tools in the classroom. Focusing on how to use digital tools in the classroom will allow educators to improve the experience of distance learning for themselves, and their students.

Mercedez here emphasises two major aspects that other students have reported as well during and after the project: first of all, learning in the framework of an international collaboration is a truly beneficial experience that today's students need in order to become professionals engaged in serious CPD (for more see also Mann & Webb, 2022 and Oesterle & Schwab, 2022, Chapters 1 and 2 in this volume, respectively). Learning how to use mobile devices and digital technology is a permanent process that requires an attitude of openness and curiosity and cannot be reduced to single training events. Second, taking part in a study programme such as proPIC, with a strong focus on digitalisation, helped her (and others) immensely during the challenges of the COVID-19 pandemic. Although none of us was aware of what would happen two years into the project period, both students and lecturers benefitted enormously from participating in the project as online learning and using a wide range of digital and online tools was no longer new to us.

A quite similar impression on the advantages of digital tools was reported by Cristina. Here, she writes about developing an online escape room and how the concept of gamification became of relevance to her. She also puts it in the light of CPD and the overall rationale of proPIC, combining the three project strands of internationalisation, digitalisation, and professionalism into one project that helps future language teachers to become experts in their field.

Cristina's vignette

proPIC's values in education: how do they help to enhance students' motivation and interest?[12]

The overall aims of proPIC are "actively engage in lifelong learning processes and to cooperatively establish a culture of self-reflection, innovation and interculturality in foreign and second language learning and teaching" (proPIC, 2020, n.p.). All these objectives are meant to "promote professionalism, innovation and transnational collaboration […] and using mobile technologies […] integrated in different curricula" (proPIC, 2020, n.p.). Promoting and enhancing all these aims among different communities of teachers can help improve professional development and, consequently, the learning processes. As

---

12. http://www.propiceuropa.com/uploads/1/0/8/0/108097905/propic_book_part_iv_cristina.pdf

a result, we achieve a more motivating educational environment and better outcomes in our students' performances. That is why experiences such as proPIC are an excellent opportunity for (future-) teachers to develop professionally, as well as personally. [...]

As part of my own research project, I created a didactic sequence of activities entitled 'Hispanic diamond: educational escape room proposal and testing for A2 contents revision' (Martín, 2020). This research project consists of a designed set of activities for Spanish as a [foreign language] students that focus on the development of language and different skills, cultural aspects, and Spanish varieties (from Spain, Argentina, Cuba, Chile, Mexico, and Colombia). This project is meant to be a revision activity for the A2 level, according to the CEFR (Council of Europe, 2001) in a format of an educational escape room that includes gamified elements (Werbach & Hunter, 2012). 'Hispanic diamond' was tested and analysed from both, teacher and students' perspectives, regarding the use of language, the gamified elements and the [information and communications technology] resources, in order to reach a conclusion on whether it had a positive impact and [benefitted] the students' learning process or not. [...]

All in all, I believe that as teachers we must be aware of the different preferences, difficulties, and backgrounds of our students. Being a language teacher does not only mean to teach linguistic content, but having the adequate tools and resources, as well as having a great pedagogical management in order to make the most of our students and having a positive impact on their learning processes.

In that sense, the Hispanic diamond project has proven to be a great asset to promote and improve our students learning process, as well as their motivation by using not only merely linguistic content, but by introducing gamified and digital elements and resources (Martín, 2020; Martín & Batlle, 2021). For that purpose, gamification is a learning approach that aims to encourage the students to learn by means of game elements. Although it offers numerous benefits for our students as previously stated, it has its downsides as well, such as challenging the teacher's skills, the teacher's need of being up-to-date in educational innovative experiences and the time-consuming effort that it entails (Chia & Hung, 2017; Lee & Hammer, 2011).

I think that many teachers regard gamification activities and escape rooms are [sic] still out of their comfort zone and therefore they are not common in language courses. However, it is worth trying them out and checking first-hand any possible improvement in terms of motivation, interest, autonomy, social, personal skills, and academic performance in our students' learning process. By taking into account the elements of the proPIC project, such as innovation, mobile technologies, development as teachers and as learners, prospective teachers, lifelong learning processes and the culture of self-reflection and interculturality we can benefit in many aspects and they can help us become better teachers, improve the learning, grow professionally, and educate covering our students' needs and interests and, therefore, motivate them.

Although gamification was not included explicitly in our project, students such as Mercedez and Cristina came across it and tried to implement it in their own teaching toolbox. They were able to identify the challenges of dealing with it in the language classroom, but also found ways of overcoming problems. Pivotal to this seems to be a clear focus on digitalisation as it may support teachers in dealing with what the future of teaching and learning in and outside the classroom could look like. This is also of great importance when looking at some key aspects of CPD – motivation and reflection.

4. Theme 3: dealing with experiences and perceptions of CPD and reflective practice

CPD can be seen as an umbrella concept for proPIC and its activities (see also Mann & Webb, 2022, Chapter 1 this volume), a topic that has not only been dealt with extensively in this book but also in our programme and structure as it was tailored to the needs of future language teachers.

Claudià's vignette

Teachers' beliefs about assessment and reflective practice: a prod to [CPD][13]

Being part of the proPIC Project in 2019 not only enriched my [information and communications technology] skills, but it also boosted my own self-regulation and made me more autonomous as a teacher, in line with my [CPD]. Reflecting upon my teaching practices was not new for me, since I had already been working on my reflective e-portfolio within my Master's degree to become a teacher of Spanish as a [foreign language]. The goal of it was basically to register my evolution by selecting relevant samples and accompanying them with a reflection. At the beginning of my portfolio I showed my initial beliefs about the didactic process, but I did not discuss my beliefs about assessment that much. It was only when I began my Master's degree thesis, defended in July 2020, that I started focusing on them. My main objective was to analyse pre-service, in-service, and teacher trainers' beliefs about [Spanish as a foreign language] assessment.

The idea to conduct this study came from my first formal contact with assessment. I [realised] that I had always thought that assessment lay merely in doing an exam, because of my own assessment experiences as a pupil. My perspective shifted notoriously thanks to formal knowledge, and when I was considering options for my thesis this curiosity to explore my colleagues' beliefs about assessment arose. Regarding its interest, beliefs are a small part of teachers' thought that, although not easily accessible, can affect teacher assessment practices. Exploring them can help me understand how teachers conceive this inseparable

---

13. http://www.propiceuropa.com/uploads/1/0/8/0/108097905/propic_book_part_iv_claudia%CC%80.pdf

part of the didactic process, but also delve into my own assessment activity. [...]

Our findings showed that all the teachers report changes in their beliefs, either as a result of training or because of their teaching experiences, and that the teaching context and the assessment experiences as language learners were related to their beliefs. Some informants disclosed that training helped them reflect upon their own assessment practices and experiences as language learners or teachers. In general, we found more similarities in the beliefs of teachers from different groups than within a specific group. Concerning teacher training in assessment, there were similarities in teachers of distinct groups, yet within a specific group each participant offered their own perspective.

Taking the findings into account, our first conclusion was that informants' assessment experiences, as well as the teaching context and formal knowledge, could cause changes in their beliefs about assessment or could be related to them. However, what teachers articulated could not correspond to their actual beliefs or practices, and at this point reflective practice stands as a possible solution to this issue. It would be interesting to carry out an investigation based on [reflective practice] to make teachers think about their beliefs and assessment practices in the classroom (Esteve & Carandell, 2009). With that, we could strengthen teachers' CPD and contribute to [reflective practice]'s main goal: to enhance teachers' pedagogical tasks.

After carrying out our investigation we were able not only to explore our colleagues' beliefs about assessment, but also to gain an insight into our perspective. We became more aware of, e.g. the fact that each assessment procedure has its purpose. In addition, we consider that it is crucial to take beliefs into account, especially during formative periods, since they evolve along with our teaching skills and experiences and are, therefore, a part of our CPD. In that sense, we encourage teachers to delve into their own beliefs about assessment and share them with their colleagues. Reflecting upon our beliefs and practices is relevant, but expressing them in a portfolio or discussing them with others is fundamental to our development.

In order to foster her own CPD, Claudià made use of the e-portfolio, an instrument of reflection used by all partners in the project (for more on this see Cuesta, Batlle, González, & Pujolà, 2022, Chapter 7 this volume). Although portfolios are considered to be a tool for individual reflective practice, they can also be used to combine one's reflections with research on a particular aspect of personal interest. Here, Claudià focused on a topic she pinpointed as relevant for herself as well as for teaching in a more general sense: assessment and beliefs about assessment procedures. She figured out how important pondering one's attitude towards evaluation and assessment is when becoming professional so that relevant changes in one's behaviour are possible if necessary. In addition to that, she also underlined another point of great importance: dialogic reflection. E-portfolios (and other tools for reflective practice) should not be restricted to oneself, but ought to be used in collaboration with colleagues and associates in the field of teaching, locally or in international projects.

In her essay, Noelia tackles the question of what CPD is about and how to achieve a professional attitude. In her vignette, the e-portfolio is taken as a starting point as she intensively reflects upon its use by looking at its advantages and disadvantages or, as she called it, 'the good and the ugly' of using such a tool.

Noelia's vignette

[CPD] through the use of portfolios: the good and the ugly[14]

As a first-time user of e-portfolio, I was hesitant on what information would be more appropriate to include in my work, and in which way content should be organised. This highlights the need for specific

---

14. http://www.propiceuropa.com/uploads/1/0/8/0/108097905/propic_book_part_iv_noelia.pdf

Chapter 13

instructions and guidance when it comes to creating and developing an e-portfolio, potentially taking away from students' creativity. Additionally, I would highlight the need for training onto the use of e-portfolio features to partially tackle the time-consuming nature of this instrument – although, the learning process of those features is time-consuming on its own.

There are certain aspects of e-portfolio I have found controversial as I developed my own skills with this tool. One of the first things I questioned was the advantage that had to do with openness and sharing knowledge and information (Tur & Urbina, 2014). This openness can be viewed as an advantage – information is available to a wide(r) audience when it is online and free of charge, it fosters collaboration and empowers the learner; or as a disadvantage since it raises several questions. Firstly, it made me consider if publishing content on the web free of charge would continue to provide big data management corporations with information they can use. If e-portfolio is used on a specific platform free of charge, who does the information the user published on that platform belong to? Another potential barrier of e-portfolios when it comes to openness is the fact that users can compare their work, potentially fostering a competitive environment. This is particularly hazardous when it comes to assessment practices, generating anxiety in students (Tur & Urbina, 2014, p. 16).

The last point I would like to raise is creativity. E-portfolios provide a plethora of opportunities in the design and presentation of student's work, with tools to exploit this creativity widely available to those who can access a computer or tablet (Allen & Coleman, 2011). From my own experience using e-portfolio, one of the main challenges was to learn how to use certain tools efficiently, for example certain software such [as] photo or video editing tools. Not only is learning how to use these tools time-consuming, there is also specific software that the user has to purchase, which might pose an accessibility threat. Not necessarily everyone has access to the required hardware and software to make the most of e-portfolio in a creative way, leading to an imbalance in opportunity and therefore, in the final work individuals might be able to produce.

As a novice and first-time user of e-portfolios, she tries to shed light on all the different aspects of using such an instrument. This includes certain critical points such as (alleged) openness, data protection, or a competitive attitude caused by presenting oneself in public. However, she also points out what positive facets can be ascribed to portfolios. Among them are (true) openness and creativity due to what she calls a 'plethora of opportunities'.

Collaboration was emphasised in Shahad's report on her experience in the project. As a student in the UK, she had the opportunity to travel to Germany during the study week and reflected upon her professional development as a future English teacher.

Shahad's vignette

Professional development through a transnational study experience[15]

[Travelling] to the University of Kiel, Germany, as a part of proPIC Europa project in 2019 was a very eye-opening experience that I have [benefitted] from in many aspects. Especially as a graduate student at Newcastle University studying for [a Master of Arts] in Applied Linguistics and TESOL, with an ambition to work as an English language instructor in the future. Thus, having the opportunity to join the study week at the University of Kiel was exciting because it gave us the chance to learn intensively about transnational language teaching and the creative use of modern technologies in teaching practices. As Godwin-Jones (2018) states there has been a major shift in the way that second language learning/acquisition is happening because of the growth of online networks and media, especially

---

15. http://www.propiceuropa.com/uploads/1/0/8/0/108097905/propic_book_iv_shahad.pdf

among young people. In the field of language learning, [utilising] computers (Johnson, Becker, Estrada, & Freeman, 2014) to assist learning has made brilliant developments in many aspects, such as computer-mediated communication, telecollaboration and even game-based learning. Hence, the study week in Kiel, was very valuable for my professional development as a teacher. [...]

The proPIC Europa project helped in many different ways, from meeting new people and listening to their different backgrounds as teachers and/or learners, to being exposed to the many different methods of teaching conducted all around the world. Additionally, I [benefitted] from the project with my university studies, and finally with professional development and teaching experiences after I graduated from the university. Even though it was only one study week, it was tailored perfectly for the benefit of teachers' development especially in the use of mobile technologies, as it is [up-to-date] with the students' current needs (Zhang, Zhou, Briggs, & Nunamaker Jr, 2006). [...]

Last but not least, the project also helped me with my professional development. The development of technology implies that the delivery of information has been gradually replaced by flexible digital formats, such as online videos and broadcasts (Bishop & Verleger, 2013). Therefore, it is only progressive for the field of education, to have technology add to its contribution to the improvement of educational outcomes (O'Flaherty & Phillips, 2015). For example, some studies have shown that video lectures outperformed face to face lectures (McNeil & Nelson, 1991; Zhang et al., 2006). Thus, having recently become a language teacher in Kuwait University I tried to implement what we learned during the study week. Accordingly, making use of technologies in teaching, and making it fun and relevant at the same time. As well as making sure to apply elements of collaborative working for the students to benefit from their sharing of ideas (Li, 2017). However, most of the things learned during the study week in Kiel, will need to be adapted in order for it to fit in the target culture, as teaching in Kuwait is very different from my experience in both Kiel and Newcastle.

In conclusion, the study week in Kiel has been advantageous for me, in both short and long-term basis. As for the short-term I have immediately benefitted from applying what I have learned in the study week to my [computer assisted language learning] course in Newcastle University, and as a student teacher the experience was very valuable and beneficial. As for the long-term, I'll be sure to participate more in self-reflectiveness during my own teaching career, and applying all that I have learned during the study week. As well as making sure to continue working on my own development as a teacher, as there is a lot of benefit to collaborating with teachers from around the world.

Shahad provides a comprehensive picture of how the study week helped her to develop skills and competences in teaching language with the help of advanced technology, but also puts this experience in the context of what she learned at her home university. Furthermore, she sees that teaching is a collaborative endeavour – for her as a (tertiary) teacher, but also her students when working on language tasks.

5. Conclusion

In all of the vignettes presented here, students dealt with an individual understanding of the overarching topics of the proPIC project: (1) developing knowledge and skills in the processes and theories of language learning and teaching, (2) developing knowledge and skills in digital mobile technologies, and (3) dealing with experiences and perceptions of CPD and reflective practice. As part of our transnational project, participants looked at these topics from different regional and national perspectives and tried to present them against the backdrop of their own experiences. The range of impressions presented here depicts only a small part of what students encountered. Thus, we decided to provide all of their essays on our website to reveal a fuller picture of what we tried to achieve with proPIC: promoting professionalism, innovation, and transnational collaboration among future language teachers.

References

Allen, B., & Coleman, K. (2011). The creative graduate: cultivating and assessing creativity with eportfolios. Changing demands, changing directions. In *Proceedings of Ascilite, Australia*, (pp. 59-69).

Baldwin, R., & Ruhtenberg, T. (2022). Student reactions to using interactive tutorials as part of the proPIC study programme. In G. Schwab, M. Oesterle & A. Whelan (Eds), *Promoting professionalism, innovation and transnational collaboration: a new approach to foreign language teacher education* (pp. 131-145). Research-publishing.net. https://doi.org/10.14705/rpnet.2022.57.1386

Bishop, J. L., & Verleger, M. A. (2013). The flipped classroom: a survey of the research. *ASEE national conference proceedings, 30*(9), 1-18. https://doi.org/10.18260/1-2--22585

Byram, M. (2008). *From foreign language education to education for intercultural citizenship*. Multilingual Matters. https://doi.org/10.21832/9781847690807

Byram, M., Holmes, P., & Savvides, N. (2013). Intercultural communicative competence in foreign language education: questions of theory, practice and research. *The Language Learning Journal, 41*(3), 251-253. https://doi.org/10.1080/09571736.2013.836343

Chia, A., & Hung, Y. (2017). A critique and defense of gamification. *Journal of Interactive Online Learning, 15*(1), 57-72.

Council of Europe. (2001). *Common European framework of reference for languages: learning, teaching, assessment*. Cambridge University Press. https://rm.coe.int/1680459f97

Cuesta, A., Batlle, J., González, V., & Pujolà, J.-T. (2022). Approaches to the development of pre-service language teachers' e-portfolios. In G. Schwab, M. Oesterle & A. Whelan (Eds), *Promoting professionalism, innovation and transnational collaboration: a new approach to foreign language teacher education* (pp. 191-212). Research-publishing.net. https://doi.org/10.14705/rpnet.2022.57.1388

Esteve, O., & Carandell, Z. (2009). La formació permanent del professorat des de la pràctica reflexiva. *Articles de Didàctica de la Llengua i la Literatura, 49*, 47-62.

Godwin-Jones, R. (2018). Chasing the butterfly effect: informal language learning online as a complex system. *Language Learning & Technology, 22*(2), 8-27.

Hoinke, U., & Clausen, K. (2022). Getting curious and gaining knowledge through transnational collaboration in foreign language teacher education. In G. Schwab, M. Oesterle & A. Whelan (Eds), *Promoting professionalism, innovation and transnational collaboration: a new approach to foreign language teacher education* (pp. 83-106). Research-publishing.net. https://doi.org/10.14705/rpnet.2022.57.1384

Johnson, L., Becker, S. A., Estrada, V., & Freeman, A. (2014). *NMC horizon report: 2014 K.* The New Media Consortium.

Lee, J. J., & Hammer, J. (2011). Gamification in education: what, how, why bother? *Academic Exchange Quarterly, 15*(2).

Li, L. (2017). *New technologies and language learning*. Palgrave Macmillan.

Mann, S., & Walsh, S. (2017). *Reflective practice in English language teaching. Research-based principles and practices*. Routledge.

Mann, S., & Webb, K. (2022). Continuing professional development: key themes in supporting the development of professional practice. In G. Schwab, M. Oesterle & A. Whelan (Eds), *Promoting professionalism, innovation and transnational collaboration: a new approach to foreign language teacher education* (pp. 15-44). Research-publishing.net. https://doi.org/10.14705/rpnet.2022.57.1382

Martín, C. (2020). *Diamante hispano: propuesta y pilotaje de un escape room educativo para la revisión de contenidos de nivel A2*. Published MA Thesis, University of Barcelona. ResearchGate. https://doi.org/10.13140/RG.2.2.26360.06409

Martín, C., & Batlle, J. (2021). Gamification: students' perceptions of an educational escape room in the context of learning Spanish as a foreign language. *REIRE, 14*(1), 1-19.

McNeil, B. J., & Nelson, K. R. (1991). Meta-analysis of interactive video instruction: a 10 year review of achievement effects. *Journal of Computer-Based Instruction, 18*(1), 1-6. https://psycnet.apa.org/record/1991-25835-001

Oesterle, M., & Schwab, G. (2022). Developing a framework of CPD for the context of foreign language teaching. In G. Schwab, M. Oesterle & A. Whelan (Eds), *Promoting professionalism, innovation and transnational collaboration: a new approach to foreign language teacher education* (pp. 45-79). Research-publishing.net. https://doi.org/10.14705/rpnet.2022.57.1383

O'Flaherty, J., & Phillips, C. (2015). The use of flipped classrooms in higher education: a scoping review. *The internet and higher education, 25*, 85-95.

proPIC. (2020). *Promoting professionalism, innovation and transnational collaboration.* http://www.propiceuropa.com/

Schwab, G., & Oesterle, M. (2022). The proPIC study weeks: experiencing transnational exchange. In G. Schwab, M. Oesterle & A. Whelan (Eds), *Promoting professionalism, innovation and transnational collaboration: a new approach to foreign language teacher education* (pp. 107-130). Research-publishing.net. https://doi.org/10.14705/rpnet.2022.57.1385

Seidlhofer, B. (2003). *A concept of international English and related issues: from 'real English' to 'realistic English'.* Council of Europe.

Siwik, F. (2019). *The intercultural speaker model: language proficiency and the "native speaker" redefined.* Bachelor Thesis, University of Education Karlsruhe.

Tur, G., & Urbina, S. (2014). Blogs as eportfolio platforms in teacher education: affordances and limitations derived from student teachers' perceptions and performance on their eportfolios. *Digital Education Review, 26,* 1-23.

Waldman, T., Harel, E., & Schwab, G. (2019). Extended telecollaboration practice in teacher education: towards pluricultural and plurilingual proficiency. *European Journal of Language Policy, 11*(2), 167-185. https://doi.org/10.3828/ejlp.2019.11

Werbach, K., & Hunter, D. (2012). *For the win: how game thinking can revolutionize your business.* Wharton Digital Press.

Zhang, D., Zhou, L., Briggs, R. O., & Nunamaker Jr, J. F. (2006). Instructional video in e-learning: assessing the impact of interactive video on learning effectiveness. *Information & management, 43*(1), 15-27. https://doi.org/10.1016/j.im.2005.01.004

Author index

B
Baldwin, Richard v, 131, 243
Batlle, Jaume v, 191, 215

C
Clausen, Kyra v, 83, 233
Cuesta, Azahara v, 191, 215

G
González, Vicenta v, 191, 223

H
Hoinkes, Ulrich vi, 83, 233

M
Mann, Steve vi, 15

O
Oesterle, Mareike vi, 1, 45, 107, 253, 263

P
Pujolà, Joan-Tomàs vii, 191, 223

R
Ruhtenberg, Tobias vii, 131

S
Schwab, Götz vii, 1, 45, 107, 263
Seedhouse, Paul viii, 147

W
Webb, Katie viii, 15
Whelan, Alison viii, 1, 147, 243, 263

www.ingramcontent.com/pod-product-compliance
Lightning Source LLC
Chambersburg PA
CBHW031135160426
43193CB00008B/151